SATHER CLASSICAL LECTURES

Volume Thirty-five

THE HEROIC TEMPER

THE
HEROIC TEMPER
STUDIES IN
SOPHOCLEAN TRAGEDY

BY BERNARD M. W. KNOX

UNIVERSITY OF CALIFORNIA PRESS
BERKELEY, LOS ANGELES, LONDON

UNIVERSITY OF CALIFORNIA PRESS
BERKELEY AND LOS ANGELES, CALIFORNIA

UNIVERSITY OF CALIFORNIA PRESS, LTD.
LONDON, ENGLAND

© 1964 BY THE REGENTS OF THE UNIVERSITY OF CALIFORNIA
FIRST PAPERBACK PRINTING 1983
ISBN 0-520-04957-8

LIBRARY OF CONGRESS CATALOG CARD NO.: 64-21684

PRINTED IN THE UNITED STATES OF AMERICA

1 2 3 4 5 6 7 8 9

To Amata Bianca

PREFACE

THE SIX chapters of this book are a slightly expanded version of the lectures it was my privilege to deliver as Sather Lecturer at Berkeley in the spring of 1963. The first two chapters attempt an analysis of the literary phenomenon of the Sophoclean tragic hero and the succeeding four treat at some length the *Antigone*, the *Philoctetes* and the *Oedipus at Colonus*.

It is a pleasure to record here my thanks for help received from so many quarters; to the John Simon Guggenheim Foundation for one of its distinguished fellowships in 1957, to Yale University and the Bollingen Foundation for travel grants in 1959, to Athens College for its lordly hospitality in 1961–62 and to the American School of Classical Studies in Athens for the privileges of its library where I spent so many happy and industrious mornings, to the University of California for its invitation and for many rewarding conversations with its scholars and students, and lastly to Helen Wadman, Vicki Zupnik, and Sandra Crowell who all served their time typing an infuriating manuscript.

BERNARD M. W. KNOX

Washington, D. C.
November, 1963.

CONTENTS

I

The Sophoclean Hero 1

THE MODERN concept of tragic drama takes for granted the existence of a single central character, whose action and suffering are the focal point of the play—what we call 'the tragic hero.' For us it is difficult to imagine *Hamlet* without the Prince of Denmark. This figure of the tragic hero is a legacy inherited by Renaissance and Neo-classical tragedy from Seneca, and so from the Greeks.[1] The literary theory which is associated with it claims as its source, rightly or wrongly,[2] the *Poetics* of Aristotle, where a famous passage seems to most critics to imply that tragedy presents the 'reversal' of a single character.[3] It was natural that Aristotle should make such an assumption, because his point of view on tragedy is primarily ethical, and the problem of moral choice is most clearly and economically presented in this way.[4] There was a firm base for such a view in the fifth-century tragedies he cites, for many of them, and especially the play he clearly regarded as the most perfect example of the tragic art, the *Oedipus Tyrannus*, do in fact center on such a single figure. This dramatic method, the presentation of the tragic dilemma in the figure of a single dominating character, seems in fact to be an invention of Sophocles.[5] It is at any rate so characteristic of his technique that we may fairly and without exaggeration call the mainstream of European tragedy since his time Sophoclean. It is Sophocles who presented us with what we know (though the Greeks of course did not use the term) as 'the tragic hero.'[6]

Even the titles assigned to Sophocles' plays suggest that this
peculiarity of his drama was recognized in the ancient world.
We do not know who assigned these titles, nor, as a rule, when
they were assigned,[7] but they clearly reflect some common
(and, on the whole, early) impression of the nature of his
dramaturgy. Of the seven extant tragedies, six are named after
the central figure; only one, the *Trachiniae*, after the chorus,
and that is the only one of the seven which is not clearly based
on the figure of a tragic hero. The titles of the seven extant
plays of Aeschylus present a different picture: the *Suppliants*,
the *Persians*, the *Agamemnon* (but here surely no one can ever
have thought that *he* is the tragic hero), the *Libation Bearers*,
the *Eumenides*. The *Prometheus Bound* is rightly named, and
does present us with a fully developed heroic and dominant
figure (though he is not a man but a god), but this play is so
unlike the rest of Aeschylean drama that it is a problem in
itself; it is a play 'to be argued to, not from' as Kitto said of
the *Heraclidae* of Euripides.[8] It must have been written late in
Aeschylus' career (later than the end of it some scholars think)
and may thus show Sophoclean influence, as the *Oresteia* does
in its adoption of the third actor.[9] The other surviving play of
Aeschylus which concerns itself with the tragic dilemma of an
individual does so in a very Aeschylean way: the bulk of the
play is made up of elaborate descriptions of the persons and
armor of the opposing champions in the final assault on Thebes,
and the play was known, as early as the *Frogs* of Aristophanes,
not as the '*Eteocles*' but as the *Seven against Thebes*.

The difference in the kind of title given the plays of the two
dramatists is of course merely a symptom of their fundamental
difference in method and outlook. For one thing, every
Aeschylean play we possess, except the *Persians* (the only play
we have where the poets deserted the myth for history), is part
of a trilogy. And every Sophoclean play is complete in itself.[10]
Sophocles' abandonment of trilogic form was probably a revolutionary step, for the fact that the Dionysiac festival continued to demand the production of three tragedies in suc-

cession by the same dramatist long after the connected trilogy had become the exception rather than the rule suggests that three was the number demanded of the dramatist when the festival was first established; and this in turn suggests that the connected trilogy was the form in which he was expected to compose.[11] Whether this revolutionary step of Sophocles produced the tragic hero or was the result of such a conception is a problem no more soluble than that of the priority of chicken or egg; all we can be sure of is that they are closely connected. The reduction of the scope allowed for the tragic subject from three plays to one led to or sprang from but in either case made possible the artistic decision to present the tragic dilemma in terms of a single personality facing the supreme crisis of his life.

It seems clear too that Sophocles was responsible for both innovations. For the step he had taken in substituting three separate plays for the connected trilogy could be developed in other ways. In Sophocles the abandonment of trilogic form and the concentration of the resulting independent play on the tragic dilemma of a single hero are different sides of the same coin, but they did not have to be. For Euripides the release from trilogic form opened up other possibilities, the full range of which he exploited with marvellous bravura. He could take a leaf from the Sophoclean book and write a *Medea* in which the central character does dominate the action, but he could also use the new form for a drama like the *Hippolytus* which brings on stage the tangled skein of a relationship between four equally important characters.[12] The *Medea*, in fact, with its Sophoclean concentration, is unusual for Euripides; he did not in his other extant plays repeat the pattern. Even plays like the *Andromache*, *Hecuba*, *Heracles*, and *Electra*, which in organization and tragic intensity are close to the *Medea* and the Sophoclean type, dissipate in various ways the unrelenting concentration on the central figure which is the Sophoclean hallmark.[13] This is not to dismiss them as failures; it is simply, as Kitto has taught us to say, that Euripides was trying to do something different, as he clearly was in such plays as *Troades*, *Phoenissae*, and *Orestes*. Plays like *Ion* and *Helen* do not concern themselves with what we would call tragic issues at all, and in the *Bacchae* it is not Pentheus, but Dionysus who dominates the action.

These are formal considerations, but there are others, which, though not divorced from form (for it is only with inferior art that the distinction between form and matter can be clearly made), yet admit of discussion in other than purely formal terms. The single Sophoclean play is the medium for a vision of human existence which differs fundamentally from that of Aeschylus, and which demands the form Sophocles found for it. In the Aeschylean trilogies (and with the help of the *Oresteia* we can see dimly the grand design of the others) the onward flow of time, οὑπιρρέων χρόνος, reveals not only the chain of causation of human action, presented through the persons of successive generations, but also the intimate and in the end clearly defined connection of all these events with the will and action of the gods. The action of the characters is an organic part of the larger design; it has its being in a hugely imagined world where the sweep of history affords us a perspective for the suffering we see on stage, and offers us consolation by giving it meaning; where also the human beings, involved in an action too great for them to understand, are warned or encouraged, judged or defended, by gods, from afar and eventually in person. Human suffering, in this all-embracing vision, has a meaning, even a beneficent purpose; it is the price paid for human progress. The violence, Aeschylus has his chorus sing, is in some way the grace of god.[14]

But the Sophoclean single play rules out the future which might serve to lighten the murk and terror of the present: the *Trachiniae* makes no reference to the eventual deification of the tortured, poisoned hero who raves in agony on the stage, the *Electra* only ambiguous references to the sequel of the matricide,[15] the *Oedipus Tyrannus* only a dark and despairing allusion to the future of the polluted and self-blinded hero. It also, in its characteristic form, cuts the close tie between men and gods. Athena appears to Ajax only in his madness and then only to mock and expose him; Philoctetes sees Heracles only when of his own free will he has embarked on a course which will prevent Troy's fall and prove the prophecies false; elsewhere the will of the gods is a distant enigma, expressed in oracles that seem to equivocate, in encouragement that seems to fail, in answers to prayers that seem to bring the opposite of what was prayed for.

In a Sophoclean drama we are never conscious, as we always are with Aeschylus, of the complex nature of the hero's action, its place in the sequence of events over generations past and future, its relation to the divine plan of which that sequence is the result. The Sophoclean hero acts in a terrifying vacuum, a present which has no future to comfort and no past to guide, an isolation in time and space which imposes on the hero the full responsibility for his own action and its consequences. It is precisely this fact which makes possible the greatness of the Sophoclean heroes; the source of their action lies in them alone, nowhere else; the greatness of the action is theirs alone. Sophocles presents us for the first time with what we recognize as a 'tragic hero': one who, unsupported by the gods and in the face of human opposition, makes a decision which springs from the deepest layer of his individual nature, his *physis*, and then blindly, ferociously, heroically maintains that decision even to the point of self-destruction.

Once again, the example of Euripides serves to reinforce the point. Except for Medea, the characteristic Euripidean hero suffers rather than acts. Heracles, Pentheus, Hippolytus, and many another are victims rather than heroes. The Sophoclean characters are responsible, through their action and intransigence, for the tragic consequences, but in Euripidean tragedy disaster usually strikes capriciously and blindly, and it comes most often, not from the reaction of his fellow men to the hero's stubbornness, but from the gods themselves: from Aphrodite, who announces Hippolytus' death sentence before the play

begins, from Hera, who sends her agent Madness against
Heracles, from Dionysus, who in person tempts Pentheus and
leads him to his hideous death at his mother's hands on the
mountains. Euripides turns his back on the characteristic
isolation of the Sophoclean tragic hero; in his tragedies man is
once more in a world where the autonomy of his action is in
doubt; the great gods walk the stage again. But now they
intervene brutally in human lives to bring events round to the
pattern of their will, and their will is no longer, as in Aeschylus,
revealed in time as beneficent. Hippolytus and Phaedra,
Heracles, Pentheus, and many another are victims of gods
whose power is exercised, as they expressly tell us, for no other
purpose than their own aggrandizement or the vindication in
the sufferings of humanity of their own wounded self-esteem.[16]
The divine action is violence, but can no longer be called 'grace.'
There is no historical perspective, either, to give meaning to
the suffering; the only consolation that can be offered the
broken victims of this unfeeling universe is the advice to suffer
with dignity. "The noble among men," says Theseus to
Heracles, "bear the calamities sent by the gods without
flinching."[17]

Between these two views of the human situation, the
Aeschylean and the Euripidean, these poles of hope and despair,
Sophocles creates a tragic universe in which man's heroic action, free and responsible, brings him sometimes through suffering to victory but more often to a fall which is both defeat and
victory at once; the suffering and the glory are fused in an
indissoluble unity. Sophocles pits against the limitations on
human stature great individuals who refuse to accept those
limitations, and in their failure achieve a strange success. Their
action is fully autonomous; for these actions and the results
the gods, who are the guardians of the limits the hero defies,
bear no responsibility. Yet the gods are presences felt at every
turn of the action, in every line of the dialogue and lyric, and
by some mysterious poetic alchemy we are made to feel, without being expressly told, that the gods have more concern and

respect for the hero, even when like Ajax or Oedipus *tyrannos* he seems to fight against them, than for the common run of human beings who observe the mean. Sophocles is no theologian; his conception of man's relation to god is presented to us only in dramatic action which is as powerful as it is enigmatic; all one can say is that the gods too seem to recognize greatness. Athena, though her mockery is bitter, treats Ajax in his madness almost as an equal, and Zeus answers his last prayer; Heracles tells Philoctetes to yield but utters no word of reproach; Antigone is justified after her death by the gods' spokesman Tiresias; Electra is given her victory at last. Even Oedipus at Thebes knows obscurely, in the hour of greatest despair, that the gods have reserved him for some special destiny, and in the last play of all they summon him to join them. The grace of god is even more violent than in Aeschylus, and more mysterious, but, though it has nothing now to do with human progress, it is there; its presence confers on Sophoclean tragedy that balance and restraint which is so conspicuously absent from the Euripidean cry of despair.

Aeschylus is indeed, as Gilbert Murray called him, the 'creator' of tragedy, but Sophocles, in his less flamboyant way, is equally original. Not only did he abandon the trilogy and add the third speaking actor, he also invented tragedy as we know it: the confrontation of his destiny by a heroic individual whose freedom of action implies full responsibility. These three 'inventions' are of course one and the same. The concentration of the dramatic spotlight on the great crisis of the hero's life demands not only the single play but the third actor too; it cannot afford that leisurely development, expressed in soaring lyric rather than the cut and thrust of dialogue, which is found in the *Suppliants* and *Agamemnon*, but must plunge into the action and maintain a breakneck pace. The swiftness of the exposition in the *Ajax* prologue, the headlong forward movement of the central scenes of the *Philoctetes*, the frantic speed of the final revelation in the *Oedipus Tyrannus*, all these depend on the presence of the third actor.

This new medium, the single play, focussed on the tragic dilemma of a single individual and technically reinforced by the introduction of a third actor, is used by Sophocles to present dramatic situations which, for all their human and dramatic variety, are surprisingly similar. In six of the extant plays (the exception is of course the *Trachiniae*) the hero is faced with a choice between possible (or certain) disaster and a compromise which if accepted would betray the hero's own conception of himself, his rights, his duties. The hero decides against compromise, and that decision is then assailed, by friendly advice, by threats, by actual force. But he refuses to yield; he remains true to himself, to his *physis*, that 'nature' which he inherited from his parents and which is his identity. From this resolution stems the dramatic tension of all six plays: from Ajax' decision for death rather than submission, from Antigone's steadfast loyalty to her brother, and Electra's to her father, from Philoctetes' bitter refusal to go to Troy, from the stubborn insistence of Oedipus at Thebes on knowing the full truth, first about Laius' murder and then about himself, and from old Oedipus' resolve to be buried in Attic soil. In each play the hero is subjected to pressure from all sides. Ajax is assailed by Tecmessa's appeal and then by his own doubts as he argues with himself, putting the case for compromise in terms so eloquent that many have believed he accepts it. Antigone is faced with the sisterly urgency of Ismene, the threats of Creon, the strong disapproval of the chorus, with imprisonment in a tomb and with the absence of any sign of approval from those gods she champions. Oedipus *tyrannos* runs into Tiresias' majestic refusal to speak, the compromising advice of Jocasta and her final desperate appeal, the agonized supplication of the herdsman at the very last moment. Later at Colonus he faces the strong disapproval of Theseus, the revulsion of the chorus, the arguments, threats, and violence of Creon, and the appeal of his son. Electra is confronted with the arguments of her sister, the call of the chorus for moderation, the threats of her mother, and above all the news that Orestes, her one hope of

rescue, is dead. Philoctetes is subjected to the threats and
violence of Odysseus as well as the friendly persuasion of
Neoptolemus and the chorus. And all of them hold firm against
the massive pressure of society, of friends as well as enemies.
The Sophoclean hero and his situation are best described in
that marvellous image which in the last play of all compares
the blind old man to "some sea cape in the North, with the
storm waves beating against it from every quarter," πάντοθεν
βόρειος ὥς τις ἀκτὰ/ κυματοπλὴξ χειμερία κλονεῖται (OC, 1240–
1241). Like the cape, the hero rides out the buffeting of the
storm and remains unmoved.[18]

In six of the extant plays, the figure of the hero is cast in the
same mold and placed in the same situation. This figure may
wear the mask of a young woman (does so in fact twice), of a
fierce and brutal soldier, a brilliantly successful and vigorous
ruler, a sick marooned outcast, or a blind filthy old beggar, but
behind all these masks remains basically the same type. The
hero faces the same situation with the same intransigence, but
this is not all. Both he and his opponents express themselves in
language that employs the same formulas from play to play.

There is of course no single definition which can contain the
variety and vitality of the six plays, the uniqueness and living
personality of the different heroes; all that is claimed here is
that there is in them a recurrent pattern of character, situation,
and language which is strongly enough marked to be called
characteristic of Sophoclean tragedy. That pattern I shall now
attempt to establish in detail, for without detailed evidence
such an assertion cannot be taken seriously. It cannot be supported solely by analysis of character, for previous attempts to
constitute a typically Sophoclean character are open to the
damning objection that interpretation of character in Sophoclean drama is too elusive and subjective a basis on which to
build.[19] It must rest on the only objective basis we have—the
words of the Sophoclean text. The proof will call for extensive
quotation, and for this my excuse is that too many theories of
Sophoclean tragedy have been based on words which are re-

markably rare in the plays Sophocles wrote.[20] In this field the
critic must, like the old-time preacher, quote chapter and verse;
his thesis stands or falls on its relation to the text, those words
which are all we have left of the original performance in the
theater of Dionysus.

The hero's decision, his resolve to act, that rock against
which the waves of threat and persuasion will break in vain, is
always announced in emphatic, uncompromising terms. "Some
enterprise must be sought ($ζητητέα$ 470) which will show my
father I am no cowardly son." "The man of birth must either
live nobly or nobly die ($καλῶς τεθνηκέναι$). You have heard all
I have to say" (479–480). "The other weapons shall lie buried
with me" ($τεθάψεται$ 577). "But I will go" ($εἶμι$ 654). "I shall
go now, where I must go" ($εἶμ'$ . . . $ὅποι πορευτέον$ 690). "I
must begin the work, and fast" ($ἀρκτέον$ 853). So Ajax speaks
of his resolve to die. The use of the verbal adjective, a form
expressing necessity, of the future tenses, above all of the tone
which brooks no argument—all this is characteristic of the
hero's resolve to act. Antigone's expression of her resolve is
just as simple and emphatic. "Be what you decide," she says
to Ismene, "but I shall bury him" ($θάψω$ 72). "If the action
brings my death, it is a noble death" ($καλόν$ . . . $θανεῖν$ 72).[21]
"I shall lie with him" ($κείσομαι$ 73); "I shall lie there forever" ($κείσομαι$ 76). And, a few lines later, "I shall go now
($πορεύσομαι$ 81) to heap up a tomb for the brother I love." So
Oedipus at Thebes makes his decision to find the murderer of
Laius; "I shall reveal" ($φανῶ$ 132),[22] and this is what he
stubbornly proceeds to do, deaf to appeals, until the whole
truth is laid bare. He repeats his inflexible determination many
times. "I could not possibly be persuaded not to learn the
truth" ($οὐκ ἂν πιθοίμην$ 1065). "This is something that could
not happen ($οὐκ ἂν γένοιτο$ 1058), that with such evidence in
hand, I should fail to find out the secret of my birth." "I must
rule," he says to Creon in the quarrel between them ($ἀρκτέον$
628)[23] and later, on the edge of the fearful revelation, "I must
hear" ($ἀκουστέον$ 1170). For Electra, mourning for her father

is, as she explains (355 ff.), a form of action against his murderers, and she makes a strong affirmation that she will never
abandon it. "I will not cease (οὐ . . . λήξω 103) from gloomy
laments, as long as I see the shining tracks of the stars and the
light of day." "I will never put a stop to these frenzied lamentations as long as I live" (οὐ σχήσω 223). When she learns the
false news of Orestes' death she proclaims her determination to
continue her demonstrations of mourning and rebellion in even
more uncompromising forms. "Never from now on will I enter
the house to live with them, rather at these gates I will sink to
the ground and friendless let my life wither away" (εἴσειμ'
. . . αὐανῶ 817-819). "I shall never," she tells her sister,
"follow your path" (οὐ . . . μὴ μεθέψομαι 1052), using a type
of emphatic future negative she has already used in a formula
of refusal.[24] "My mind is made up," she says (δέδοκται 1049),
and when Chrysothemis refuses to help her she "must do the
deed alone" (δραστέον 1019). Philoctetes too has his mind made
up (δέδοκται 1277); "even more firmly than I can express," he
answers when the question is put to him.[25] And his refusal to
go to Troy is absolute. "Never (οὐδέποτέ γε 999). No matter if
I have to suffer every evil." "Never, never (οὐδέποτ' οὐδέποτ'
1197), not even if the firebearing thunderbolt comes flaming
on me." "Never" (οὐδέποθ' 1392), he repeats the word to
Neoptolemos, "never of my own free will shall I see Troy." The
blind old man at Colonus announces his resolve so unexpectedly
and emphatically that his interlocutor is astounded. "There
is no possibility that I shall leave this place" (οὐχ . . . ἂν
ἐξέλθοιμ' 45). "What does that mean?" asks the confused
native of Colonus, who thought he was dealing with an abject
suppliant. The old man's announcements grow more emphatic
still. "They will never have control of me," (οὐκ . . . μὴ
κρατήσωσιν 408), he says of the Thebans and again, "They
will never have me on their side" (οὐ . . . μὴ λάχωσι 450).

This heroic resolve, announced in absolute and forbidding
terms, is nevertheless put to the test. The form of attack on the
hero's resolve which he finds hardest to resist is the emotional

appeal of those who have claims on his affections. Tecmessa appeals to Ajax in the name of her love for him and of his son. "Pity your son, my lord" (510). She speaks with the urgency and abject desperation of the suppliant. "I beg you" (λίσσομαι 368). "I implore you" (ἀντιάζω 492). "On my knees I supplicate you" (ἱκνοῦμαι 588). Ajax is indeed moved, as we learn from his famous speech—"I pity her" (652)—but these appeals do not turn him from his chosen course. Chrysothemis similarly implores Electra (λίσσομαι 428, ἀντιάζω 1009) but with even less effect. Jocasta, who cannot argue with Oedipus, for she dare not reveal the truth she has just come to understand, implores him not to continue the search for his identity, "I beg you, do not do this" (λίσσομαι, μὴ δρᾶν τάδε 1064). Earlier in that same play the chorus implores the *tyrannos* to reconsider his death sentence on Creon: "Consider, we beg you" (λίσσομαι 650). And Polynices, associating his sister with him in his appeal to his blind father at Colonus, begs the old man as a suppliant (ἱκετεύομεν 1327) to join him against his brother.[26]

But the assault on the hero's will usually takes the form of argument, of an appeal, not to emotion, but to reason. The attempt to move the hero is described as 'advice' (παραινῶ) or 'admonition' (νουθετῶ). "Even though I am young to advise you" (παραινέσω 1181), says Antigone as she tries to persuade her father to listen to his son. "How shall I distrust his words, this man who gives me friendly advice?" (παρῄνεσεν 1351), says Philoctetes, when Neoptolemos makes his final appeal, and when he rejects it, he repeats the word: "You who give me this terrible advice" (αἶνον αἰνέσας 1380).[27] So Jocasta tries, unsuccessfully, to 'advise' Oedipus (παραινοῦσ' 918).[28]

Sometimes the word used is νουθετῶ which has a stronger sense: 'reprove, admonish, warn, correct.' "Others too have bad sons," says Antigone to her father, "and a sharp anger, but admonished by the incantations of those that love them (νουθετούμενοι 1193) their natures are charmed." "When you learn what I have to say, *then* reprove me" (νουθέτει 593), says Oedipus to Theseus, earlier in the play. "And even so, you

reprove me" (νουθετεῖς 1283), cries Philoctetes indignantly after
Neoptolemos has made his appeal; later Neoptolemos repeats
the word: "If anyone admonishes you in friendly style, (νουθετῇ
1322), you loathe him." So Electra is reproved by her sister.
"All this reproof of me (νουθετήματα 343) you learn from *her*,"
says Electra to Chrysothemis; "You have no right to reprove
me" (νουθετεῖν 595), she says to her mother. And when
Chrysothemis rejects her plan for an attack on Aegisthus, she
says: "Your reproof (νουθετεῖς 1025) shows that you will not
act with me."

The advice or admonition is an appeal to reason. "Consider,
think" (φρόνησον 49), says Ismene to her sister, and again,
"Reflect" (σκόπει 58). "Consider this" (σκέψαι δὲ τοῦτο 584),
says Creon to Oedipus *tyrannos*; "Consider, we beg you"
(φρονήσας 649), says the chorus to him later and Jocasta bids
him, "Consider" (σκόπει 952). "Now is the moment for
thought" (φρονεῖν 384), says Chrysothemis to Electra.[29]
"Consider well" (φρόνησον εὖ 371), says the chorus to Ajax.
Neoptolemos leaves his sailors with Philoctetes in the hope that
he may have some 'better thought' (φρόνησιν . . . λῴω
1078), and the sailors repeat the phrase, "You could have
thought under a better inspiration" (λῴονος ἐκ δαίμονος
1099).[30] Theseus sternly bids the blind old man 'consider'
(σκόπει 1179) whether he should listen to his son, and Antigone,
taking up the task where Theseus fails, uses the same word
(ἀποσκόπει 1195).

The method of rational argument is persuasion, and this
word, πείθω, and its middle form, πείθομαι, with its harsher
meaning 'obey,' occurs in every confrontation of the hero with
his friends and his adversaries. "Will you not be persuaded?"
(σὺ δ' οὐχὶ πείσῃ; 592), says Tecmessa to Ajax, as the tent is
closed on him and his resolve to kill himself, and Chrysothemis
uses exactly the same words to Electra in the first argument
between them (σὺ δ' οὐχὶ πείσῃ; 402). "I beg you to be persuaded by me" (πιθέσθαι 429), she says to her sister again; and
later the chorus, which has been whole-heartedly on Electra's

side so far, momentarily supports Chrysothemis against
Electra's resolve to act alone with the same word: "Be persuaded" (πείθου 1015). Oedipus *tyrannos*, too, is urged to accept
persuasion: by Tiresias—"if you will be persuaded by me"
(ἤν ἐμοὶ πίθῃ 321); by the chorus—"Be persuaded" (πιθοῦ 649);
and in the last desperate appeal of Jocasta—"Yet be persuaded" (ὅμως πιθοῦ μοι 1064).

For Antigone a special related word is used: ἀπιστέω, to
refuse persuasion, to disobey. "Do not coöperate with those
who disobey this decree" (τοῖς ἀπιστοῦσιν 219), says Creon to
the chorus, and soon Antigone is brought on stage by the
guards. "Do they bring you as one who disobeyed the royal
law?" (ἀπιστοῦσαν 381), the chorus asks her. And Creon
refers to her as "the only one in the city who disobeyed"
(ἀπιστήσασαν 656). There can be no question of persuading
her, nor of her obeying; she has already by her irrevocable act
of defiance made such words irrelevant. It is Ismene who says,
"I shall obey" (πείσομαι 67), and later, much later and too late,
Creon will say the same thing (πείσομαι 1099). Philoctetes "will
never be persuaded" (οὐ μὴ πίθηται 103), says Odysseus in the
prologue, and so he must be deceived. Philoctetes hears the news
that Odysseus will come to persuade him to go to Troy with
scornful incredulity. "Is it really true that *he* . . . swore he
would persuade me and ship me off to the Achaeans?" (πείσας
623). "I shall as soon be persuaded, when I am dead, to come
back from Hades to the light," he goes on (πεισθήσομαι 624).
"You must obey" (πειστέον 994), a triumphant Odysseus tells
him later, but when force fails to move him, Neoptolemos tries
persuasion, with no better result. "I was persuaded by your
words before" (πεισθεὶς λόγοις 1269), says Philoctetes bitterly.
"I wish you could have been persuaded by my words"
(πεισθῆναι 1278), says Neoptolemos, and later, acknowledging
failure, "I seem to persuade you not at all" (πείθειν . . . μηδὲν
1394). Creon comes to Colonus, so he says, "to persuade this
man" (πείσων 736). "Be persuaded by me" (πεισθεὶς 756), he
says to Oedipus later. But Oedipus is not moved. "This will be

most pleasant for me," he tells Creon, "if you are unable to persuade either me or these men here" (πείθειν 803). Later his daughter Antigone (πιθοῦ 1181) and his son Polynices (πιθέσθαι 1334), use the same word.

The hero, as his friends and enemies see him, needs to learn, to be taught. "If you could learn," says the chorus to Electra, "to benefit from her words" (μάθοις 370), and Chrysothemis says to her sister, "There is no capacity to learn in you" (μάθησις 1032). "Listen and learn from me," she says again (ἄκουσον . . . μαθοῦσα 889). "You are not willing to be taught" (διδαχθῆναι 330), she tells her but Electra fiercely rejects such teaching. "Don't try to teach me to be a traitor to those I love" (μή μ' ἐκδίδασκε 395). "Judge me when you have learned" (μαθών 544), says Creon to Oedipus at Thebes, but Oedipus replies, "I am no good at learning—from you" (μανθάνειν 545). "Listen to me and learn . . ." (μαθ' 708), says Jocasta to him later, and, much later still, in the depths of degradation, self-blinded, helpless, he tells the chorus, "That what I have done was not the best thing to do—do not try to teach me . . ." (μή μ' ἐκδίδασκε 1370). "We shall learn," says Ajax in his great speech, "to feel reverence for the Atridae" (μαθησόμεσθα 667), but his earlier estimate of himself was truer: "You are a fool if you think you can educate my nature so late in the day" (παιδεύειν 595). "Do not lament," says Neoptolemos to Philoctetes, "before you learn . . ." (πρὶν μάθης 917). "What lesson?" (μάθημα 918), asks the hero. It is a lesson he will not learn from any mortal man. "My good man," says Neoptolemos to him in exasperation, "try to learn not to be overbold in your misfortunes" (διδάσκου 1387).

What the hero is really asked to do, the demand behind the appeal to reason and emotion, the advice to reflect and be persuaded is—to yield, εἴκειν. This word (with its compounds) is the key word of the Sophoclean tragic situation; it occurs in every one of the six plays in the significant context of the attack on the hero's resolution.[31]

It seems to be a favorite Sophoclean word; not only is

Sophocles unique among the dramatists in his use of the aorist formation εἰκαθεῖν,[32] but also the use of this word group to characterize the demand made on the hero of the play is almost exclusively Sophoclean. In Aeschylus such a use is found only in the *Prometheus Bound*,[33] a play which in vocabulary and style differs sharply from the rest of the Aeschylean corpus;[34] in Euripides the word is used in the context of attack on a heroic resolution only in the *Hippolytus*, where the Nurse urges Phaedra to yield to her passion for Hippolytus (τὸν μὲν εἴκονθ' ἡσυχῇ μετέρχεται 444), and even there it is not directly addressed to or said of the person concerned, nor, for that matter, is Phaedra the 'hero' of the play.[35]

It is a word which has a long history in Greek poetry, and one of its meanings in Homer is 'to give ground, to retreat.' That basic meaning of 'retreat,' of giving ground before the enemy, pervades its transferred meaning of 'concede, permit.' What it means in Sophoclean tragedy is spelled out for us in a famous passage of the *Antigone*. Haemon is trying to persuade his father to spare Antigone's life. "You see how by the bank of the winter stream in flood, many of the trees give way (ὑπείκει 713) to preserve their branches, but those that resist are destroyed root and branch. In the same way, the man who stretches the sheet sail taut and does not give way at all (ὑπείκει μηδέν 716), turns over and sails the rest of his voyage with the decks below the keel. No, give way (εἶκε 718), retreat from your passionate temper."

This is the appeal made to all the Sophoclean heroes. To yield, to give ground, to retreat. "She does not know how to give in to misfortunes" (εἴκειν δ'οὐκ ἐπίσταται 472), says the chorus of Antigone in the same play. They are right, it is something she does not know how to do, and that is true for all of them. "A hard saying, one that does not give way to misfortunes" (φάτιν . . . κοὐχ ὑπείκουσαν κακοῖς 1046), says the chorus of Philoctetes' reply to Odysseus' brutal orders; later, when Philoctetes debates with his own pride and anger the offer made to him by Neoptolemos, he uses the same word.

"Well then, shall I give in?" (ἀλλ' εἰκάθω δῆτ'; 1352). "What do you want me to concede to you?" (εἰκάθω 651), says Oedipus *tyrannos* to the chorus, when they implore him to reconsider his death sentence on Creon. It so happens he does make this concession, but in such a way that Creon tells him, "You are hateful in your yielding" (στυγνὸς μὲν εἴκων 673).[36] "Do not force me to give in to you in this" (τάδ' εἰκαθεῖν 1178), cries Oedipus to Theseus when asked to listen to his son's appeal. "Yield to us, let our brother come" (ὕπεικε 1184), says Antigone and repeats the word: "Yield to us" (εἶκε 1201). He does consent to listen, but to Polynices' appeals to give in, "Withdraw your grievous anger" (μῆνιν . . . εἰκαθεῖν 1328), "I urge you to be persuaded, to give in" (παρεικαθεῖν 1334), he replies with a terrible curse. "Oh in the gods' name, give in" (ὕπεικε 371), says the chorus to Ajax, and in the great speech later he puts the case for surrender. "We shall learn to give in to the gods (θεοῖς εἴκειν 667). . . . things strange and most enduring give in to authority" (ὑπείκει 670).[37] But Ajax does not give in. Nor does Electra. "Even if they gave me all the gifts in which you now live luxuriously, I would never give in to them" (ὑπεικάθοιμι 361), she tells her sister; it is in vain that Chrysothemis urges her twice, in exactly the same words, to "give in to those who have the power" (τοῖς κρατοῦσιν εἰκαθεῖν 396, 1014).[38]

The hero refuses to yield. And in his reply to the demand that he should, he uses another word characteristic of the Sophoclean tragic situation, ἐᾶν 'to leave alone, allow, let.' "Let me be thus distraught" (ἐᾶτέ μ'ὧδ'ἀλύειν 135), says Electra to the chorus when they try to moderate her mourning for Agamemnon. "Leave me alone, get out" (οὔκουν μ'ἐάσεις 676), shouts Oedipus *tyrannos* to Creon, and later, a broken man but still of the same heroic temper, he says to Creon, "Leave me to live on the mountains" (ἀλλ'ἔα με ναίειν 1451). "Reprove me," says Oedipus at Colonus to Theseus, "when you learn what I have to say, but now let me" [speak] (τανῦν δ'ἔα 593), and later in the same speech he repeats the word: "Leave me alone in the decision I made to start with" (ἔα μ'ἐν οἷσιν ἠρξάμην 625). "Leave me to live here," he says to Creon (ἡμᾶς δ' ἔα ζῆν 798). And so too, later still, as he goes off to his mysterious death: "Do not touch me, but let me find by myself the holy burial place" (ἐᾶτέ με 1544). So Philoctetes to Neoptolemos: "Let me suffer this, whatever I am to suffer" (ἔα με . . . 1397).[39] And Antigone too uses the word: "Leave me and my ill-counsel to suffer this dreadful fate" (ἀλλ'ἔα με 95).[40]

It is no easy task to urge surrender on the hero, in fact it is difficult to tell him anything at all; he will not listen. "Speak to those who listen to you" (τοῖς ἀκούουσιν 591), says Ajax to Tecmessa as she pleads with him not to kill himself. "He never at any time would listen to my words" (λόγων ἀκοῦσαι 1070), says Menelaus, when Ajax is dead. "The good man must listen to those in authority" (κλύειν 1352), says Agamemnon, arguing against Odysseus' defense of Ajax. And Menelaus says the same thing: "It is the mark of an evil man, that a man of the people should not recognize that he should listen to his masters" (κλύειν 1072). These words, κλύειν and ἀκούειν, often have in Sophocles this sense of 'be subject to authority, obey'—precisely what the heroic nature will not admit. So Chrysothemis, defending her hypocritical surrender to Clytemnestra and reading her sister a lesson in conduct, makes the marvelously paradoxical statement, "If I am to be free, I must listen to the powers that be in everything" (ἀκουστέα 340). So Creon proclaims that when the city has set a man in authority, "one must listen to him" (κλύειν 666), and Ismene advises her sister: "We must listen to these things and things even more painful than this" (ἀκούειν 64). But the words do not always have this extra sense of 'submission'; usually the problem is to get the hero to listen at all. "Hear an equal reply" (ἀντάκουσον 544), says Creon to the *tyrannos*; and immediately afterwards, again; "Listen to what I am going to say" (ἄκουσον 547). "Listen to me" ('πάκουσον 708), says Jocasta; "Listen to this man and as you listen, reflect" (ἄκουε . . . κλύων 952). The hero does not want to hear. "Who would not be angry listening to such words?" (κλύων 340), says Oedipus as Tiresias evades his questions; and later: "It is intolerable to hear such things from him" (κλύειν 429). "Listen to me in the gods' name, so that you may learn" (ἄκουσον 889), says Chrysothemis to Electra. Philoctetes will not listen to Odysseus: "I would sooner listen to the serpent, my mortal enemy" (κλύοιμ' 632). And Neoptolemos knows that it is no easy thing to tell him what he must know: "Do not be angry as you listen" (μὴ θυμοῦ κλύων 922). When he makes his final attempt at persuasion he makes the same appeal: "Hear my words" (λόγους δ'ἄκουσον 1267); "Listen" (ἄκουσον 1316). "Listen to me and come home" (κλύων 740), says Creon to Oedipus at Colonus. When Oedipus realizes that the suppliant he is asked to hear is Polynices, he calls him, "the man of all men whose voice I could least bear to hear" (κλύων 1174). "Can you not listen to him?" (ἀκούειν 1175), says Theseus. "Why is this so painful to you, to hear him?" (κλύειν 1176). And Antigone repeats the argument. "What harm in hearing what he says?" (ἀκοῦσαι 1187). They are all the same. They have to be implored to listen, and even when they do the words fall on deaf ears.[41]

The hero will not listen, but he hears enough to know that he is under attack. And his reaction is violent and swift. The role of those who try to advise him is not easy. Ajax, when Tecmessa begs him for her sake and the child's not to kill himself, uses language that would be harsh even to an enemy: "Get out. Go back to where you came from . . . You have said too much already . . . You are a fool." Ajax of course is a savage warrior but the princess Antigone is not much gentler with her sister: "You be whatever you decide—*I* will bury him." "Don't fear for me; make a success of your own life." "All right, that's your excuse. But I shall go and bury the brother I love." "If you talk like that I shall hate you." Later when Ismene makes a distraught attempt to share Antigone's fate she is treated even more contemptuously: "Don't appropriate what you had no part in." "Save yourself. I don't begrudge you your escape."

"You chose to live." Ismene's sincere and pathetic question,
"What pleasure will there be in my life, deprived of you?" is
answered brutally: "Ask Creon. He's the one you care for."
The sister she once tried to enlist in her enterprise she now
treats as an enemy; she has in fact earlier told Ismene to
denounce her to the authorities. "I will hate you all the more,
if you keep silent." Electra is no kinder to her sister Chryso-
themis: "I loathe you ($\sigma\tau\upsilon\gamma\tilde{\omega}$ 1027) for your cowardice." "You
seem vile ($\kappa\alpha\kappa\dot{\eta}$ 367) to people, traitor to your father and
your family."[42] Like Antigone, she treats the sister who will
not join her desperate action as one of the enemy: "Go to your
mother and tell her everything" (1033). Oedipus at Thebes is
no easy person to advise either. True enough, Tiresias' obstruc-
tive silence is enough, as Oedipus says, to make a rock angry,
but his anger surpasses the worst the prophet could foresee and
actually provokes him to reveal what he had intended to keep
hidden. "Vilest of the vile" ($\kappa\alpha\kappa\tilde{\omega}\nu$ $\kappa\dot{\alpha}\kappa\iota\sigma\tau\epsilon$ 334), Oedipus calls
Tiresias, and later Creon fares no better: "I have found you my
enemy, a burden to me" (546). "Do not try to tell me you are
not vile" ($\kappa\alpha\kappa\dot{o}\varsigma$ 548). "You were born vile" ($\kappa\alpha\kappa\dot{o}\varsigma$ 627).[43]
And when he does grant Creon a reprieve from the death
sentence, he shows no lessening of repugnance: "This man, no
matter where he may be, will have my loathing" ($\sigma\tau\upsilon\gamma\dot{\eta}\sigma\epsilon\tau\alpha\iota$
672). Then, like Ajax: "Get out." Philoctetes, even after the
bow has been restored to him, is not much more conciliatory:
"You wish to betray me to my enemies." "You will destroy me
with those words of yours, I know you." Neoptolemos describes
him accurately: "If anyone reproves you, speaking in your best
interests, you loathe him" ($\sigma\tau\upsilon\gamma\epsilon\tilde{\iota}\varsigma$ 1323). Oedipus at Colonus
is cast in the same mold. The appeal of Creon is met with the
same invective (he calls him 'vile,' $\kappa\alpha\kappa\dot{o}\nu$, 783) and with a
baleful curse; that of Polynices with demonic rage and a father's
curse, and the same epithet ($\kappa\dot{\alpha}\kappa\iota\sigma\tau\epsilon$ 1354, $\kappa\alpha\kappa\tilde{\omega}\nu$ $\kappa\dot{\alpha}\kappa\iota\sigma\tau\epsilon$
1384).[44] Even Theseus is fiercely put in his place: "When you
learn from me, *then* reproach me" (593). All of them treat
advice and objections in the same fierce way;[45] friendly advice

is met with the same imperious rejection as hostile threat.[46]
Their watchword is: 'he who is not with me is against me.'

The attempt to sway or hinder them provokes their anger;
they are all angry heroes. Long before we see the culmination
of old Oedipus' rage in the curse he pronounces on his son,
there has been anger enough in the play. "You gratify that
anger which has always been your bane" (ὀργῇ χάριν δούς 855),
says Creon to the blind old man, and Ismene tells him the
oracles speak of a Theban defeat "stemming from your anger
when they take their stand at your tomb" (τῆς σῆς ὑπ'ὀργῆς
411). The fierce anger the old man displays towards his son, expressed first as a refusal to speak to him, is twice described with
the word that recalls the baleful wrath of Achilles (μῆνιν 1328,
μηνίεις 1274)—a word which is used in the earlier play (OT 699)
to describe the wrath of the tyrannos towards Creon. Philoctetes
too rages in anger against Neoptolemos, who tells him later,
when he has returned the bow: "There is no ground now for
you to be angry at me" (ὀργὴν ἔχοις ἄν 1309). Antigone's
anger at Ismene, at Creon, at the chorus, is plain to see: "Your
self-willed temper has destroyed you" (αὐτόγνωτος . . . ὀργά
875), the chorus tells her. "I know," says Electra to the chorus,
"I know, I am aware of my own passion" (οὐ λάθει μ'ὀργά
222). "Nothing in anger, in the gods' name" (πρὸς ὀργήν 369),
says the chorus to her later, and Chrysothemis tells her: "Re-
strain your temper" (κατάσχες ὀργήν 1011). The chorus earlier
spoke of her 'too bitter wrath' (ὑπεραλγῆ χόλον 176), the same
word Athena used of the wrath of Ajax—'made grievous with
wrath' (χόλῳ βαρυνθείς 41).[47] Of the wrath of Oedipus at
Thebes little needs to be said; the word ὀργή in the sense of
'anger' occurs in various forms seven times in less than two
hundred lines.[48]

To the rest of the world, the hero's angry, stubborn temper
seems 'thoughtless, ill-counselled.' Chrysothemis twice urges
her sister not to come to grief through 'lack of thought, ill
counsel' ('ξ ἀβουλίας, ἀβουλίᾳ 398, 429). Jocasta calls the furious quarrel Oedipus provokes with Creon 'ill-advised' (ἄβουλον

634). And Antigone ironically adopts this term for her own conduct: "Leave me and my ill-counsel to suffer this dreadful fate" (τὴν ἐξ ἐμοῦ δυσβουλίαν 95). So Ajax is called 'ill-calculating'[49] (δυσλόγιστος 40) by Odysseus, though he shows later that he is perfectly capable of reflection and calculation (λογίζεσθαι 816), in his own terms. But the hero's temper seems more often not merely a failure to think out the right course of action, it appears to the surrounding world as something to be denounced in stronger terms, as 'mindless, senseless, mad' (ἄνους, ἄφρων). Ismene tells her sister that excessive, extraordinary action has no sense (νοῦν οὐδένα 68), and ends by calling her 'senseless' (ἄνους 99), the same word Creon applies to her later (ἄνουν 562). The chorus, when she is brought in under arrest, fears that she has been taken in 'madness' (ἀφροσύνῃ 383), and later attributes her daring action to 'foolishness of speech' (λόγου τ' ἄνοια 603). Calchas, the prophet, reported by the messenger in the *Ajax*, speaks of 'mindless bodies' (κἀνόητα σώματα 758). He means of course Ajax, and a few lines later we are told that Ajax proved 'senseless' (ἄνους 763), when his father gave him good advice, which he rejected 'mindlessly' (κἀφρόνως 766).[50] Chrysothemis, at the climax of her argument against Electra's determination to attack Aegisthus single-handed, bids her 'have some sense' (νοῦν σχές 1013), and the chorus, with its exhortation to Electra to be 'persuaded' by her sister, adds the sentiment that the best profit for human beings to acquire is forethought and a wise mind (νοῦ σοφοῦ 1016). "If you think that self-willed obstinancy without sense (τοῦ νοῦ χωρὶς OT 550) is a prized possession," Creon says to the *tyrannos*, and later at Colonus taunts the old Oedipus with an insulting phrase, "a mind like yours" (ὅτῳ γε νοῦς ἴσος καὶ σοὶ πάρα 810). The hero can even be described as μῶρος, 'foolish.' Even the gentle Theseus, appalled at Oedipus' rage against his own people, reproves him harshly with this word, "You fool" (ὦ μῶρε 592). Antigone knows that Creon will think her a fool (μῶρα δρῶσα τυγχάνειν 469) and casts the word back at him in advance (μώρῳ μωρίαν ὀφλισκάνω 470).[51]

But the condemnation of the heroic temper is moral as well as intellectual. To friends and enemies the hero's mood appears as 'overboldness, rashness, insolence, audacity'—τόλμη and θράσος. "Did you then have the audacity to break these laws?" (ἐτόλμας 449), says Creon to Antigone, and Antigone knows that in Creon's eyes she has shown 'dreadful daring' (δεινὰ τολμᾶν 915).[52] "Even the bold try to escape when they see death near" (χοἰ θρασεῖς 580), says Creon of Antigone, and the chorus tells her she has "advanced to the last limit of audacity" (ἐπ' ἔσχατον θράσους 853). So Odysseus speaks of Ajax' attempt on the chieftains as 'daring and rashness of heart' (τόλμαις . . . καὶ φρενῶν θράσει 46), and Teucer of Ajax' suicide as 'bitter rashness' (τόλμης πικρᾶς 1004). Neoptolemos, his patience ebbing, tells Philoctetes not to 'grow overbold' in his misfortunes (μὴ θρασύνεσθαι κακοῖς 1387). "You will not escape the consequences of this rash insolence" (θράσους/ τοῦδ' 626), says Clytemnestra to her daughter, and Chrysothemis asks her sister how she can "arm herself with such rash daring" (τοιοῦτον θράσος 995). Aegisthus, thinking he has won the day, gloats over Electra's defeat: "You who were so insolent and rash before this" (τὴν ἐν τῷ πάρος χρόνῳ θρασεῖαν 1446). Even stronger terms are used: ἄγριος, 'wild' like a beast; ὠμός, 'raw, savage'; σκληρός, 'hard' like metal.[53] "You have turned savage," says Neoptolemos to Philoctetes (σὺ δ' ἠγρίωσαι 1321), and Tiresias challenges Oedipus to rage 'in the wildest anger' (ἥτις ἀγριωτάτη 344) he can muster. Antigone's retort to Creon calls from the chorus the comment that she is "savage by birth as her father was" (ὠμὸν ἐξ ὠμοῦ πατρός 471), and Ajax is repeatedly described with this word (205, 885, 930) and proudly adopts it for himself (548). Polynices speaks of the 'hard' (σκληρά 1406) curses of his father; and Creon, with Antigone in mind, speaks of "tempers that are too hard" (σκλήρ' ἄγαν 473).

There is one word that is applied to them all, to describe their character and their action; δεινός, 'strange, dreadful, terrible.' "Dreadful to see, dreadful to hear" (δεινὸς μὲν ὁρᾶν, δεινὸς δὲ κλύειν 141), sings the chorus at their first sight of blind Oedipus in the grove of the Eumenides, and Philoctetes is described by the chorus as the 'strange and dreadful wayfarer' (δεινὸς ὁδίτης 147).[54] Antigone knows that Creon considers her attempt to bury her brother 'strange and dreadful daring' (δεινὰ τολμᾶν 915), and Creon, in the *Oedipus Tyrannus* speaks of the 'dreadful' words of accusation leveled at him by Oedipus (δειν' ἔπη 512), and tells Jocasta that Oedipus assumes the right to do 'dreadful things' (δεινὰ . . ./ δρᾶσαι 639) to him. "In strange and terrible circumstances," says Electra to the chorus, "I am constrained to strange and dreadful expedients" (δείν' ἐν δεινοῖς ἠναγκάσθην 221). Ajax is called by the chorus the 'dreadful, great, raw-powered Ajax' (δεινὸς μέγας ὠμοκρατής 205), and his speech to Athena is described as a 'dreadful word' (δεινὸν . . . ἔπος 773).[55]

They are δεινοί, strange, terrifying, because they have no sense of proportion, no capacity for moderation. "Your mourning," says the chorus to Electra, "abandons moderation for the impossible" (ἀπὸ τῶν μετρίων ἐπ' ἀμήχανον 140), and she answers them later with a cognate word, justifying herself with the claim that there is no measure, no proportion in the evil which surrounds her (τί μέτρον κακότατος ἔφυ; 236). The chorus sympathizes with Philoctetes, a man whose life is 'illproportioned' (οἷς μὴ μέτριος αἰών 179), but later, appalled at his stubbornness, they say to him sharply: "Show some moderation" (μετρίαζ' 1183). But this is what the heroes cannot do. They and their actions are 'outsized, extraordinary, prodigious'—περισσός.[56] "Outsized and mindless bodies" (περισσὰ κἀνόητα σώματα 758) is the phrase of the prophet Calchas for Ajax, and the chorus, trying to calm Electra, tells her that she is not the only human being to suffer loss. "You are not unique, singled out from your sisters in the house" (πρὸς ὅ τι σὺ τῶν ἔνδον εἶ περισσά 155). "Extraordinary action," says Ismene to Antigone (περισσὰ πράσσειν 68), "is senseless," and Creon uses the same word in a slightly extended sense when he condemns Antigone to a prison tomb: "Let her

learn there that reverence paid to Death's kingdom is labor
lost" (πόνος περισσός 780).

There is no dealing with such incorrigible natures. All that
can be hoped for is that in time they will realize what is good
for them. And this too is a formula which appears in every
confrontation of the hero with his advisers, a hope or threat
that the hero will be taught by time, and change his stubborn
mind, that he will 'realize' the truth—an idea frequently conveyed by the future or aorist dependent forms of γιγνώσκω
(γνώσομαι, γνῷ, etc.)—forms which have this special sense of
'realize that one is wrong, recognize the unwelcome truth.'[57]
Creon at Colonus is amazed that the blind beggar has apparently learned nothing in all the long years since he ruled
Thebes in power: "Not even time, it seems, has grown brains
in your head" (οὐδὲ τῷ χρόνῳ φύσας . . . φρένας 804). But
later he appeals to time: "In time, I know, you will realize this"
(χρόνῳ γὰρ . . . γνώσῃ τάδε 852). Antigone too speaks to him
in these same terms, when he refuses to listen to Polynices:
"You will realize what the final result of evil wrath is" (γνώσῃ
1197). In the earlier play Creon appeals to the tyrannos with
the same formula: "But in time you will realize this surely"
(ἐν χρόνῳ γνώσῃ 613). And when Creon condemns Antigone to
imprisonment he foresees that she will either die in the tomb
or "realize, at last though late, that reverence for the realm of
Hades is labor lost" (γνώσεται γοῦν ἀλλὰ τηνικαῦθ' 779).
"Realize, realize your situation well" (γνῶθ' εὖ γνῶθ' 1165), the
chorus sings to Philoctetes, and when Neoptolemos leaves him
he too hopes that time will change him. "Wait," he says to the
chorus, "so long a time as is needed for us to prepare the ship for
sea . . . and perhaps this man will meanwhile find a better
attitude towards us" (χρόνον τοσοῦτον . . . φρόνησιν . . .
λῴω 1076ff). "You refuse to be taught by the passing of time,"
says Chrysothemis to her sister (ἐν χρόνῳ μακρῷ διδαχθῆναι
330), and much later she tells her: "Get some sense even though
the time is late" (ἀλλὰ τῷ χρόνῳ ποτέ 1013). "Long time,"
she says in the argument against her sister's plan to attack

Aegisthus, "is left to judge between us" (χὠ λοιπὸς χρόνος 1030). But time is on Electra's side. And in her moment of victory she lures Aegisthus to his death with an ironic repetition of this phrase: "For in time I have got sense, so as to accommodate myself to my superiors" (τῷ γὰρ χρόνῳ 1464). When Ajax states the case for retreat and submission, he begins with the famous lines: "All things long uncounted time brings forth from darkness and hides again from light" (ὁ μακρὸς . . . χρόνος 646). "How shall we not realize that we must observe discipline?" he says later (πῶς οὐ γνωσόμεσθα σωφρονεῖν; 677). And the chorus, misled by his words, later echoes them. "All things the long expanse of time withers . . . Ajax has repented of his passion" (ὁ μέγας χρόνος . . . Αἴας μετανεγνώσθη θυμοῦ 717).

But the hope that time will teach the hero is never fulfilled; he remains unchanged. Oedipus *tyrannos*, it is true, does come to realize that he has been unjust to Creon (1420–1421), but by the end of the play he is the same imperious figure as he was at the beginning, issuing requests to Creon that are phrased like commands, rejecting persuasion, insisting on his own way; he even has to be reminded, in the last line of the play, that he is no longer *tyrannos* in Thebes.[58] Ajax, who states the case for time's dominance over man's life with such force and beauty, defies it; he goes passionately to his death to perpetuate a timeless hatred which will not be changed even in death's kingdom. Antigone, far from realizing in her dark prison that she was wrong to show reverence for the dead, hangs herself and thus brings about the utter ruin of Creon her enemy. Electra, triumphant in victory, can even mock the prophecy that time will teach her. Philoctetes, who was granted time by Neoptolemos so that he could 'come to a better frame of mind,' turns the tables and ends by persuading Neoptolemos to abandon his own dream of glory as the sacker of Troy and take him home to Oeta instead. And Oedipus at Colonus who in the first scene is a resigned, humble, feeble, old man, taught, as he says, by time (7), ends by condemning his enemies to defeat and his sons to death at each other's hand before he transcends human stature and time alike in his mysterious god-directed death.

Time and its imperative of change are in fact precisely what the Sophoclean hero defies; here is his real adversary, all-powerful Time, the master of us all, which, as Oedipus tells Theseus, dissolves all human things, man's body, his intellect, the work of his hands, the creations of his brain. Time is the condition and frame of our human existence, and to reject it is 'to be in love with the impossible.' But in Sophocles it is through this refusal to accept human limitations that humanity achieves its true greatness. It is a greatness achieved not with the help and encouragement of the gods, but through the hero's loyalty to his nature in trial, suffering, and death; a triumph purely human then, but one which the gods, in time, recognize and in which they surely, in their own far-off mysterious way, rejoice.

II

The Sophoclean Hero 2

To those who face him, friends and enemies alike, the hero seems unreasonable almost to the point of madness, suicidally bold, impervious to argument, intransigent, angry; an impossible person whom only time can cure. But to the hero himself the opinion of others is irrelevant. His loyalty to his conception of himself, and the necessity to perform the action that conception imposes, prevail over all other considerations.

These conceptions vary from one hero to another. Antigone justifies her defiance of public opinion and the polis in terms of εὐγένεια (38),[1] the claims of noble birth, of κλέος (502), her desire for glory, of εὐσέβεια (924, 943) her religious feelings. Electra's view of herself is similar, and she uses the same words: εὐγενής 257, εὔκλεια, κλέος 973, 985, εὐσέβεια 250. Ajax too cites the claims of noble birth (εὐγενῆ 480)[2] and mourns his present loss of glory (εὔκλειαν 436, 465) though he does not claim religious reverence.[3] Oedipus *tyrannos* is loyal to his own conception of himself as the man of action,[4] the revealer of truth (132), the solver of riddles (393 ff.). And at Colonus he sees himself as one who fulfills the oracles of Apollo and so satisfies his own desire for vengeance on Thebes and his sons. Philoctetes too has wrongs to revenge; he cannot contemplate the prospect of going to Troy, because it will help the enemies he has hated for so long.[5]

Their motives may differ, but the mood is the same in all of
them; they are driven by passion, θυμός, a rage of the soul.
Plato derives this word from θύω,[6] to seethe, to rage, a word
used of winds, fire, and the sea. It is the dominant element in
the heroes; passionate intensity deafens them to the appeal to
reason.[7] Not that they cannot use their minds; on the contrary,
Oedipus, for one, has a brilliant intellect, and even Ajax can
debate the case for life or death with eloquence and force. But
they do not *want* to listen to reason; they obey instead the deep
imperative of their passionate natures. "You fool," says
Theseus to Oedipus, "passion (θυμός 592) is no advantage in
misfortune." It may be no advantage, but it cannot be restrained. Oedipus speaks of his θυμός in former days as 'boiling'
(ἔζει 434) and 'running out of control' (ἐκδραμόντα 438), but
it is still as fierce now, and Creon says bitterly that there is no
old age for the θυμός (954) of Oedipus but death.[8] Creon speaks
of Antigone as a 'spirited horse' (θυμουμένους 477), and both
Creon and Tiresias speak of the θυμός of Oedipus *tyrannos*.
"Rage in your anger," says the prophet to him (θυμοῦ 344),
and Creon calls him "harsh, when you reach excess of passion"
(θυμοῦ περάσῃς 674).[9] "Ajax," sings the chorus in its ignorance,
"has repented of his passion" (μετανεγνώσθη/ θυμοῦ 717). "Do
not give way to passion when you hear" (μὴ θυμοῦ 922), says
Neoptolemos to Philoctetes, and Electra is told not to 'gratify
her passion' (θυμῷ . . . χαρίζεσθαι 331) by her sister, and by
the chorus that she generates 'new wars' with her 'harsh-
passioned soul' (δυσθύμῳ . . . ψυχᾷ 218–219).

Their passionate nature is exasperated by the feeling which
all of them have (and with some grounds) that they are treated
'disrespectfully,' ἀτίμως. Their sense of their own worth, of
what is due them from others, is outraged; they are denied
τιμή—not so much 'honor,' which in English has a connotation
of extra consideration for achievement, as simply 'respect,' the
consideration due to the individual's rights and stature as a
human being. This word ἄτιμος is a recurring feature of the
description of the hero's situation. Philoctetes, who, as he

proudly says, sailed a volunteer for Troy with seven ships, voices his indignation at the Atridae with this word: "They threw me ashore, without consideration" (ἄτιμον 1028). So Ajax cries in anger: "Here I lie, without respect" (ἄτιμος 426); "I perish, disregarded by the Achaeans" (ἄτιμος 440). When he thinks in his mad fit that he has killed his enemies, he boasts: "Those men will never treat Ajax disrespectfully again" (οὔποτ' . . . ἀτιμάσουσ' ἔτι 98). Oedipus at Colonus, denied the sanctuary he was promised, calls on the chorus not to show 'disrespect' (μηδέ . . . ἀτιμάσῃς 286); later he claims that he was expelled from Thebes 'so disrespectfully' (οὕτως ἀτίμως 428), and curses his sons so that they may learn "not to treat their father without respect" (μὴ 'ξατιμάζητον 1378).[10] Antigone tells Ismene that Creon has treated their brother 'without respect' (ἀτιμάσας 22),[11] and Tiresias later tells Creon that he has 'disrespectfully' (ἀτίμως 1069) settled a living soul, Antigone, in the tomb. Orestes is appalled at his sister's appearance, so 'ruthlessly misused'[12] (ἀτίμως . . . ἐφθαρμένον 1181), and after the murder of Clytemnestra tells Electra that her mother's fierce spirit will never 'treat her disrespectfully' again (μηκέτ' . . . ἀτιμάσει ποτέ 1427). Even Oedipus *tyrannos*, who is at first treated with all the respect due to a successful and autocratic ruler, accuses Tiresias of 'disrespect' (ἀτιμάζεις 340), and speaks of Creon's supposed conspiracy as an attempt to expel him 'unrespected' (ἄτιμον 670) from the country. Later he fears, as he probes closer to the dreadful truth, that he will lose the respect of others when that truth is known. He comforts himself: "I shall not be held in disrespect" (οὐκ ἀτιμασθήσομαι 1081).

Worse than the general lack of respect for their acts, persons, and attitudes, is the extreme expression of it: mockery, laughter; even if the hero does not experience this face to face he imagines it in his moments of brooding despair.[13] Philoctetes is obsessed with the thought that he is a laughingstock for his enemies, for the Atridae (γελῶσι 258), for Odysseus (γελᾷ μου 1125), for Neoptolemos (γελώμενος πρὸς σοῦ 1023). Ajax' greatest torment is the thought of his enemies' laughter at the ignominious failure of his attempt on them[14] (οἴμοι γέλωτος 367, ἐπεγγελῶσιν 454), especially the laughter of Odysseus (πολὺν γέλωθ' 382); his partisans, the chorus (198, 959, 1043) and Tecmessa (969) harp on the same theme. Electra in her grief at the news of Orestes' death is tormented by the thought of the laughter of her enemies (γελῶσι 1153), and she has actually seen the smile on the face of her mother (ἐγγελῶσα 807).[15] Antigone turns from the chorus with a bitter cry, "I am mocked" (οἴμοι γελῶμαι 839). And Oedipus *tyrannos* in his fall fears the mockery of Creon, who magnanimously disclaims any such intention (οὐχ ὡς γελαστής 1422) but cannot refrain from sarcasm a few moments later (1445).[16] Only the dreadful figure of the blind, cursing, prophetic old man at Colonus is an exception; he neither fears nor inspires laughter in those who face him.[17]

The disrespect and mockery of the world lock them even more securely in the prison of their passionate hearts, fill them with fierce resentment against those they regard as responsible for their sufferings. Their anger takes the form of appeals for vengeance, of curses on their enemies. Ajax in his last speech calls on the Erinyes to punish the sons of Atreus, and then, his wrath widening, he calls on them to feed on the whole Greek army, to spare none (835–844). Electra calls on them too, repeatedly, to avenge her murdered father and herself (112 ff., cf. 276, 491), and Oedipus at Colonus invokes the Eumenides in his curse on Creon and the even more terrible curse he pronounces on his son. Antigone, the guard tells Creon, cursed those who disturbed the dust she sprinkled on her brother's corpse, and at the end, no longer sure the gods are on her side, she accepts her fate, if they approve (925), but prays that if she is right, Creon will suffer the same injustice he has used against her (927–928). Philoctetes mouths curses from one end of the play to the other; he curses the Atridae and Odysseus many times (315, 791, 1019, 1035, 1040, 1112 ff.) and Neoptolemos twice (962, 1286).[18] And Oedipus at Thebes hurls his curse at the man who saved his life for such a dreadful destiny (1349 ff.). For most of them no more dreadful curse can be imagined than that their enemies should experience exactly what they are suffering in their own persons. Antigone wishes Creon "no more evil than what he unjustly inflicts" on her (927–928). Philoctetes prays that Odysseus and the Atridae may feel the pain of his own sickness (791 ff.) and the long years of his suffering (1114), and that the Atridae may be, as he has been, abandoned on a desert island and given the rags and scant food they left him (275).[19] Ajax prays that the Atridae may die, like him, by their own hands (840 ff.), and Oedipus at Colonus provokes from Creon a furious outcry by wishing him an old age like his own (869–870).

The hero is a lonely figure; he is $\mu\acute{o}\nu os$ 'alone,' $\acute{e}\rho\tilde{\eta}\mu os$ 'abandoned, deserted.' The consequence of his intransigence is that isolation which has so often been described as the mark of the Sophoclean hero. Antigone is alone in her attitude, as Creon tells her in front of the chorus, which does not contradict him ($\mu o\acute{v}\nu\eta$ 508); she is the 'only one' ($\mu\acute{o}\nu\eta\nu$ 656) in the city to disobey him; she is finally buried alive, alone ($\mu\acute{o}\nu\eta$ 821, cf. 887, 919, 941, $\acute{e}\rho\tilde{\eta}\mu os$ 773). Electra is alone in her defiant mourning for her father and her opposition to her mother ($\mu o\acute{v}\nu\eta$ 119); more alone still when she decides to do Orestes' work, and attack Aegisthus ($\mu\acute{o}\nu\eta$ 1019, $\mu\acute{o}\nu a$ 1074). Oedipus at Thebes cuts himself off from Tiresias, then Creon, is finally deserted by the chorus (873 ff.) and Jocasta (1071), but pushes on alone to the discovery of the truth. And at Colonus he is at first rejected with horror by the chorus (226), reproved by Theseus (592), threatened by Creon (874 ff.), and ends his earthly career by cursing his sons, before he goes off to die, alone ($\acute{e}\rho\tilde{\eta}\mu os$ $\acute{e}\theta a\nu es$ 1714). Ajax' whole career has been that of a man who acts and fights alone ($\mu\acute{o}\nu os$ 29, 47, 294, 1276, 1283), and he goes off in the last moments of his life to find a deserted place, untrodden ($\dot{a}\sigma\tau\iota\beta\tilde{\eta}$ 657),[20] to die, alone. Philoctetes is of course the loneliest of all; he has lived for almost ten years abandoned and alone on a desert island ($\beta\rho o\tau o\tilde{\iota}s$ $\dot{a}\sigma\tau\iota\pi\tau os$ 2), and to the physical loneliness, imposed on him by others, which he has so long endured (μόνος 172, 183, 227, 286, ἐρῆμος 228, 265, 269, 1018), he now adds the loneliness he deliberately chooses (μόνος 954, ἐρῆμος 1070).

The hero is isolated, but not only from men; he also abandons, or feels himself abandoned by, the gods. Ajax knows that Athena is his enemy: "I am hateful to the gods" (457), he says, and "I owe nothing to them in the way of service any more" (590, cf. 397 ff.). Oedipus *tyrannos* scorns the prophecies of Apollo's oracle (964), and counts himself the "son of Chance" (1080). Philoctetes, faced with the depressing catalogue of the deaths of all the Achaeans he admired and the triumphs of those he hated, finds the gods 'base, evil' (κακούς 452, cf. 1020). Even Electra's faith that the gods will avenge her father falters at the news of Orestes' death; when the chorus calls on the thunderbolts of Zeus and the shining sun she starts to protest and they warn her to say nothing rash: "No big words" (830).[21] Antigone in her final speech doubts that the gods are on her side: "Why should I in my misfortune look to the gods any more?" (922). And even Oedipus at Colonus, though confirmed in his belief that he has come to his destined place of rest, shows signs of bitterness towards heaven; told by Ismene that the gods who were working his ruin before now raise him up, he replies: "It is a paltry thing to raise up in old age a man who fell in his youth" (395).[22]

This isolation is so total that the hero, in his moments of deepest despair, speaks neither to man nor to gods, but to the landscape, that unchanging presence which alone will not betray him.[23] Philoctetes, when his appeal to Neoptolemos meets only with embarrassed silence, speaks to the island, which, as his beautiful last farewell speech shows, he has come to love. "You harbors, headlands, you wild beasts of the mountains, my companions, you jagged rocks, to you I appeal, accustomed presences, for I do not know who else to speak to . . ." (οὐ γὰρ ἄλλον οἶδ' ὅτῳ λέγω 938). "You cleft in the hollow rock, hot in summer, cold in winter, so I was never to leave

you, you will be present at my death"[24] (1081 ff.). So Ajax
addresses his last words to the sun, the light, the rock of
Salamis, to Athens, and to the streams, plains, and rivers of
Troy which have seen his glory in battle. "Farewell, you who
raised me. This is his last word, Ajax says it to you" (864).[25]
Electra first appears singing her song of mourning (and not for
the first time, as she tells us—πολλὰς . . . ᾠδὰς 88)—to the
elements: "O holy light and air, you two equal partners who
share the earth between you" (ὦ φάος ἁγνὸν/ καὶ . . .
γῆς ἰσόμοιρ᾽ ἀήρ 86 ff.). Oedipus at Thebes, when his hard-won
knowledge of his identity makes him the loneliest man on earth,
speaks to Mount Cithairon, to the three roads and the hidden
valley where he killed his father (1391, 1398 ff.).[26] Antigone,
just before she is led off to her living tomb, mocked, as she
proclaims, by the chorus, addresses the streams and groves of
her native city (844 ff.), and a few moments later, the tomb in
the rock which is to be her marriage chamber (ὦ τύμβος ὦ
νυμφεῖον ὦ κατασκαφὴς οἴκησις 891).

In his total alienation from the world of men the hero turns
his back on life itself and wishes, passionately, for death. This
is the constant refrain of Ajax, the subject of all his intense and
brooding speeches. He begs the chorus to kill him (361), invokes Zeus to fulfill his heroic prayer that he may kill his
enemies and then die himself (387 ff.), and calls on the darkness
of Erebos to give him a home (394 ff.). He decides, in a reasoned
discussion of the possibilities open to him, for death (479), and
comes to the same conclusion after Tecmessa's appeal for pity
has moved him to reconsider (684 ff.). He is a man 'intent on
death' (ὃς σπεύδει θανεῖν 812), 'in love with death' (ὦν γὰρ
ἠράσθη τυχεῖν . . . θάνατον 967), his heart yearns for death
(τοὐμὸν ὦν ἐρᾷ κέαρ 686)[27] and he sees his sword, in his farewell
speech, as his greatest friend (εὐνούστατον τῷδ᾽ ἀνδρί 822).[28]
He calls on Death himself (ὦ θάνατε θάνατε, νῦν μ᾽ ἐπίσκεψαι
854), inviting him to come and 'oversee' his suicide. Ajax of
course is a man who, given his proud nature and the ignominious failure of his attack on his enemies, can contemplate no

other course, but other Sophoclean heroes, gentler in character
and in circumstances less urgent, echo his words. Electra, when
she believes that Orestes is dead, speaks of the 'favor' (χάρις
821) that would be granted her if someone would kill her; she
has no desire for life (τοῦ βίου δ' οὐδεὶς πόθος 822). When she
resolves to act alone, the chorus praises her contempt for her
own life; she "cares nothing for death, she is ready to leave life"
(οὔτε τι τοῦ θανεῖν προμηθὴς τό τε μὴ βλέπειν ἑτοίμα 1078-
1080). And in the excess of her mourning over the urn which
she believes contains Orestes' ashes, she wishes to join him in
death, to share his tomb (1165 ff.). Antigone makes light of the
death she risks, dismissing it in a sarcastic phrase to Ismene—
"what you call dreadful" (τὸ δεινὸν τοῦτο 96)—and accepts it
as a glory (72); she even tells Creon that for her to die young
is a 'gain' (κέρδος 462), and proudly reminds Ismene: "You
chose life but I chose death" (555). Oedipus at Thebes, the only
powerful and successful figure in the entire gallery of Sophoclean heroes (and the only one who fits Aristotle's definition—
a man in high repute and good fortune), wishes for death when
it begins to appear that he may be the murderer of Laius (βαίην
ἄφαντος 832); later he calls for a sword (1255), though he stops
short of suicide. In his agony after he has blinded himself he
wishes that he had died, a crippled infant, on the mountain
long ago (1349), and begs now to be left to dwell on the mountains, to die (1451). Philoctetes, in the spasms of pain brought
on by his disease, begs twice to be killed (749, 800), attempts
suicide when he realizes he has been trapped by Odysseus
(1001), begs the sailors of the chorus for a sword, an axe, any
weapon, to kill himself (1207), and when Neoptolemos, restored
to his confidence, tries to persuade him to do what is best for
him, reproaches his 'hateful life' for keeping him on earth
(1348-1349). He too, like Ajax, calls on Death in person: "O
Death, Death, why is it that though I call on you continually
you never come . . . ?" (ὦ θάνατε θάνατε, πῶς ἀεὶ καλούμενος
. . . 796). Oedipus at Colonus has come there to die; he recognizes his promised place of rest. And in his last moments on

stage, as he goes off to meet his longed-for end, the speed and sureness of his movements and the urgent exaltation of his language show us a man utterly transformed from the stumbling, complaining old man of the opening scenes.

The hero chooses death. This is after all the logical end of his refusal to compromise. Life in human society is one long compromise; we live, all of us, only by constantly subduing our own will, our own desires, to the demands of others, expressed as the law of the community or the opinion of our fellowmen. We learn this lesson in childhood or, more expensively, later; those who fail to learn it end as criminals or madmen. But in Sophoclean tragedy the hero faces an issue on which he cannot compromise and still respect himself. Surrender would be spiritual self-destruction, a betrayal of his *physis;* the hero is forced to choose between defiance and loss of identity. And in the Sophoclean hero the sense of identity, of independent, individual existence, is terribly strong. They are, all of them, exquisitely conscious of their difference from others, of their uniqueness. They have a profound sense of their own worth as individuals, and this exasperates the anger they feel at the world's denial of respect. In the crisis of their lives, abandoned by friends, ringed by enemies, unsupported by the gods, they have nothing to fall back on for support but this belief in themselves, their conception of their own unique character and destiny.

This point has to be emphasized because much modern criticism of Sophoclean tragedy tends to deny its validity. There has been a reaction, necessary and desirable, against nineteenth-century psychological analysis which in the discussion of Sophoclean characters (and Shakespearian too) went to such excess of depth analysis that it could even discuss, seriously and at length, feelings and motives not referred to in the text, which had to be 'reconstructed,' inferred from a full imaginary biography of the dramatic character.[29] The pendulum has swung back, and of course it began by swinging back too far (the influential book of Tycho von Wilamowitz came close to denying cohesion of character altogether); but it has still not yet righted itself entirely. In the work of some of the subtlest and most imaginative modern critics the prevailing tendency is still to smooth down the jagged individuality of the Sophoclean characters, and to exclude the modern idea of dramatic character completely. Albin Lesky, whose brilliant critical insight and immense learning have combined to produce what are perhaps the most important modern judgments on Sophocles, has discussed this problem at length and with great subtlety; he quotes with approval two formulas which attempt to find a midpoint between the extreme views of Sophoclean figures, as 'types' and 'characters.' The first is the view of Wilhelm Humboldt, who says of Sophoclean characterization: "Everything too individual is despised and deliberately avoided. Not the individual but the human being is to appear, in the precisely distinguished but simple traits of his character."[30] And the second is Gerbert Cysarz' formulation of the 'classic concept of personality': "Personality instead of just interesting individuality, norm instead of the eccentric and bizarre."[31] Both formulations are at first sight attractive; they seem to exactly differentiate the Sophoclean characters from those of Euripides, and to fit the Sophoclean figures into the frame of that classic ideal embodied in the sculptures of the Parthenon. They are subtle formulas of compromise between the misguided attempt to construct from the plays what Lesky wittily dismisses as 'mosaic-type character portraits' and the opposing view that Sophoclean heroes, like "most women" in Pope, "have no characters at all."[32] And yet they do not suffice. "Nicht der einzelne sondern der Mensch," is a phrase that does not leave enough room for Ajax' unrepentant glorification of the violence that has brought him to the necessity of suicide, for Oedipus' terrible curse on his son, for Antigone's last speech, which has seemed to many critics to show exactly what Cysarz excludes—'Apartheit und Bizarrerie.' The formulas leave little place for that irreducible center of particularity, of uniqueness, which in the last analysis (and Antigone's speech is precisely that) is the only source of the heroic will to defy the world.[33]

This uniqueness, this sharply differentiated individuality, is something of which the Sophoclean heroes are fully aware, indeed, they insist on it. Ajax has no doubt of his difference from the Greek chieftains. He claims to be "a man such that Troy saw no other like him in the host which came from Greek soil" (οἷον οὔτινα Τροία στρατοῦ δέρχθη 423–425). He has no doubt that Achilles, a rebel like himself, would have recognized his superiority (441 ff.). He is so sure of his rightness and greatness that even in disaster, surrounded by the mangled animals he has tortured and butchered in his fit of madness, he has no other wish for his infant son than this: that he should be like his father. "He must without delay be broken and trained in his father's wild ways, be made like him in nature. My son, may you be luckier than your father, but in everything else the same" (τὰ δ' ἄλλ' ὁμοῖος 551). Later he tells Tecmessa she is a fool if she thinks she can "educate his character" (ἦθος . . . παιδεύειν 595). And others recognize his individuality. "His death," says Tecmessa, "is bitter for me, sweet for his enemies, but joy for him" (αὐτῷ δὲ τερπνός 967). "What he yearned to have, he has got for himself"—(ἐκτήσαθ' αὐτῷ 968)—"the death he wanted." And to his first speech with its resolve for death and its harsh conclusion—"you have heard all I have to say"—the chorus replies: "No one could say that it was not a genuine speech of yours; it was from your own heart" (ὑπόβλητον λόγον[34] . . . ἀλλὰ τῆς σαυτοῦ φρενός 481–482). The speech is 'in character.'

Electra, the most self-analytical of all the Sophoclean heroes, is fully aware of her uniqueness; she can feel shame at the outrageous conduct to which it sometimes drives her (254, 616 ff.), but also a fierce pride in her independence of spirit. She loses no chance to emphasize the difference between herself and her sister: "*You* can cringe and fawn. Those are not *my* ways" (οὐκ ἐμοὺς τρόπους λέγεις 397). "I do not want to live by *those* laws" (τούτοις . . . τοῖς νόμοις 1043), she says when Chrysothemis urges prudence. She casts scorn on her sister for not being herself: "Your reproof of me," she says, "is a lesson you learn from *her;* nothing you say is from yourself" (ἐκ σαυτῆς 344). Oedipus *tyrannos* too is aware of his own extraordinary character and capacities; he announces himself as "Oedipus whom all men call famous" (ὁ πᾶσι κλεινὸς Οἰδίπους καλούμενος 8). He reminds Tiresias that the riddle of the Sphinx, a problem for prophets, was solved instead by an untrained amateur; "But *I* came, know-nothing Oedipus, and put a stop to it" (ἐγὼ μολὼν ὁ μηδὲν εἰδὼς 396 ff.). When Jocasta leaves him with the wish that he may never find out who he is, he proudly proclaims his nature and his identity. The son of Chance. "With such a parentage, I shall never turn out to be someone else, so as not to learn the secret of my birth" (οὐκ ἂν ἐξέλθοιμ' ἔτι ποτ' ἄλλος 1084–1085). Even in the agony of his new-found knowledge and his ruined eyes, he asserts his individual responsibility. "It was Apollo . . . who brought these evils to completion. . . . But the hand that struck my eyes was mine alone" (ἔπαισε δ' αὐτόχειρ νιν οὔτις ἀλλ' ἐγώ 1331–1332). And later he sees himself as one apart, reserved for some mysterious destiny. "No disease, nor anything else can wreck me. For I would never have been saved from death, except for some dreadful evil" (1455 ff.). Antigone too is fiercely protective of her independence and quick to resent any affront, real or fancied, to her personality.[35] She speaks of Creon's decree as a personal insult. "He has made a proclamation to you and to me, yes I say to *me*" (λέγω γὰρ κἀμέ 32), she says to Ismene, and like Electra she stresses at every point the difference between herself and her sister. "You be what you decide, but *I* . . ." (ἀλλ' ἴσθ' ὁποῖά σοι δοκεῖ . . . 71), she says to her, and, "You chose to live but I to die" (555). She later justifies her attempt to bury Polynices with arguments so strange that many scholars have been driven to question their authenticity; she is indeed 'a law unto herself' (αὐτόνομος 821) as the chorus says of her. Philoctetes, a man who has for ten years lived by his wits on a desert island and brooded on his wrongs, is very conscious of his own identity. He is proud of the courage and endurance which have kept him alive (ὥς τ' ἔφυν εὐκάρδιος 535),[36] and aware too of his uniqueness in those qualities. "No one but me could have stood even the sight of what I have suffered," he tells Neoptolemos (οἶμαι γὰρ οὐδ' ἂν ὄμμασιν μόνον θέαν/ ἄλλον λαβόντα πλὴν ἐμοῦ τλῆναι τάδε 536–537). Deceived and deprived of the bow he cries indignantly: "He would not have taken me if I had my health—not even sick like this, except by treachery" (947–948). He sees that the young man who deceived him is not acting from his own impulse, but contrary to his nature; "Be yourself" (ἐν σαυτοῦ γενοῦ 950), he says to him. And in the final interview between them, when the truth is told him, his resentment at the wrongs done him by his enemies, the idea that he will have to work and fight side by side with them, is too much; he asks his eyes: "How will you be able to stand the sight of me associating with the sons of Atreus?" (1354–1355). Oedipus at Colonus, who begins with little or no personality at all, a resigned humble old man, swiftly rises to such heights of anger, authoritative prophecy, and vindictive imprecation that even his friends and daughters are appalled; not content with proclaiming himself a savior, he obstinately defends not only his present resolution to die on Attic soil but also the fearful actions of his past; he is indeed, to use his own words, a 'dread nature' (αἰνὰ φύσις 212).

They all have the fierce sense of independence of the thorny individual; they will not be ruled, no one shall have power over them, or treat them as a slave, they are free. Electra's complaint is that she is 'ruled' (κἀκ τῶνδ' ἄρχομαι 264) by her enemies, that she is enslaved to them by force (τοῖσδε δουλεύω βίᾳ 1192). Orestes was her hope of freedom, but the report of his death means she 'must be a slave again' (δεῖ με δουλεύειν πάλιν 814), and she appeals to her sister to act with her and 'be called free in future' (ἐλευθέρα καλῇ 970).[37] Ismene tells her father that the Thebans will bury him where he will not have power over himself (μηδ' ἵν' ἂν σαυτοῦ κρατῇς 405), but he protests, "Then they shall never have power over me" (οὐκ . . . ἐμοῦ γε μὴ κρατήσωσίν ποτε 408), and later appeals to Theseus: "Let no one have power over my life" (μηδεὶς κρατείτω 1207). Antigone is urged by Ismene to remember that "we are ruled by the stronger" (ἀρχόμεσθ᾽ ἐκ κρεισσόνων 63), but she is later described by Creon as wanting "to give orders to those in authority" (τοὐπιτάσσειν τοῖς κρατύνουσιν 664), although she is 'the slave' (δοῦλος 479) of others.[38] Ajax, in his argument for surrender, speaks of the Atridae as "rulers, so we must give in to them" (ἄρχοντές εἰσιν 668), but nothing is farther from his thoughts. Teucer claims repeatedly that Ajax was not under the orders of the Atridae; he was 'commander himself' (αὐτὸς ἄρχων 1234), he was 'in command of himself' (αὐτοῦ κρατῶν 1099).[39] The Atridae admit that they could never rule him. "We shall rule him dead" (θανόντος γ᾽ ἄρξομεν 1068) . . . "we could not control him living" (βλέποντος . . . κρατεῖν 1067). Philoctetes, faced with the brutal "You must obey" of Odysseus, bursts out: "My father brought me into the world as a slave, I see, not a free man" (δούλους . . . οὐδ᾽ ἐλευθέρους 995-996), and tries to take his own life by leaping from the rocks.

The choice, as the hero sees it, is between freedom and slavery. In these circumstances, to give way is 'intolerable.' To go home from Troy without glory is for Ajax 'unbearable' (οὐκ ἔστι . . . τλητόν 466); death is better. Philoctetes reacts to Odysseus' threats in similar terms, "Unbearable!" (ταῦτα δῆτ᾽ ἀνασχετά; 987), and later, when he rejects the arguments of Neoptolemos, asks his eyes how they will be able to 'bear' (ἐξανασχήσεσθε 1355) the sight of him associating with his enemies at Troy. "If I had borne (ἠνσχόμην 467) to leave my brother's corpse unburied," says Antigone to Creon, "*that* would have given me pain." Oedipus at Colonus speaks of his son's voice as the one voice among all those in the world that he could 'bear' to hear only with the utmost pain (ἐξανασχοίμην κλύων 1174). And at Thebes he finds Tiresias' words 'intolerable' (ταῦτα δῆτ᾽ ἀνεκτά; 429).[40]

All of us at times may find the advice of others or the demands of a situation 'intolerable,' may assert our will in the face of opposition. But the hero does so all the way, to the absolute end of such a defiance, which is death. It is no accident that the plays of Sophocles contain so many suicides. In all the seven plays of Aeschylus which have been preserved there is not one (though the Suppliants threaten suicide and Ajax, in a lost play, certainly committed it); in all the surviving plays of Euripides there are only four;[41] but in the seven plays of Sophocles there are no less than six: Ajax, Antigone, Haemon, Eurydice, Deianira, and Jocasta—and in addition Philoctetes attempts suicide on stage, Oedipus *tyrannos* asks for a sword to kill himself, and Oedipus at Colonus prays for death in the opening scene of the play and goes swiftly and joyfully to it at the end. The world as it is, life as it is lived, refuses them freedom to be what they are, and they are ready to leave it rather than to change.

The Sophoclean hero sets his own conditions for existence. "Your father should have begot you on previously agreed terms" (ἐπὶ ῥητοῖς 459), says the Nurse to Phaedra in the *Hippolytus* of Euripides, "if you will not acquiesce in these laws." The phrase could be applied to the Sophoclean hero too. They will live only on their own terms. They are, to use Ismene's phrase to Antigone, "in love with the impossible" (ἀμηχάνων ἐρᾷς 90).[42]

"The man who is incapable of working in common," says Aristotle in a famous sentence of the *Politics* (1253a), "or who in his self-sufficiency has no need of others, is no part of the community (πόλεως), like an animal, or a god" (θηρίον ἢ θεός). Most of the Sophoclean heroes are referred to in words that implicitly or explicitly compare them to wild animals. Ajax is presented to us in the images used by Odysseus and Athena in the prologue as a wild beast tracked to his lair (κυναγῶ etc. 5, 37; ἴχνη etc. 6, 20, 32) or in the trap (ἕρκη 60); he is repeatedly described as ὠμός 'wild, savage' (205, 885, 930) and himself adopts and glorifies in the word (548) and its implications.[43] Antigone too has this word applied to her by the chorus after her violent dismissal of Creon's decree (γέννημ' ὠμὸν 471).

Philoctetes begs the startled Neoptolemos and his sailors not to be frightened at his 'wild' appearance (ἀπηγριωμένον 226), and later Neoptolemos tells him he has 'turned savage' (σύ δ᾽ ἠγρίωσαι 1321). So Tiresias tells Oedipus to rage "in the most savage anger you can muster" (ὀργῆς ἥτις ἀγριωτάτη 344), and the chorus in that same play, speculating on the identity of the murderer of Laius (it is of course Oedipus himself) sing of him as a wild bull of the rocks roaming in the wild forest among the caves (ὑπ᾽ ἀγρίαν ὕλαν . . . πετραῖος ὁ ταῦρος 478). Clytemnestra talks to Electra as to a wild animal that has escaped from the cage: "So you are at large and roaming loose again?" (ἀνειμένη μὲν . . . αὖ στρέφῃ 516),[44] and Creon uses the same word of Antigone and her sister: "They must be tied up, not allowed to run loose" (μηδ᾽ ἀνειμένας 579). Ajax, the chorus sings, is "marked as a victim to a hateful destiny" (ἀνεῖται στυγερῷ δαίμονι 1214); the word means literally 'allowed to roam free' like a sacrificial beast that is loosed to graze in a compound until its hour comes.[45] Creon expects to break Antigone's resistance and expresses his confidence in the phrase, "with a small bridle the most spirited horses are broken" (477), and he speaks too of his opponents as men who will not bow their necks beneath the yoke (291).[46]

"A beast," says Aristotle, "or a god" (θηρίον ἢ θεός). The heroes refuse to accept the limitations imposed on human beings by their mortality, resist the strong imperatives of time and circumstance—all things change, but they will not—and this is an assumption of divinity. Only the gods are eternal and unchanging; "everything else," as Oedipus tells Theseus, "is confounded by all-powerful time" (OC 609). Ajax is twice emphatically described as one who "does not think according to his limitations as a man" (οὐ κατ᾽ ἄνθρωπον φρονῶν 777 cf. 761). Antigone is reproved by the chorus for her attempt to compare herself with "those who are equal to the gods" (τοῖς ἰσοθέοις 837), with that Niobe whom Electra also emulates and whom she "counts as a god" (σὲ δ᾽ ἔγωγε νέμω θεόν 150). Oedipus at Thebes in one way after another assumes the tone and language of a god[47] and ends by proclaiming himself the 'son of Chance,' own brother to the months, the peer of Time (1080 ff.). Philoctetes by his obstinate refusal to go to Troy seems, just before the end of the play, to have changed the course of history, falsified divine prediction, and thwarted the will of Zeus; it takes a god in person, descending from his heavenly abode, to set matters right. And we do not need the hint contained in Theseus' question to Oedipus at Colonus— "What is this more than human suffering you are subject to?" (μεῖζον ἢ κατ' ἄνθρωπον 598)—to feel that the blind man is turning before our eyes into something that can no longer be measured in human terms.

Such is the strange and awesome character who, in six of the Sophoclean tragedies, commands the stage.[48] Immovable once his decision is taken, deaf to appeals and persuasion, to reproof and threat, unterrified by physical violence, even by the ultimate violence of death itself, more stubborn as his isolation increases until he has no one to speak to but the unfeeling landscape, bitter at the disrespect and mockery the world levels at what it regards as failure, the hero prays for revenge and curses his enemies as he welcomes the death that is the predictable end of his intransigence. It is an extraordinary figure, this Sophoclean tragic hero, and though it is clear that it was in the drama of Sophocles that it 'found its natural form,' to use Aristotle's phrase, we shall expect to find its source in the work of his predecessors.

It is often stated that the first extant play which introduces to us the figure of the tragic hero is the *Seven Against Thebes* of Aeschylus.[49] Certainly Eteocles dominates the action, but it is hard to find in this play the germ of the Sophoclean conception. Apart from the fact that the bulk of the play, the description of the champions, is not action in the Sophoclean sense of the word at all,[50] Eteocles is not placed in the Sophoclean situation of resistance to persuasion and threat. In fact, he makes his resolution (the decision to fight Polynices), at the end of the play, and the short scene in which the chorus attempts to dissuade him (677–719) is couched in language which has almost no point of contact with the typical formulas of such a scene in Sophocles.[51] And so in the *Suppliants*, the *Persians*, and the *Oresteia*; the situation of the hero is not the same, and though of course many verbal parallels occur[52] they are even less than might be expected in view of the facts that the two dramatists were contemporaries, competitors in fact, that they wrote in the same high, formal style appropriate to the genre, that they presented in one case the same mythical material in extant plays,[53] and lastly that many of the words we have described as Sophoclean formula are common basic elements of the vocabulary. Nowhere in these plays does one find a real parallel; there is no scene where one recognizes over an extended passage the Sophoclean situation and the language associated with it.

But there is one Aeschylean play, the *Prometheus Bound*, which does show a remarkable resemblance to Sophoclean tragedy. Though the central scenes of the play, the long descriptions of Prometheus' services, first to Zeus and then to mankind, the even longer descriptions of the past, present and future of Io, are not action in the sense Sophocles conceived it, the dramatic framework of all this narrative and prophecy shows a striking resemblance to Sophoclean character and dramaturgy. The hero, like Philoctetes, like Oedipus at Colonus, is fixed, in this case literally, in one place; the action is a sequence of visits by others who come to deceive, persuade, or threaten.[54] The dramatic power of the play has its source in the efforts to break his resolution and their failure. But the resemblance is even more striking. Many of the Sophoclean formulas for this situation appear in the *Prometheus Bound*, used exactly as they are used by Sophocles, and this is the only Aeschylean play of which this can be said.[55]

The hero is isolated, more so even than Philoctetes; Lemnos is sometimes visited by sailors off their course,[56] but Prometheus is impaled on a neighborless, deserted rock (ἐρήμου . . .

ἀγείτονος πάγου 270)[57] in the 'uninhabited wilderness' (ἄβροτον . . . ἐρημίαν 2) of Scythia. He is punished 'so that he may be taught' (ὡς ἂν διδαχθῇ 10) to 'acquiesce' (στέργειν 11) in the overlordship of Zeus, so that he 'may learn' (ἵνα μάθῃ 62) that sophistes though he is, he is weaker than Zeus. When his tormentors have left him, the hero adresses the landscape: "O shining air and swift-winged breezes, you river springs, the uncounted rippling flash of the ocean waves, Earth, mother of us all, and the all-seeing circle of the sun, I call on you" (88 ff.).[58] He suffers at the thought of his enemies' rejoicing (156 ff.); he wishes (though later he states that it is impossible) for death, "If only he had hurled me below the earth to Tartaros, unbounded realm of Hades, host of the dead" (152–155). And he states his resolve, to keep the secret on which the fate of Zeus depends, "I shall never, cowering before his threats, reveal this" (οὔποτ' . . . καταμηνύσω 175)—a resolution repeated at high points of the action in ever more defiant terms (989 ff., 1002 ff., 1043 ff.). He rejects in advance the persuasion of Zeus (πειθοῦς 172), and the chorus calls him 'rash' (σύ μὲν θρασύς 178) and 'too free of speech' (ἄγαν δ' ἐλευθεροστομεῖς 180). He is tortured, he says, 'dishonorably, disrespectfully' (οὕτως ἀτίμως 195), and tells the chorus that when Zeus decided to annihilate the human race no god would oppose him, "but I dared" (ἐγὼ δ' ἐτόλμησ' 235). The chorus advises caution but he rejects their advice: "It is a slight thing for one who has his foot set outside of suffering to advise and reprove" (παραινεῖν νουθετεῖν τε 264). Another friend comes to advise him, Oceanus.[59] "I wish to advise you what is best" (παραινέσαι γέ σοι θέλω τα λῷστα 307–308). The advice is couched in familiar terms. "Abandon your present angry temper" (ἃς ἔχεις ὀργὰς ἄφες 315). "You do not give way to misfortune" (οὐδ' εἴκεις κακοῖς 320). "Treat me as your teacher" (ἔμοιγε χρώμενος διδασκάλῳ 322). The hero rejects the advice to 'yield' (οὐδ' εἴκεις 320) with the Sophoclean reply: "Leave this matter alone" (καὶ νῦν ἔασον 332). "Save yourself" he tells

Oceanus (σεαυτὸν σῷζ' 374) with the same contempt Antigone shows for her sister.[60] This confrontation of hero and advisors is followed by the long recital of Prometheus' services to mankind, during which dramatic action comes to a stop, but, in the choral ode which follows, the chorus returns to the attack. They reprove him for his 'self will'[61] (ἰδίᾳ γνώμᾳ 543). Then the long Io scene again suspends the dramatic development, which however reaches its climax with her exit. Prometheus restates his resolve in the strongest, clearest terms he has so far used and defies the power of Zeus (939). Hermes enters at once to threaten and demand surrender. In the dialogue between them the tortured hero wishes his enemies may suffer the same penalties they inflict on him (χλιδῶντας ὧδε τοὺς ἐμοὺς ἐγὼ ἐχθροὺς ἴδοιμι 972),[62] and proclaims again that no force or guile of Zeus will move him from his resolve. His mind is made up, long since (πάλαι . . . βεβούλευται τάδε 998).[63] Hermes pleads with him to 'show good sense' (ὀρθῶς φρονεῖν 1000) and tells him what will happen if he is not 'persuaded' by what is said to him (ἐὰν μὴ τοῖς ἐμοῖς πεισθῇς λόγοις 1014). He ends his description of the new and terrible sufferings which obstinacy will bring with an appeal to reason: "Consider" (φρόντιζε 1034). "Do not count self-will as better than good counsel" (εὐβουλίας 1035). The chorus joins Hermes and repeats the phrase, "He bids you search out the wisdom of good counsel" (τὴν σοφὴν εὐβουλίαν 1038). "Be persuaded" (πιθοῦ 1039). But he will not. And goes down below the earth with a final cry of defiance, "I am wronged" (ἔκδικα πάσχω 1093).

Here, it would seem, is the model for the Sophoclean hero. The *Life of Sophocles* tells us that "he learned tragedy in the school of Aeschylus"[64] (παρ' Αἰσχύλῳ δὲ τὴν τραγῳδίαν ἔμαθε), and this analysis seems to suggest strongly that in fact he found in the *Prometheus Bound* the prototype, already clear in outline, of that tragic pattern he was to make peculiarly his own.

But, of course, it is not so simple. These resemblances to
Sophoclean character, situation, and language in the *Prometheus Bound*, are to be found only there in Aeschylean drama;
we cannot trace a development of this particular form through
Aeschylean tragedy to Sophocles. The *Prometheus Bound* appears to be, in this respect, a totally new departure in the work
of the older poet. Such a thing of course is entirely possible—
Aeschylus was after all the creator of tragedy, an innovator on
the grand scale—but the trouble is that the *Prometheus Bound*
seems to be a totally new departure in his work in every other
respect too. The play, for all its Aeschylean grandness of
conception, seems out of place in the context of the *Oresteia*,
the *Seven*, the *Persians* and the *Suppliants*. In vocabulary, in
the ease and clarity of its style, in the caution of its imagery,
in the shortness and relative unimportance of its choral odes,
it does not sound like the work of the poet whose mantic style
demands such wealth of explanation as Fraenkel's 832 large
pages of commentary on the 1673 lines of the *Agamemnon*. Its
content is no less incongruous; the presentation of Zeus in the
play can be reconciled with Aeschylean religious ideas only by
assuming that the rest of the trilogy showed us an evolution of
the supreme god—an idea which it is difficult to buttress by
reference to Greek, and above all to early Greek, thought. As
if this were not enough, the play seems to show acquaintance
with ideas and formulations associated with the sophistic
teachers and their impact on Athenian thought; not only the
use of the word *sophistes* to describe Prometheus in a context
which imposes the derogatory meaning of 'trickster' so common
in the later fifth century, but also, as has recently been pointed
out,[65] the use of the contrast ἔργῳ—λόγῳ,[66] which is, again,
a cant phrase of the last half of the century, but unattested for
the first. All this is not enough, as Lesky says in his magisterial
discussion,[67] to justify those who deny Aeschylean authorship,[68]
but it does constitute a difficult problem, which cannot be
lightly dismissed.

The resemblance to Sophoclean tragic practice[69] is then a

new problem added to what was already, in Lesky's phrase, 'the most problematical of all Greek tragedies.' In this problem there is no certainty to be attained, and no agreement to be expected; more than one scholar has publicly reversed his stand on the question. Each reader is thrown back on the hypothesis which seems to explain most of the facts (and in the light of the discrepancies between this play and the other six the simple attribution to Aeschylus must also be regarded more as a hypothesis than a fact). There is one possible explanation of the 'Sophoclean' nature of the play which also explains some of the other problematical features: it is here advanced as a hypothesis, no more. It is possible that the play was written by Aeschylus very late in his career under the influence of Sophoclean innovations in the drama.[70]

The date of the *Prometheus Bound* like everything else about it is a matter for dispute. But in spite of Mette's attractive early dating on the basis of the relationship between Fragments 181, 320, and 334 and the apparent echoes of the *Prometheus Bound* in the *Triptolemos* of Sophocles (468 B.C.), the later the date of the play the more possible it is to explain the acquaintance with sophistic language and thought, especially the clearly Protagorean cast of Prometheus' account of human progress. True, we have no means of determining the date at which such ideas became current in Athens, but, again, the later the date of the *Prometheus Bound*, the more plausible that Aeschylus could reflect them. The latest possible date is after the *Oresteia* (458 B.C.) and before the poet's death in Sicily (456/455 B.C.).[71] If it was written during those years, it was written when Sophocles had already for more than ten years (since 468 B.C.) been producing plays in the theater of Dionysus. Aeschylus adopted from Sophocles the third actor and used him in the *Oresteia*. The *Prometheus Bound*, it is now agreed more and more widely,[72] also requires a third actor for the prologue. If Aeschylus could learn from his younger rival in this respect, is it not possible that he could adopt other features of Sophoclean drama? In the simplicity of the dialogue, the short-

ness and style of the choral odes, above all in the character of
the hero, his situation and the formulas used to express that
situation, can we perhaps see another Aeschylean adaptation of
new dramatic resources he found in the work of his young
competitor?

This is advanced as a question, not a statement; we are in
the dark here. But even if the *Prometheus Bound* is the germ of
Sophoclean tragedy, the originality of Sophocles is still patent,
for there is one important difference between Prometheus and
the Sophoclean heroes, a difference which affects the essence of
their tragic nature, the greatest difference in the world. Prometheus is immortal; he cannot die. "You would find it difficult
to bear my sufferings," says Prometheus to Io, "for my fixed
destiny ($\pi\epsilon\pi\rho\omega\mu\epsilon\nu\sigma\nu$ 753) is—not to die." And he confidently
challenges Zeus to hurl the thunderbolt, loose the winds, shake
the earth, and stir the sea, "for no matter what he does he will
not put me to death" ($\epsilon\mu\epsilon\ \gamma'\ o\dot{\upsilon}\ \theta\alpha\nu\alpha\tau\dot\omega\sigma\epsilon\iota$ 1053). The god does
not have to face that last extremity which awaits the Sopho-
clean human hero, death—that leap into the unknown dark
at which the flesh even of the bravest recoils instinctively.[73]
This difference is like that between the battles of men and those
of the gods in the *Iliad*; when gods fight each other we cannot
take them seriously, for they risk at most temporary pain or
loss of esteem (and in fact Homer's treatment of the battles of
the gods is the only comic relief in the *Iliad*).[74] But when
Hector, heavy with the foreknowledge of his death, takes his
hopeless stand before the Skaian gate, when Achilles hears his
horse Xanthos prophesy his death soon after Hector's but still
goes out to kill his enemy, the true tragic note is struck. Only
the fact of death can make action heroic; heroism and tragedy
are the peculiar province and privilege of mortal man.

And in any case the model for both Prometheus and the
Sophoclean heroes lies farther back, in the poetry Aeschylus
and Sophocles learned as children, the poetry on which the
education of both their generations was firmly based, in Homer,

and particularly in the *Iliad*. Achilles[75] chooses early death
with glory when he might have had long, but undistinguished,
life, is injured in his self-esteem by Agamemnon's insults,
threats, and oppressive action, retreats into self-absorbed fury
to bring defeat and death on his former allies and comrades and
in the end destruction on himself. When they beg him to relent,
he refuses harshly and bitterly; even old Phoinix whom he
loves cannot move him. His anger which once was leveled at
Agamemnon now includes the whole Achaean army; their losses
and defeats stir him only to mockery. His stubborn refusal to
help them leads to the death of Patroclus and this in turn to the
death of Hector which, as Achilles knows when he kills him,
shortly precedes his own. And many of the Sophoclean formulas for the hero's situation, mood, and action, have their
origin here.

Achilles is 'treated disrespectfully' (ἄτιμος e.g., 1.171, 9.648);
his passion (θυμός e.g., 1.192, 217) and wrath (χόλος 1.283,
9.260, 678 μῆνις 1.1) make him impervious to supplication
(λίσσομαι says Nestor 1.283) and appeals to reason (νόει φρεσί
9.600). He will not be persuaded (1.296 οὐ . . . πείσεσθαι
. . . ὀίω, 9.345, οὐδέ με πείσει cf. 386); he will not yield
(1.294 ὑπείξομαι), he is wild (9.629 ἄγριον), terrible (11.654
οἷος ἐκεῖνος δεινὸς ἀνήρ), and 'impossible' (16.29 σὺ δ᾽ ἀμήχανος
ἔπλευ). He warns Phoinix not to argue with him "so that I
will not hate you" (9.614 ἵνα μή μοι ἀπέχθηαι)—it is the same
word Antigone uses to Ismene (93); like Electra, he has no use
for life if he cannot have his way (18.90 οὐδ᾽ ἐμὲ θυμὸς ἄνωγε
. . . ζώειν) and he accepts death at once, since that is the price
(18.98 αὐτίκα τεθναίην). "Now I shall go . . ." (18.114
νῦν δ᾽ εἶμ᾽), he says, "to find Hector" and sums up his heroic
and fatal choice in words which Antigone echoes much later:
"I shall lie there, when I die. But now I shall win fair glory"
(κείσομ᾽ ἐπεί κε θάνω· νῦν δὲ κλέος ἐσθλὸν ἀροίμην 18.121).[76]
And like the Sophoclean hero he states his resolve with passionate emphasis, in absolute terms:

not if he gives me ten times as much and twenty times over
as he possesses now, not if more should come to him from elsewhere,
or gave all that is brought into Orchomenos, all that is brought in
to Thebes of Egypt . . .
not if he gave me gifts as many as the sand or the dust is,
not even so would Agamemnon have his way with my spirit.

> (*Iliad* 9.379–386, trans. by Lattimore)

He does finally rejoin the battle, but not as a concession to
Agamemnon; it is only because his fury has now been turned
against Hector, whose appeal for burial he rejects in the same
hyperbolic terms:

not if they bring and set before me ten times
and twenty times the ransom, and promise more in addition,
not if Priam son of Dardanus should offer to weigh out
your bulk in gold, not even so . . .

> (22.349–352, trans. by Lattimore)

In the baleful wrath of Achilles, his self-absorbed brooding
on the affront to his self-esteem, his anger against those who
have wronged him and those who would turn him from his
chosen path, in the fatal consequences of his obstinacy and in
his acceptance of death, above all in that magnificent ninth
book where the three different assaults on his resolve are
delivered and repulsed—here is to be found the model and even
the formulas of the Sophoclean tragic situation. Sophocles
might have taken for himself the Aeschylean claim that his
tragedies were 'slices from the banquets of Homer.'[77]

Both poets drew from the same great source but the results
are very different. Aeschylus transformed the capricious gods of
the Homeric epic into beneficent powers who through suffering
brought man and his *polis* (something that hardly exists in the
Iliad), to a higher stage of understanding and civilization. The
Zeus, Apollo, and Athena of the *Oresteia* recall those same
figures in the *Iliad* only in their outward characteristics; the
gods of Aeschylus are new creations, inspired by the ideals and

aspirations of that Athenian democracy which, barely twenty years old, checked the Persian advance into Europe at Marathon and ten years later stopped it forever at Salamis. But Sophocles writes as if this magnificent synthesis of old and new had never been attempted or achieved; he turns away from the Aeschylean adaptation of the heroic spirit to the conditions of the *polis* and goes back to the irreconcilable Achilles sulking in his tent. In his heroes who assert the force of their individual natures against their fellow men, their *polis*, and even their gods, he recreates, in a community now even more socially and intellectually advanced than that of Aeschylus, the loneliness, terror, and beauty of the archaic world.

To discuss the reasons why he did so brings us into an area where nothing can be proved and even conjecture is presumptuous; the sources of great art lie too deep for such exploration. But there is one important thing we know about Sophocles which does seem to be connected with his partiality for the irreconcilable hero as a tragic subject and which may, tentatively and with all due humility, be cited as relevant to his conception of tragedy.

It is his religion. I do not mean by this the conception of the Olympian gods and their ordering of the world which can be constructed (though not without grave difficulties) on the basis of the seven plays. Not only would the argument smack of the circular, it would also inevitably be too subjective, for the 'religion of Sophocles,' as demonstrated in the plays, varies with the eye of the beholder; it has been confidently identified with the two extremes of literal-minded fundamentalist piety and intellectual humanism, and almost everything in between. Only one thing seems undeniable about the religious view which informs the plays: that Sophocles did not share Aeschylus' belief in a Zeus who worked through the suffering of mankind to bring order out of chaos, justice out of violence, reconciliation out of strife. There was little in the age he lived in to support such a conception. As a youth he had danced in the celebration for the victory of Salamis, a victory of the Greeks

united against Persia, but in his manhood he saw the dis-
solution of that unity, the growing hostility between Athens
and Sparta which moved inexorably towards the disastrous
war in which he was to pass the last years of his life. The
Olympian gods in Sophoclean drama are enigmatic, masked
figures whose will humanity can for the most part only guess
at, and only identify with justice by a kind of heroic, defiant
faith.

But the Olympian gods were only one aspect of his religion.
The cult of these gods was not so much a private as a public
matter; they were so closely identified with the city that the
gold on the stature of Athena in the Parthenon was 'removable,'
and is reckoned in with other Athenian financial resources in
Pericles' account of the Athenian war funds. As an Athenian
citizen, Sophocles could feel pride in and thankfulness to such
a goddess, but it is difficult to see how anyone could have felt a
personal religious relationship to her, or indeed to Zeus, of
whom Aristotle remarks that there would be something absurd
about the idea of loving him. The worship of the Olympians
was not enough; men felt also a need for what one of my
predecessors in these lectures has aptly called a 'personal
religion'[78]—some religious relationship and practice which
brought them into a more consoling and intimate communion
with God than the Olympians, enthroned in their temples,
could ever provide.

In the case of Sophocles we know what this was. He was
devoted to the cult of the heroes. It was he whom the city
designated to welcome the hero-god Asclepios when (presumably in the shape of a sacred snake) he was brought from
Epidaurus to Athens. He was actually a priest of the cult of the
hero Halon (about whom unfortunately we know nothing—
even the name is a matter for controversy). He established,
according to a strange story in the Life, a shrine of the hero
Heracles the Denouncer.[79] And after his death he was himself
honored with worship as a hero by his fellow citizens: an annual
sacrifice was officially voted, and a hero shrine was set up for

his worship under the name Dexion, 'the welcomer,' because he had welcomed the hero-god Asclepios.[80] The site of this shrine has been discovered on the west slope of the Acropolis; it is identified by an inscription which shows that the worship of Dexion continued well into the fourth century.[81] There are many puzzling and disputed details in the fragmentary accounts that have survived, but one thing is clear: there is firm and almost contemporary evidence for Sophocles' close connection with, and participation in, the cult of the heroes.

Aeschylus' 'personal' religious connection, our sources indicate fairly clearly, was with the mysteries of Eleusis, where he was born.[82] Sophocles was born in Colonus where there was a grave of the hero Oedipus, and his personal religion was hero cult. There could hardly be a more striking contrast. For though both cults were concerned with death, the mysteries offered a vision of a blessed life beyond the grave, while the worship of the hero was concentrated on the grave itself. The rites of Eleusis were an occasion for joy—the procession, the ribald banter at the bridge, the rapt ecstasy of the initiates who had witnessed the revelation; the rites of the heroes were a grim ceremonial compounded of fear and lamentation—the blood sacrifice offered to the grave, a feast in which the human worshippers did not share. Eleusis was a revelation of light; the hero was worshipped only after the sun was down, in darkness.

These heroes, who were worshipped at the site of their burial (real or supposed), with offerings of black victims, the blood poured into a trench dug in the earth, were of many different kinds: faded divinities, healing powers, historical figures, founders (real or imagined) of cities, even local goblins or earth spirits.[83] But most of them were heroes in the other sense too— the famous heroes of Greek saga and especially of epic poetry. These were men who by the awesome force of their personality, the greatness of their achievement, their suffering, and in most instances their passionate anger, seemed in life to exceed the proportions of ordinary humanity and even in the grave continued to compel the fear and admiration of mankind. Their graves were holy places, sources of strength and prosperity to the land, or of danger to it if their cult should be neglected. The thing that distinguishes nearly all of them is their irreconcilable temper; the greatness of their passion brought them into conflict with men and even with the gods, and rather than accept the slightest diminution of that high esteem their pride demanded, they were ready to kill and die. Even in death their anger was alive and terrifying; the cult of the hero was a ceremony which aimed to appease his wrath, and the sacrifices were called μειλίγματα 'propitiatory offerings.' "The hero cult," says Nilsson, "is, more than any other, apotropaic; it is designed to appease the mighty dead who are by no means slow to wrath."[84] And the hero himself might have no other claim to worship than this unrelenting anger with the world. "A hero"—Nilsson again—"is recognized not because of his services but because there stems from him some special strength, which does not need to be of a benificent kind"; the hero's claim has "no relation to moral or higher religious ideas but is an expression of naked power or strength."[85]

The Greek admiration and fear of such natures sometimes led to extraordinary results, such as the cult of Cleomedes of Astypalaea, whose story is told by Pausanias[86] and Plutarch.[87] Cleomedes, a brilliant athlete, had the misfortune to kill his opponent in a boxing match at the Olympic games. He was convicted by the judges of 'wrongdoing' (ἄδικα εἴργασθαι) and his victory was annulled (ἀφῃρημένος τὴν νίκην). He went mad (ἔκφρων) of grief and returned home. There he attacked a school which had about sixty children in it; he pulled down the pillar that supported the roof, and it fell in and killed the children. When the citizens began to stone him he took refuge in the shrine of Athena. He got into a chest which was lying there and pulled the lid shut on himself. The citizens in spite of their concerted efforts were unable to open it. When they finally broke open the planks they found no Cleomedes, alive or dead. They sent envoys to Delphi to ask what had happened to him and the priestess of Apollo replied: "Last of the heroes is Cleomedes of Astypalaea. Honor him with sacrifices as one no longer mortal." The citizens of Astypalaea must have been relieved to hear that he was the last, but they established his cult as directed by Apollo, and it was still observed when Pausanias wrote in the second century A.D. To the ancient Greek mind there seems to have been something almost divine in passionate self-esteem, no matter how slightly justified and no matter what crimes it led to.

This strange phenomenon of Greek religious feeling is of course very old, but its continued existence in the fifth century (the Cleomedes incident falls between the battles of Marathon and Salamis) and later, and above all the fact that Sophocles was a priest of a hero cult, make it difficult to dismiss as a mere survival of primitive savagery. And, in those same Mediterranean countries where the hero's bones were guarded and his fierce spirit placated and invoked, later centuries were to see similar honors paid to the tombs and relics of the saints, and, for that matter, many of the early saints were as strange, impossible, and awe-inspiring as the heroes, and shared with them the readiness to die rather than surrender. The hero offered the ancient Greeks the assurance that in some chosen vessels humanity is capable of superhuman greatness, that there are some human beings who can imperiously deny the imperatives which others obey in order to live. It is not that the hero is worshipped as an example for human conduct; he is no guide to life in the real city man has made or the ideal city he dreams of.[88] But he is a reminder that a human being may at times magnificently defy the limits imposed on our will by the fear of public opinion, of community action, even of death, may refuse to accept humiliation and indifference and impose his will no matter what the consequences to others and himself.

And there are occasions when the hero *is* an example to be followed. In war, for example, when the virtue demanded of every man is precisely the heroic virtue, that he will value his own life as nothing. And in great crises of the soul, when a man's

whole life work is challenged and threatened, when loyalty to
the guiding principle of his life means suffering or even death.
When Socrates, whose life of patient intellectual probing for
moral definitions seems as far removed from the careers of the
heroes as north is from south, seeks in his defense in court for
comparisons with his own case, it is Achilles and Ajax whom
he cites.[89] Strange authorities for a philosopher—and yet, not
so strange. For in his refusal to abandon what he considers his
mission, imposed by the god, he shows the familiar heroic
stubbornness, and in his ironic but outrageous proposal that his
punishment should be that entertainment at the public ex-
pense offered to Olympic victors he shows the defiant arrogance
which is the mark of the heroic temper. In his deliberate choice
of death rather than surrender he enters the ranks of the heroes
himself.

It seems likely, then, that Sophocles' close connection with
hero cult had a part in his creation of the tragic hero,[90] and
certainly the plays reflect this preoccupation. The *Oedipus at
Colonus* is a mystery play which deals with the transition of
Oedipus from human to heroic stature,[91] and the burial of a
hero is the point of conflict in the last part of the *Ajax*. And
of course, many of the heroes of the plays were worshipped
with these rites in Athens and elsewhere during Sophocles'
lifetime.[92]

But this explanation is really a restatement of the problem in
a different form. In the Athens of Anaxagoras and Protagoras,
where hero cult must have seemed to many of the young an
embarrassing survival of the unenlightened past—the Athens
of Periclean democracy where the rebellious temper of an
Achilles or an Ajax had little relevance to the new democratic
ideal of the individual's position in the *polis*—why did Sophocles serve as the priest of a hero cult and fill his tragedies with
these recalcitrant, uncoöperative heroes who seem to have
stepped out of the *Iliad* to reassert against friends, enemies,
city and gods their unquestioning faith in their own superiority?
One thing, at least, is certain: Sophocles was not attempting a

historical reconstruction of the heroic age, as many nineteenth-
century critics thought (hence their frequent citation of his
'anachronisms'). Sophocles' Ajax is not really a Homeric hero
any more than Shakespeare's Richard the Second is a four-
teenth-century monarch (as Queen Elizabeth was quick to
realize).[93] All great drama must be contemporary in thought
and feeling, immediate in its impact on the audience; the hero
must be as Aristotle says 'a man like us,' not a historical
reconstruction. Sophocles' obsession with the Achillean temperament and situation must stem not from an interest in the past
but from a deep conviction that this temperament and situation
are the true, the only possible, dramatic expression of the
tragic dilemma of his own place and time.

The relevance of the heroic temper to the splendid achieve-
ments and brilliant prospects of Periclean democracy can be
found only in the great events of the century in which Sophocles played his full part as citizen, statesman, and soldier. His
life spans almost the whole course of the heroic saga of Athens'
rise to a height where the mastery of the whole Greek world
seemed within its grasp, and of its catastrophic fall.

For Aeschylus, the Marathon fighter, who had lived under
the tyranny, seen the establishment of Athenian democracy,
and taken a soldier's part in its triumphant vindication in the
war against Persia, the future was full of hope. The *Oresteia*,
produced within two years of his death, is a pageant of man's
advance, blind and violent, but still an advance, from savagery
to civilization, under the mysterious guidance of a stern but
benevolent Zeus. The pattern of the trilogy is the thrust and
counterthrust of apparently irreconcilable opposites, ending
in their reconciliation, and this reconciliation is the basis for a
new and better dispensation. In the democratic institutions of
his city, so hardly won and so valiantly defended, Aeschylus
saw the prototype of his reconciliation of opposites among men
as among gods; force is superseded by persuasion, armed
vengeance by the court of law, civil war by debate in assembly.
There would be more strife, new opposites to be reconciled, new

suffering to be endured for new progress made, but the strife and the suffering he saw as creative—that 'violent grace' of the gods which the chorus celebrates in the *Agamemnon*.

But Sophocles, in the years of his maturity, lived in a different age. The political power and material wealth of Athens reached a level which Aeschylus, confident though he was of Athens' future greatness,[94] could hardly have foreseen; but the future became darker with the years. Athenian imperial policy enforced membership in what had started as a league of free cities for the liberation of Greece but was now an empire which even Pericles compared to a *tyrannis*, an autocratic, despotic power.[95] Sophocles himself took part on more than one occasion in punitive operations against cities which had once been free allies and were now Athenian tributaries.[96] The fear and hatred of Athens, the 'tyrant city,' grew with the years; all over Greece the cry was once again for liberation, but this time from Athens, and it was achieved in the long and destructive war which Sophocles, now an old man, saw almost to its bitter end. I have argued elsewhere that Athens itself, its heroic energy, its refusal to retreat, to compromise, was the inspiration for the figure of Oedipus *tyrannos*.[97] But, as we have seen, Oedipus is cast in the same mold as the other Sophoclean heroes. The choice of such a heroic figure, the fascination it exerted on the poet's mind through the long years of his career as a dramatist, may owe more than a little to his participation as soldier and statesman in the great heroic drama of his time—the attempt of the small city of Athens to dominate the whole of the wide-spread Hellenic world, to impose its political will, as it was already imposing its art and thought, on all Hellas, the islands, the mainland, even, in a megalomaniac venture worthy of an Ajax, on rich, powerful, distant Sicily. Undaunted by losses and defeats, impervious to advice or threat, finding always fresh sources of energy in its passionate conviction of superiority, Athens pursued, throughout the course of Sophocles' manhood and old age, its stubborn, magnificent course to the final disaster. It was, like a Sophoclean hero, in love with the impossible.[98] "You must realize," says Pericles to the Athenians, in the last speech reported by Thucydides, "that Athens has the greatest name among men because it does not give in to misfortunes (διὰ τὸ ταῖς ξυμφοραῖς μὴ εἴκειν 2.64, 3), has expended lives and labor beyond all others in war, and acquired a power which is greater than any up to our time; and of this power, even if some day we lose (for all things are born to be diminished) a memory will be left forever to those who come after us." The tone ("for all things are born to be diminished"), the phrases ("does not give in to misfortune"), and the proud acceptance of loss for glory ("a memory will be left") are those of Sophoclean tragedy.

In all these epic events and discussions Sophocles played his part, and no small one, in the battle fleets and the council chamber; this was the context of his life and action, the air he breathed.[99] The greatness and tragic destiny of Athens must have been not only in his mind but also in his heart and soul and every fiber of his being when he created for the theater of Dionysus those imperious, heroic figures who go the same passionate way.

III

Antigone 1

"LISTEN, I tell you, it is the hard, stubborn will that comes to defeat, it is the strongest iron, fire-heated to toughness, which you most often see smashed and shattered. And I know that with a small bridle the most spirited horses are broken" (*Ant.* 473 ff.). This is Creon, speaking of Antigone. Until the end he maintains this confident expectation: that Antigone's defiant mood will be subdued, her rebellious spirit tamed. He is wrong. She goes to her death unrepentant. It is Creon whose will is smashed and broken. It is Creon who gives in.

In this play two characters assume the heroic attitude, but one of them is in the end exposed as unheroic. Unlike Antigone, whom even death cannot move, Creon surrenders. The collapse of his apparently unshakable resolution throws into sharp relief the heroism of Antigone, who, in the face of opposition from friend and enemy alike, stands her ground and goes, still defiant, to her death. The *Antigone* is a tragedy which raises great questions, social and religious, but it is also a striking presentation, through the contrast between these two figures, of the true nature of the Sophoclean hero.

When Antigone first appears, at the opening of the play, her resolve is already formed. She is going to bury her brother. She knows what penalty she risks—death by stoning (36)—but is undeterred. She asks her sister Ismene to "take part in the labor and the work" (εἰ ξυμπονήσῃς καὶ ξυνεργάσῃ 41). For she intends to 'lift up' (κουφιεῖς 43)[1] her brother's body.

Ismene's attempt to dissuade her begins with an appeal to reason: "Think!" (φρόνησον 49). What Antigone is to 'think' of is the deaths of their mother, father, and brothers; not only are the two sisters left alone in the world, but, if they defy Creon, their deaths will be 'the worst of all' (κάκιστ' 59). This is no mere rhetoric. Oedipus died self-blinded, Jocasta 'disfigured her life' (54) by hanging herself, the brothers killed each other, but the sisters risk stoning, a public, shameful, ugly death. What Antigone proposes, she goes on to say, is defiance of the state. "If, in violence to the law, we overreach the vote or authority of absolute power . . ." (59–60); Sophocles has chosen these words with great care. The word τυράννων emphasizes the absolute power of Creon, conferred on him by the *polis* in the emergency, and at the same time, by its plural form, generalizes the expression and thus lessens the suggestion that he is a 'tyrant.' The word 'vote' (ψῆφον) suggests that Creon's proclamation is no capricious gesture but the expression of a deliberate policy—as we see later the suggestion is correct— and it also, with its democratic associations, hints that Creon speaks for the whole body of the citizens. The word κράτη, another generalizing plural, emphasizes the fact that Creon has the full power of the state at his command, and the phrase 'in violence to the law' marks Antigone's attempt as criminal. These are weighty objections, and they are followed by another. Antigone must 'reflect' (ἐννοεῖν 61) that they are women, incapable by nature of fighting against men. The final argument is a fresh reminder that they face the power of the state, this time couched in language which emphasizes Creon's naked power rather than his right: "we are ruled by those who are stronger" (ἀρχόμεσθ' ἐκ κρεισσόνων 63). Ismene goes on to emphasize the harsh necessity of obedience (ἀκούειν 64) not only to this but perhaps to even more painful orders. For her part, she will beg the dead for forgiveness, but "I shall obey those in authority" (πείσομαι 67). "For excessive, extraordinary action has no sense at all" (νοῦν οὐδένα 68). This speech makes clear the choice which Antigone faces. Submission, or failure and death. But as Ismene sees it there is no choice at all. For, as the chorus says later when Creon proclaims the penalty for disobedience: "No one is such a fool as to be in love with death" (οὕτω μῶρος ὃς θανεῖν ἐρᾷ 220).

Ismene's refusal to help is a blow to Antigone, for she needed help badly. "To share the labor and the work with me . . ." she said, and the words are not metaphorical. For she intended to 'lift' the body of her brother, to raise it up and lower it into a grave, and this she cannot do alone. The real burial they might have successfully completed together must now be replaced by a symbolic burial which Antigone will carry out alone; perhaps a sense of the inadequacy of the first attempt is what brings her back a second time, in daylight, to pour libations on the corpse she has only managed to cover with a light film of dust (256). Ismene's refusal means that she must change her plan, and this perhaps helps to explain the bitterness of her attitude to her sister later. But it makes no difference to her resolve now; like Electra, she will do alone what she had hoped to do with her sister's help. For her too, there is no choice. She does not condescend to answer Ismene's arguments. She regrets that she asked for her help and rejects in advance any offer of coöperation should Ismene later change her mind. She accepts death: "If I do this and die for it, it is καλόν" (72) —that untranslateable word, 'good, glorious, fine, beautiful,' is at any rate the opposite of what she told Ismene she would be if she refused to help—κακή (38), 'bad, ugly, cowardly.' At the end of the scene she repeats her choice of death: "I shall suffer nothing so great as not to die gloriously" (καλῶς θανεῖν 97). This is the watchword of Ajax too.[2]

From this high resolve she never retreats. In the short glimpse we are given of her in the guard's account of her capture, the same defiant self-confidence is emphasized. Caught red-handed, she was 'not at all disturbed' (οὐδὲν ἐκπεπλεγμένην 433), and when charged with this and the earlier attempt to bury Polynices she 'denied nothing' (435).[3] Face to face with Creon she speaks just as boldly: "I say I did it. I do not deny it"

(443). Creon's next question offers her an excuse, a way of retreat. "Did you know my proclamation forebade it?" (447). But she refuses to accept the offer. "I knew. How could I fail to? It was public" (448). The defense of her action which follows destroys forever any possibility of compromise, excuse, or pardon. It is an acceptance of death rather than surrender and ends with words no ruler, however tolerant, could forgive: "If what I am saying seems foolish to you, let's say (σχεδόν τι 470) I am convicted of folly by a fool." No wonder the chorus speaks of her as the "savage offspring of a savage father" (γέννημ' ὠμὸν 471).[4] This is Ajax' word again, and Antigone is in fact more like Ajax than any of the other Sophoclean heroes. Like him, too, she will not yield. "She does not understand," says the chorus, "how to give in to misfortunes" (εἴκειν . . . κακοῖς 472).

Creon's furious reply, with its claims that her spirit will be broken, that she is his slave (479), that she has broken the law, she does not even answer: in words packed with personal distaste and contempt,[5] she claims from him only the swift fulfillment of the death penalty he has proclaimed (499 ff.). She claims that death as 'glorious' (502). In the dialogue which follows she is just as harsh to Ismene as she was to Creon. This is of course partly due to the fact that she is trying to save Ismene's life by impressing on Creon that her sister had no part in the defiance of his orders. In this, as we see later, she succeeds.[6] But the bitter tone of her rejection—"justice will not allow this" (538); "Ask Creon what to do; he's the one you care for" (549)[7]—also expresses genuine anger. She keeps her promise (70), that she would not accept Ismene as an ally even if she changed her mind; Antigone is resentful of the sister whose cowardice forced her to abandon her plan for a proper burial of the body, and furious at the thought that the glory for which she gives her life might be shared with an unworthy sister. For this glory is all she has. Like Achilles she has chosen a short life with glory. "You chose to live, and I to die" (555). And like Achilles the one thing she finds intolerable is that this glory, so dearly bought, should in any way be diminished.

"If only," says Achilles to Patroclus, "if only not one of all the
Trojans could escape destruction, not one of the Argives, but
you and I alone could emerge from the slaughter so that we
two alone could break Troy's hallowed coronal" (*Il.* 16.97 ff.,
trans. by Lattimore). Antigone's dream of glory is like this;
she wants no other participants to lessen her full possession of
the thing for which she gives her life.

Our next view of her is our last. She laments her death.
There is no hint of surrender; she is performing her own funeral
lament since, as she says, there is no *philos*, no friend or relative,
who will do it for her (881–882). There is no relative left but
Ismene, whom she has repudiated as a member of the family.
The chorus shows no sympathy and places the full responsibility for her imminent death on her own head.[8] She is
αὐτόνομος (821), they tell her, a word which is generally applied
to cities—'independent, living under their own laws'—but is
here applied, in a bold figure of speech which contains the
essence of the play's conflict, to an individual—she 'lives by
her own law.'[9] They go on to say still harsher things. She compares her fate to that of Niobe—the point of comparison is
made clear elsewhere by Electra, who speaks of Niobe 'weeping
in a tomb of rock' (*El.* 151)—but the chorus reproves her for
her presumption.[10] "Niobe was divine, born of a god,[11] and we
are mortal and born to die." And then they sympathetically
excuse her exaggeration: "And yet (καίτοι) it is a great thing
for a dying girl to hear, that in life as later in death, she has an
inheritance bordering on that of those who are equal to the
gods." She turns angrily away from them and what she calls
their 'mockery' (γελῶμαι 839) with bitter reproach. The exchange is revealing. The distinction they make between her
mortal state and Niobe's divine parentage is 'mockery' because
the hero, pitting himself alone against man's city and its demand for submission to time and change, can find consolation
only in some kind of immortality, the quality of the gods; the
stubborn refusal to compromise, to accept defeat, to change,
is godlike. The reply of the chorus is a severe censure. "You

have advanced to the extreme limit of audacity (θράσους 853) and smashed hard against the high pedestal of Justice.[12] Your self-conceived passion has destroyed you" (αὐτόγνωτος ὀργά 875).

Two words in this long, lyrical dialogue precisely define the character of Antigone and the heroic temper in general: αὐτόνομος 'a law unto itself' and αὐτόγνωτος ὀργά 'passion self-conceived.' The force which drives the hero on to assert his independence, like a sovereign state, is something which stems from his inner being, his *physis*, his true self: it is not to be explained by outside circumstances.

And now Antigone faces the execution of her sentence, a living death in an underground prison. She makes her last long speech, not in lyrical song but in spoken iambics, the medium of reflection, discussion, analysis. She tries to reason out her own motives, to clarify for herself, now that the consequences are irrevocable, the motive and nature of her action. The reasoning is certainly 'autonomous' and 'self-conceived' but it contains not the slightest hint of surrender. "The same fierce blasts of the same winds of the soul have her in their possession" sings the chorus (929–930). Still defiant, she is led off to her tomb. Her last action too is defiant. Once in the prison-tomb where Creon has placed her to 'realize' that she was wrong, she hangs herself. And this action triggers the series of hammer blows which strike Creon down at the end of the play. Antigone shares with Electra the distinction of being the most intransigent of the Sophoclean heroes. Ajax and Philoctetes at least discuss the possibility of surrender, Oedipus at Thebes and at Colonus makes minor concessions, but Antigone, like Electra, never for one second or in one detail wavers from her fixed resolve.

Her stubborn, self-willed, insistence on her own way and on her rightness is made all the more striking by her appearance opposite the figure of Creon. Creon seems at first sight to be the hero of the play. He is the one who, like the Aristotelian tragic hero, is a man of eminence, high in power and prosperity, who comes crashing down from the pinnacle of greatness, and it is he who speaking in terms of the length and importance of his role (especially in the second half of the play) is the protagonist. But he lacks the heroic temper. [In Creon we are presented with the spectacle of a man who displays every symptom of heroic stubbornness, who is placed in the classic situation of the Sophoclean hero, expressed in the appropriate formulas, but who is swayed by advice, makes major concessions, and collapses ignominiously at the first real threat.]

Creon, like Antigone, makes a firm resolve at the beginning (in fact, before the beginning) of the play, and from that resolve follow the consequences which are the play's events. He decides that the corpse of Polynices shall be left to rot unburied, torn by the dogs and birds. He reinforces that decision with a decree that any opposition to it is to be punished by death. This resolve is couched in the formal terms, excluding argument, of a political decree: "It has been proclaimed to the city that no one shall pay him funeral rites, or mourn him; he is to be left unburied" (ἐκκεκήρυκται 203). The perfect and the impersonal form of the verb (contrasted with the "I have proclaimed"—κηρύξας ἔχω—of verse 192) express the resolution as an objective and permanent fact. The usual simple futures of the heroic resolve follow at once: "Never through my action will the base have more respect than the just" (τιμῇ προέξουσ' 208); "the man who is well-disposed to the city shall be respected by me in death as in life" (τιμήσεται 210). Sentries are already posted over the body (217); he expects opposition. His expectation is justified; the guard arrives to tell him that his edict has been defied almost simultaneously with its announcement.

Creon is now in the position of the hero whose will is thwarted, whose claim to respect for that will is denied, whose right to independent action is challenged. And there follows at once, as with Antigone in the prologue, as with Achilles in the council of the Achaeans,[13] the advice to compromise. The chorus is impressed by the mysterious details of the burial: the absence of any trace of human activity (249–252), the fact

that no bird or beast had come near the body—a sign perhaps
of that divine protection which kept untouched the bodies of
Sarpedon (*Il.* 16.667) and Hector (*Il.* 24.18 ff.).[14] They suggest
to Creon, not as a sudden inspiration but as an idea that has
taken shape in their minds since the beginning of the guard's
report (πάλαι 279), that the burial of Polynices is 'divinely
caused' (θεήλατον 278). This is a strong word; literally it means
'driven on by a god.'[15] The implication of the chorus' suggestion
is clear: not only is it impossible to resist the divine will shown
in the apparently miraculous burial of Polynices, but also the
nature of the opposition to Creon's order gives him an excuse to
retreat and still save face.

The compromise is rejected in heroic style: "Stop, before
you fill me with rage" (ὀργῆς 280). "What you say is intolerable" (οὐκ ἀνεκτά 282). He rejects the idea of divine intervention and prefers to see in the burial the hand of political
enemies. But he can take no action against them. There is only
the guard on whom to indulge his rage, and this he does, accusing
him of the crime (322), but finally ordering him, under threat
of torture before death, to produce the real criminal.

He is soon faced with the entirely unforeseen and appalling
consequences of his action. He spoke of political opponents, of
rebels, of bribed criminals; it never for a moment occurred to
him that he would have to face as his opponent and victim, as
now he does, his own sister's child, a princess of the royal house.
His attempt to offer her a way out is contemptuously refused;
he is met with a proud admission of full responsibility and
with scathing, contemptuous defiance which leaves him no way
to go but forward to the execution of the penalty he has
decreed. He is mocked (γελᾶν 483). His rage flames up to
heroic proportions. He will put her to death "whether she is
my sister's child or more closely related in blood than all my
family put together[16]—she shall not escape, she and her sister."
His rage at the affront to his τιμή, his self-respect, swells to
include together with the main object of his wrath all those
connected with it, as Ajax (844) and Philoctetes (1200) wish

for the destruction of the whole Greek army, and Achilles for the death of all the Trojans and all the Greeks except himself and Patroclus. Creon will not be moved by the appeals of Ismene and the chorus. He will not be 'ruled' by a woman (οὐκ ἄρξει γυνή 525); his mind is 'made up' (δεδογμέν' 576). He orders the two girls to be bound, still convinced that Antigone's spirit will break at least enough for her to attempt escape from the death sentence he has now publicly and officially pronounced.

And now he is again urged to compromise, this time at greater length and by a more persuasive advisor than the chorus. Haemon begins (he knows his father) in the most conciliatory tone imaginable: he professes complete acceptance of his father's wishes (635–638). But after Creon's exultant speech, full of obvious relief at the unexpected ease with which this difficult first moment of their interview has passed, Haemon slowly and carefully presses the assault on his father's resolution. The speech shows diplomatic talent of the highest order. Haemon does not presume to say that his father is wrong (685–686), but another view is possible (687). The necessary attempt to excuse or even partially to justify Antigone's action is put forward as the view of the citizens, not as Haemon's own (693 ff.). He speaks for those who dare not speak directly to Creon, who fear the 'dread countenance' (ὄμμα δεινόν 690) of the king. The advice he is about to give is prompted, he says, not by his feelings for Antigone (he makes no mention at all of his betrothal to her) but by concern for his father (701–704). The advice is the classic appeal to reason and uses the familiar phrases of the attempt to sway the heroic will. It is full of expressions which precisely delineate the nature of that self-centered, inflexible temper which is the central theme of Sophoclean tragedy. "Do not carry one disposition alone in yourself" (ἕν ἦθος μοῦνον 705); the hero is single-minded, obsessed with one objective, incapable of change, of assuming another ἦθος, another disposition or character.[17] And this disposition is defined as one which holds "that what *you* say, and nothing else, is right" (706). It is that of a man who believes that he alone has intelligence (φρονεῖν 707), that he has a tongue and a soul (ψυχήν) which others do not have. "Such people," says Haemon, in a violent metaphor, "when spread open [like a letter] are at once revealed to be empty" (διαπτυχθέντες ὤφθησαν κενοί 709).[18] Creon must learn. "Even a man who is wise, will find nothing disgraceful in learning many things" (μανθάνειν 710).

There follow the famous lines on the trees which yield to the winter flood and those which do not, the sailor who refuses to shorten sail and capsizes. The passage recalls the similar images of stubbornness which Creon used in his reply to Antigone (473–478). But the tone is different. Creon affirmed brutally that precisely the most unyielding tempers are most easily broken, the hardest iron smashed, the wildest horses brought to heel. The speech was a refusal to credit Antigone with the full strength of the heroic resolution, not an attempt to persuade her to abandon it. Rather than reason with her he will use force to break her defiant mood. This is all he *can* do, for her action, which made a mockery of his decree, is irrevocable; the most he can hope to do now is to reduce her to penitence, to fear, to an appeal for mercy. But Haemon is still in time to prevent 'the incurable' (τὸ ἀνήκεστον), and his images emphasize the alternatives of destruction or survival. To yield (ὑπείκει 713, 716) is to save oneself. And he ends with an appeal to 'give way'—"Retreat from your passion" (εἶκε θυμοῦ 718)— and to 'learn' (μανθάνειν 723), an appeal which the chorus, though in a characteristically neutral formula, repeats after him (μαθεῖν 725).

Creon's reaction to the advice is the same as Antigone's, the customary violent response of the hero. "Shall I be taught . . . ?" (διδαξόμεσθα δὴ 726), he begins, and before long calls his son 'completely vile' (ὦ παγκάκιστε 742). Like Antigone he ranks his friendly advisor with his enemies (740 cf. 549); like

all the heroes, he will not listen (μηδὲν κλύειν 757). He ends with
a repetition of his resolve: "he [Haemon] shall not rescue the
two girls from death" (οὐκ ἀπαλλάξει μόρου 769).
And then, quite unexpectedly, he changes his mind. On two
points, both of them of major importance. One question from
the chorus (770) is enough to bring a reprieve for Ismene: only
Antigone is to be put to death. And here, too, there is a significant change of plan. The original penalty was death by stoning, and a few moments previously he threatened to have her
killed in front of Haemon, but now he decides to imprison her
in an underground cell, with a little food. The words he uses
(ἄγος μόνον etc. 775 ff.) have never been satisfactorily explained; all we can be sure of is that he is referring to some
primitive belief that such a method of execution (presumably
because it avoids actual bloodshed) absolves the city (776) and
himself (889) from ritual pollution.[19] But there are other reasons
behind the sudden change of plan. For one thing he is surely
influenced by Haemon's emphatic claim that the people of
Thebes praise Antigone's action (693 ff.). If there is any truth
to this at all, the execution of Ismene would be a foolish
provocation, and the execution of Antigone by stoning might
produce a situation beyond his control, for it is a measure which
requires the coöperation of the people, a sort of legal lynching,
reserved for objects of universal hate. He speaks of avoiding
a situation in which the whole city (πᾶσ' ὑπεκφύγῃ πόλις 776)
would have Antigone's blood on its hands; perhaps what he
really fears is that no one would cast the first stone.[20] But this
is not all. He has in fact granted her a kind of reprieve; her
death is to be delayed. And in his words, as he pronounces
sentence, there is a hint that he expects her, once she has begun
to brood in fear and solitude on her fate, to collapse and surrender. "And there perhaps, as she prays to Hades, the only
one of the gods she reveres, she will find some way to escape
death, or she will realize, though late, that worship of Hades
is labor lost" (777–780). Later he says: "whether she is to die
or to live, entombed in such a dwelling-place . . ." (887–888).

As long as she remains alive there is still a chance that Creon will break the hard iron of her will.

This change of plan is the first indication that Creon is not, after all, cast in the heroic mold. That characteristic phenomenon of heroic anger, its widening to include peripheral and even totally innocent objects, reached its limits in Creon's condemnation of Ismene and his quarrel with his son, but now has begun to work in reverse. There is a calculating and fearful head behind that heroic mask. The point is reinforced by the contrasting scene which follows. Antigone is dragged off to her doom. Abandoned by all, mocked, as she sees it, by the chorus, no longer sure of the support of the gods, doubtful now even of her own motives, she is still irreconcilably defiant. To the threatening figure of Creon *instans tyrannus,* who cuts short her farewells to the light with brutal threats, she does not address one single word.[21]

And now comes the real test of Creon's resolution; he must face a more formidable adversary than his own son. The parallel between Antigone and Creon is maintained. Just as she rejected first the friendly advice of a sister who could do no more than appeal to reason, so he rejected the advice of his son, who had no more than the power of his arguments to make him formidable. And just as Antigone next had to face the authority and terrifying threats of Creon, so he is now confronted with the authority and even more terrifying threats of the blind seer Tiresias.

Tiresias begins with an appeal to reason, couched in the classic formulas. "I shall teach you, and do you obey the prophet" (ἐγὼ διδάξω . . . τῷ μάντει πιθοῦ 992). "Reflect" (φρόνει 996) "that you are poised on the razor edge of chance." "You will realize" (γνώσῃ) . . . "as you listen" (κλύων 998). And at the end of his awesome description of the omens which show the gods' anger at Creon's exposure of the body, he returns to the familiar formulas. "Consider this, my son" (φρόνησον 1023). "The man who falls into trouble and tries to heal himself is not illcounselled" (ἄβουλος 1026). "Give in to

the dead man" (εἶχε τῷ θανόντι 1029). "Learn" (μανθάνειν
1031). Creon reacts with fury. He repeats his resolve, and in
more hyperbolical terms than ever. "You will not bury him in
the grave (οὐχὶ κρύψετε 1039) not even if the eagles of Zeus
seize his flesh and carry it up to the throne of Zeus, not even
so." Tiresias maintains his reasonable tone; he urges 'good
counsel' (εὐβουλία 1050). But then, spurred on by Creon's
angry insults, he launches into a direct prophecy of the dis-
asters Creon will soon bring down on his own head: the mourning of men and women in the royal house, the hatred of the
cities whose champions have been left unburied. He leaves with
the familiar appeal to time to bring the wrathful hero to his
senses. "Lead me home, boy, so that he can vent his passion
(θυμόν 1088) on younger men than me, and come to realize (γνῷ
1089) that he must keep a gentler tongue in his head and a
mind (νοῦν 1090) better than the one he harbors now."

The hope that time will change the hero's mind, as we have
seen, is always vain. Ajax rejects the world of time and change,
Philoctetes will 'never' go to Troy of his own free will, Electra
will 'never' cease her lamentations until time brings her victory
over her enemies, Oedipus at Thebes will not give up the search
for his own identity and at Colonus will not change his decision
to die on Attic soil. And Antigone in her prison has already by
her suicide sealed Creon's doom. But Creon is the exception.[22]
And he does not even need much time. The chorus speaks four
lines of warning, no more, and Creon breaks. "I have realized it
myself" (ἔγνωκα καὐτός 1095), he says when the chorus reminds him that Tiresias has never been proved wrong. "It is
a terrible thing to give in (εἰκαθεῖν 1096) but terrible too to
resist and smite my passionate temper (θυμόν 1097) with
destruction." The chorus tells him that he needs 'good counsel'
(εὐβουλίας δεῖ 1098) and he asks their advice. "What must I
do? Tell me. I shall obey" (πείσομαι δ' ἐγώ 1099). It is Ismene's
word (67), not Antigone's. Release the girl, they tell him, and
bury the man; but he hesitates once more. "You think I should

give in?" (παρεικαθεῖν 1102). But give in he does, completely.
"I who bound her will release her in person" (1112).

There is no other scene quite like this in all Sophoclean
drama. It is true that the blind prophet is an awe-inspiring
figure and his prophecies terrifying, but Oedipus *tyrannos* was
faced by the same prophet and even more dreadful prophecies;
far from breaking his spirit, the confrontation served only to
raise him to new heights of self-assertion and obstinacy. But
Creon surrenders unconditionally, snaps like the iron heated to
toughness in the fire, accepts the bridle, yields to the winter
flood and shortens sail. It is a situation unique on the Sophoclean stage, and its effect is heightened when it is followed
immediately by the news of the final act of intransigence of the
powerless, condemned girl, whose revenge is now to come. Our
last sight of Creon is the almost unbearable spectacle of a
strong man utterly broken by calamity. Again the comparison
with Oedipus *tyrannos* is instructive. Oedipus in his blindness,
pollution, and misery asserts himself again as a powerful imperious personality,[23] but Creon at the end of the *Antigone* is a
wailing wreck of a man, stripped of dignity. Haemon's words
are prophetic. He has been 'laid open,' and there is nothing
there.

The clash between Antigone and Creon is of course much
more than a confrontation of the true hero with the false. The
conflict raises political and religious questions of the highest
importance; in fact it is set in these terms from the very first
scene. These questions have been much discussed. The prevailing view of them is that the play presents a contrast between a
religious (Antigone's) and a political point of view (Creon's).
But this is oversimplified. Antigone's defiance of the *polis* is a
political as well as a religious action, and Creon's exposure of
the body of Polynices stems from religious as well as political
convictions. The motives of these characters are complex.

Creon's political view is clearly and elaborately presented
(and will be discussed later) but in what sense can we speak of

Antigone's action as political? The question calls for an examination of the words in which she defends her action to Ismene
and before Creon.

"You will soon show," she says to Ismene, "whether you were
born noble (εἴτ' εὐγενὴς πέφυκας) or, though your parents were
princely, a coward" (εἴτ' ἐσθλῶν κακή 38). "He is my brother,
and yours too" (45–46). "I shall go and heap up a gravemound
for the brother I love" (80–81). And to Creon she says: "If I
had endured to leave unburied one born from my own mother,
that would have caused me pain." (466–468). And later: "There
is nothing disgraceful in showing reverence for those who come
from the same womb" (511).

In these statements (which have of course been separated
from those in which she appeals to the gods), the sanction she
invokes for her act is the claim of family, of blood relationship.[24]
Antigone's loyalty to this relationship overrides any claims that
the *polis* can make. She speaks of this loyalty to blood relationship in exactly the terms a citizen would use of his loyalty to
the *polis*, in political terms, in fact. When Ismene asks her:
"Do you really intend to bury him, though it is forbidden to
the city?" she answers: "He is my brother . . . I shall not be
convicted of treachery" (οὐ προδοῦσ' ἀλώσομαι 46). And she
asks Creon what "glory more glorious" (502) she could win
than by burying her brother. This loyalty of hers is in fact a
political loyalty not only because the particular circumstances
force her to choose between family and *polis*, but also because
historically the strong, indissoluble tie of blood relationship
had in earlier times, through the *genê*, the 'clans,' been the
dominating factor in the citizen's social and political environment. It was much older than the *polis*, and in democratic
Athens still showed on every side signs of its continued power
as a rival and even a potential danger to the newer civil
institutions and forms of organization. It is no accident that
the foundation of Athenian democracy was Cleisthenes' re-
organization of the citizen body in local as opposed to family
units. "The substitution of the deme for the clan meant in effect

the transition from a principle of kinship to that of locality. . . . Athens after the reforms of Cleisthenes was no longer a 'federation of kindreds' " (γένη).[25] Since those words were written, historians have tended more and more to question and even to deny such an estimate of the purpose and effect of the reforms, but there is good ancient evidence for this view. Aristotle, for example, in a discussion of the methods of safe-guarding democratic institutions, mentions "regulations like those passed by Cleisthenes at Athens, when he wanted to increase the power of the democracy . . . fresh tribes and brotherhoods should be established; the private rites of families should be restricted and converted into public ones; in short, every means should be adopted which will mix the citizens one with another and get rid of old connections" (*Pol.* 1319). The new constitution even changed the way a man identified himself; henceforward, in his official designation, his name was followed no longer by his patronymic, with its proud emphasis on his family, but by the name of his deme.[26] Such radical incursions by political reformers into the sphere of what we would regard as private relationships show that the old loyalty to the family was strong enough to be reckoned with as a challenge, perhaps as a danger, to the new democratic institutions, and in fact the history of the Greek *polis* bears eloquent testimony to the fact that in moments of crisis many a man would often stand by his blood relatives even if it meant civil war or betrayal of the *polis*.

This historical opposition between family and *polis* was no new subject for the theater of Dionysus; it is one of the many threads in the complex fabric of the *Eumenides* of Aeschylus. In that play the primitive justice of the old family organization, a personal justice administered by the relative of the murdered man, has resulted in the insoluble dilemma of Orestes' murder of his mother. The way out is found in the creation of a new system of justice, and this system is inaugurated by the goddess Athena and administered by the Athenian *polis;* the state assumes what had been the age-old responsibility of the blood relative. The court of the Areopagus asserts, in its first decision, the priority of the civil institution of marriage, a link between two people of different blood, over the ancient tie of blood relationship; it judges that the murder of a husband by a wife is a more heinous crime than the murder of a mother by a son. And this judgment is firmly set in a political context; in the speeches of Athena the dominant theme is Athenian democracy, its institutions, its problems, and its great future. Aeschylus presents the rejection of the supremacy of blood-relationship as a crucial stage in the development of Athenian democracy. And it is remarkable that in his grand design the old, primitive blood loyalty is associated throughout with the female: with Clytemnestra and the Erinyes on stage, and in the imagery of the trilogy with all the monstrous creatures of pre-Olympian divinity, who are mostly female—Sphinxes, Gorgons, Harpies. The central stasimon in the *Choephoroe* (central also in the trilogy), explores the theme of the dark, sexual violence of the female as the dominant force in the world of primitive man, a time when "many are the dreadful horrors of fear which earth breeds and the inlets of the deep sea teem with hostile monsters" (*Cho.* 585–588). The new dispensation, which begins with the first decision of the *polis*, asserting the priority of the marriage tie to that of blood, is on the other hand associated throughout with the male, with the reassertion of Agamemnon's greatness which is so marked a feature of the *Eumenides*, with Apollo, the male god *par excellence*, with Athena's male birth and her declared preference for the male. What anthropological, historical basis there may be for this presentation of human progress as a product of the struggle between male and female, *polis* and the family, is a controversial question hotly discussed and never likely to be fully or unanimously answered, but the idea is there—it exists for all to see in the structure, action, and imagery of the *Oresteia*. And it must be concluded, since Attic tragedy was so public and communal a form of art, that this idea was thoroughly familiar to the Athenian audience of the fifth century. In the *Antigone* the same basic opposition is expressed in the same terms. It is a woman, who, in defiance of the *polis* (βία πολιτῶν 79, 907) asserts the paramount nature of her duty to a blood relative; it is a man who proclaims the right of the *polis* to cut clean across such obligations, to demand loyalty to the *polis* even if it means betrayal of the age-old, sacred duty to bury a blood relation.

The devotion of Antigone to those of her own blood, an over-riding loyalty which allows no rival, is urged upon us from the start by a host of phrases (many of them containing words which seem to be fresh coinages of Sophocles)[27] which empha-size the physical intimacy, the near unity, of those born of the same mother. The untranslatable first line of the play —ὦ κοινὸν αὐτάδελφον 'Ισμήνης κάρα 'common own-sister Ismene'—preludes in the opening note of the overture the theme which is to be fully developed in her language and that of her sister throughout the first half of the play. "The son of my own mother," she calls Polynices (466–467) and "my own brother" (αὐτάδελφον again 503);[28] she sees no disgrace in honoring "those from the same womb" (τοὺς ὁμοσπλάγχνους 511)—this word, found only here in Sophocles, stresses the intimate physical bond between brother and sister.[29] She brushes Creon's claims aside with the phrase: "He has no part in this, to keep me from my own" (τῶν ἐμῶν ⟨μ'⟩ εἴργειν μέτα 48); the expression dismisses Creon's action as interference in a relationship which is exclusive. And in her last speech she speaks of going to join 'my own' (πρὸς τοὺς ἐμαυτῆς 893).

The closeness of the blood relationship is emphasized also by the profuse employment of the dual number in the speeches of the sisters. They speak of themselves in the dual throughout the first scene (there are seven instances of these forms used by the sisters of themselves in the first sixty-three lines of the play); they think of themselves as a unit.[30] (Significantly, the dual form is not used by either of them in this connection after Ismene has refused to help her sister bury Polynices' body.)[31] And the brothers too are referred to consistently in this old form which blurs the distinction between identities, or rather, emphasizes the close connection of two as opposed to the rest of the world.[32] For Antigone and Ismene the brothers are an inseparable entity,[33] and the use of this form to refer to them makes clear the gulf between the sisters, who cannot think of the brothers apart from each other,[34] and Creon, who distinguishes the patriot brother from the traitor. Antigone points the contrast when she quotes Creon's proclamation: "Has not Creon, in the matter of the burial of our (νῷν, dual form) two brothers (κασιγνήτω, dual again) honored the one (τὸν μὲν) and dishonored the other?" (τὸν δ' 21–22). In these two lines the resources of grammar and syntax are used with brilliant linguistic economy to present the difference between a family loyalty which regards the brothers as one and the loyalty to the *polis* which separates and opposes them.

The word which above all reveals Antigone's preoccupation is '*philos*,' 'beloved,' 'dear.' This word has a very wide range of reference, extending beyond that of loved object or person to 'friend' in the most superficial sense. But its basic and original meaning is 'a person or thing loved and close,' as is clear from its use in Homer as a sort of possessive adjective: φίλον ἦτορ 'my heart'[35] because the one closest and dearest to me.[36] The extension of this sense to a man's nearest relatives[37] is a natural and easy process and so too is the further extension to 'friends.' By Sophocles' time the word could mean either 'close relative' or 'friend,' depending on the context. This ambiguity is brilliantly exploited in the speeches of Antigone and Creon. For with the meaning 'relative' it describes a situation not only arbitrarily imposed by birth (not dependent on choice, as is the case with 'friends') but also unchangeable ('friends' may turn into enemies but no matter what a relative does the relationship remains the same). For Antigone, Polynices, who is *philos*, her own brother, can never be an enemy, *echthros*, but Creon cannot admit that Polynices, an enemy, *echthros*, should be treated as *philos*, a 'friend.'

In Antigone's speeches the word always refers to the blood relationship. "Don't you see," she asks Ismene, "that our

friends are threatened with the doom of our foes?" (πρὸς τοὺς
φίλους στείχοντα τῶν ἐχθρῶν κακά; 10). This is Jebb's translation, and his explanation of the line is right: that Polynices is
to share the fate of the enemy Argive champions, to be left
unburied.[38] But *philous* here cannot mean 'friends.' If ever
Thebes had an implacable enemy it was Polynices. What makes
him *philos* is that he is the blood-brother of Antigone and
Ismene. And Ismene uses the word in exactly the same sense in
her reply (οὐδεὶς μῦθος . . . φίλων 11). But though she recognizes the validity of the claim of blood relationship and will ask
her dead brother for pardon, Ismene has not the courage to defy
the *polis*. Antigone, who has, states her purpose with an emphatic repetition of the same word: "I shall lie beloved with
him I love" (φίλη μετ' αὐτοῦ κείσομαι, φίλου μέτα 73); she will
go to make a grave for her 'most beloved brother' (ἀδελφῷ
φιλτάτῳ 81). And Ismene recognizes her loyalty with the same
word: "You are senseless, but a true loving sister to those you
love" (τοῖς φίλοις δ' ὀρθῶς φίλη 99).[39] In Antigone's farewell
speech the word is heavily emphasized again. "I am in hopes,"
she says, "to come as one beloved (φίλη) to my father and
dear to you, mother (προσφιλής), and beloved to you (φίλη)
brother" (898-899); she is going, as she says to join 'her own'
(πρὸς τοὺς ἐμαυτῆς 893). The threefold repetition in a context
where she speaks of returning to the closed circle of the family,
complete, but for her, in the world of the dead, shows what the
word means to her. So earlier, in her lament for her death,
which she must perform herself, as she says, because no relative
remains to perform that family office over her tomb, she sees
herself as 'unmourned by *philoi*' (φίλων ἄκλαυτος 847), she is
aphilos (876) 'friendless,' 'relationless,' "none of my dear ones
wails for me" (οὐδεὶς φίλων στενάζει 882). It is in the light of
all this that we must understand her famous reply to Creon's
claim that the patriot brother Eteocles would resent funeral
honors paid to the traitor Polynices: οὔτοι συνεχθεῖν ἀλλὰ
συμφιλεῖν ἔφυν (523). "I was born"—the literal force of ἔφυν is
important here; it is not citizenship but birth that determines

one's allegiance—"I was born not to join in their political hatred for each other but in their love for each other as blood brothers." To her mind, even the fact that they killed each other does not cancel the relationship of *philia* between them; she is convinced that Eteocles, if he had lived, would have buried his brother and that, dead, he approves her deed. There is in fact only one case in which the tie of blood relationship can be cancelled: the betrayal of the sacred obligations that tie imposes. And there is one member of the family whom she in fact repudiates. It is Ismene. "I cannot feel affection for a *philê* (a loved one), a relative—who shows love in words only" (λόγοις φιλοῦσαν . . . οὐ στέργω φίλην 543), she says bitterly, and from this point on she talks as if Ismene had ceased to exist. She has no *philoi* to mourn her death, she calls herself the 'last' of the family (λοισθία 895), she is the 'only remaining' (μούνην λοιπήν 941) daughter of the royal house.

The nature of her loyalty is recognized and clearly stated by her opponent, Creon. "I shall kill her," he tells Haemon, "and in answer let her sing her hymns to Zeus of the kindred blood" (ἐφυμνείτω Δία ξύναιμον 658-659);[40] this word ξύναιμος he has already used of the brothers (198) and the sisters (488).[41] And he also states clearly and consciously that in putting Antigone to death he is repudiating that blood loyalty for which she stands. "Even if she is my sister's child, even if she is more close in blood than all those under the protection of Zeus of the family enclosure (τοῦ παντὸς . . . Ζηνὸς ἑρκείου), she shall not escape death" (486-488).

In her devotion to family, she ignores completely the rights of the *polis*. The first six lines of her opening speech, in their syntax as in their vocabulary, imply, as we have seen, a mentality which is confined within the limits of the blood relationship. When, in verse 7, the first reference to the *polis* appears, it is presented as the threat, the enemy. Antigone does not use words that, like τύραννος, for example, might have justified her disobedience of Creon's order in political terms; her description of the edict she intends to defy is couched in phrases which would recall to the audience the legal powers and methods of their own democracy. She speaks of a proclamation made 'to the whole people' (πανδήμῳ πόλει 7) by the 'general' (τὸν στρατηγὸν 8), a word which would suggest to the Athenians the position held in the fifth century by the democratic leader, the προστάτης τοῦ δήμου—it was in fact the office held year after year by Pericles himself.[42] To Ismene's objection that the burial is forbidden to the city (ἀπόρρητον πόλει 44) she answers simply: "He is my brother." To her emphatic statement of the official nature of the decree (νόμου βίᾳ . . . ψῆφον τυράννων 59–60) Antigone makes no reply at all, and Ismene's confession that she finds it impossible to act 'in defiance of the citizens' (79) she dismisses as an 'excuse' (80). Her loyalty is extreme and exclusive; far from admitting that the *polis* has any claims on her, she practically ignores its existence.

But the opening scenes of the play make it clear that now, if ever, the *polis* needs loyalty. The prologue is of course designed to show us Antigone's point of view, but even in the prologue we are made aware of the danger Thebes has so narrowly escaped and the critical situation which it still faces. The Argive army has only just withdrawn ἐν νυκτὶ τῇ νῦν (16), in the night which still waits for dawn; the conversation between the two sisters is the whispering of conspirators in the dark (κρυφῇ 291) of the very night in which the city has escaped sack and slaughter but is left leaderless by the death of its king in battle.[43]

With the entry of the chorus we sense fully for the first time the mood of the *polis*, and see Polynices through the eyes not of his sisters but of his fellow citizens. He is a traitor who brought a foreign army to sack his own city. The chorus has no doubt what the result would have been if he had won; he was beaten off, they sing, "before his jaws could be sated with our blood, before fire could lay low our crown of towers" (120 ff.).[44] Antigone and Ismene passed over in silence the fact that Polynices was guilty of a crime which was for the Greeks of the fifth century the most heinous imaginable, and the most savagely punished; in Sophocles' Athens the traitor to the city was in fact denied the right of burial in the land he had betrayed (though we have no record of a case in which the relatives were forbidden to bury the body elsewhere).[45] This stasimon prepares our minds for the entry of Creon, who now comes to speak for the *polis*.

His speech, a sort of inaugural address announcing the principles which will guide his management of the state, asserts the claims of the *polis* as predominant over and exclusive of all others. The city, he says, "is what preserves us" ($\H{\eta}\delta'\ \dot{\varepsilon}\sigma\tau\grave{\iota}\nu\ \dot{\eta}$ $\sigma\dot{\omega}\zeta o\upsilon\sigma\alpha$ 189); the ship of state on which we sail must at all costs be kept upright and afloat ($\dot{o}\rho\theta\H{\eta}s$ 190). In its interest we must sacrifice private friendship ($\varphi\acute{\iota}\lambda o\nu$ 183) and—for, as we shall see, he is conscious of the other meaning of the word—family obligations.

For us in the twentieth century this speech, especially the now hackneyed and much abused image of the ship of state, does not have anything like the force it exerted on the fifth-century audience. The claims of blood relationship are not so strong for us; we have no fresh history of conflict between family and state. But more important still, the state, for us, is very old, and, over many centuries of our history, great and monstrous crimes have been committed in its name. We are the children of generations which came early in our history to regard the state's claim to supremacy as the chief danger to individual freedom; and we ourselves live in constant fear of Leviathan, the huge spreading bureaucratic apparatus of the democratic state, still more in fear of the monolithic dictatorships which in Germany and Russia have twice in our lifetimes demonstrated the ease with which state power, used with cunning and cruelty, can extinguish the light of freedom. We instinctively distrust the speaker who appeals to reasons of state against individual liberty, even though, in critical situations, we may admit his argument. For us the pressing danger is not the anarchy that might result from the weakening of government, it is the growth of the state's power to the point where our freedom as individuals would vanish. "The man," says Creon, "who thinks a friend (*philon*) more important than his own country, I count as nothing." In 1939 E. M. Forster, who knows his Sophocles well and surely had an eye on Creon's speech, wrote the famous and scandalous sentence: "I hate the idea of causes, and if I had to choose between betraying my country and betraying my friend, I hope I should have the guts to betray my country."[46] This is of course a polemical statement, inspired by bitter memories of the crass propaganda used in the First World War, and deliberately couched in shocking terms, but it none the less expresses, in extreme form, a feeling which has its place in the consciousness of civilized modern man.

It could not have been written, much less said in public, in fifth-century Greece; its author would have been treated as criminally insane. Loyalty to the *polis* was not an abstract 'cause'; it was a practical necessity. War between one city state and another was a normal and accepted condition, and defeat in such a war might well mean massacre and enslavement; until Alexander's conquests replaced the small independent city with the huge kingdoms of the Hellenistic age, every Greek citizen knew that his individual freedom, property, and even life could be preserved only by the constant efforts and sacrifice of the citizen body as a whole. The devoted loyalty the modern state demands in emergencies—'*la patrie en danger*' —was in the small Greek *polis*, perpetually at war with its neighbors, a permanent need; the country was always in danger. But the *polis* was not only the community which afforded the individual defense from constant external danger. It was also the form of organization which preserved his civilization and distinguished him from the barbarian tribes that in the north were his close neighbors. The institutions of the *polis* were the guardians of all that he had won and constructed —of the Spartan *eunomia*, the discipline of law, of Athenian *parrhesia*, the precious freedom of speech. Behind the Athenian democratic constitution lay a long history of violence, anarchy and tyranny; that constitution had been dearly bought in blood and effort, heroically defended against foreign invaders and traitors at home. The *polis* was the sole guarantee of the civilization Athens now enjoyed. That same Pericles who in the Funeral Speech gloried in the individual liberty Athens gave its citizens could also later remind them that the *polis* is more important than the individual.[47] "I consider that if the city as a whole is on a successful course (ὀρθουμένην—Creon's word),[48] this is of more benefit to the private individuals of which it is composed than if it is prosperous in the individual fortune of each citizen, but on a wrong course as a community. For the man whose private affairs flourish when the city is in danger of destruction perishes with it just the same, but if the city prospers while he himself is subject to misfortune he is none the less preserved" (διασώζεται—Creon's word again).[49]

The Athenian *polis* seemed to its citizens to be the high point of a long development from savagery to civilization. In the famous ode which follows Creon's proclamation, the chorus sings of man's progress from helplessness to mastery of his environment, a progress culminating in the creation of the *polis*. He conquers the sea and land, the birds, fishes, and beasts, he teaches himself speech and ἀστυνόμους ὀργάς 'attitudes that enable him to live in a community.' And this community, the *polis*, preserves the progress he has made and makes possible still further advance.[50] The *polis* is the ship on which man makes his voyage forward, and at all costs it must be kept upright and afloat.

Creon's inaugural address is made to an extraordinary meeting of the assembly (σύγκλητον 160) which he has summoned to propose a matter for discussion (προύθετο λέσχην 161). These phrases suggest strongly Athenian constitutional procedure[51] and emphasize that he speaks as a representative of the *polis*.[52] "I have no respect," he says, "for one who thinks a friend (*philos*) more important than his own country." He applies this general principle to himself; he would not keep silent if he saw destruction coming on the city, nor would he count as *philos* a man who was an enemy of the country (185 ff.). The word *philos* is ambiguous; his intention to forbid burial to Polynices, his sister's son, shows that under the general meaning of his public statement—'friend'—there lurks the private meaning 'blood relation.' He proceeds to justify the action he has not yet announced. The city is what saves us, and sailing on this ship, keeping it upright, "we make our friends" (τοὺς φίλους ποιούμεθα 190). Here there is no ambiguity; we make, we choose our friends, we cannot, for better or for worse, choose our relatives. The city's interest dictates our choice of friends; we adopt as ours the city's friends and repudiate her enemies. The point is emphasized by the use of the word ποιούμεθα; it is the phrase used of 'adopting' a child. The friendships we make under the aegis of the city and in her interest present us with a new family, one that cannot bring us into conflict with the state.

And now, "in accordance with these principles," he goes on to announce the decree. But the words he uses (ἀδελφὰ τῶνδε 192), literally, 'brothers, to what I have said,' were carefully chosen by the poet. This is a metaphor which is rare in Greek poetry;[53] used here to introduce a decree which splits the duality of the two brothers, it suggests that Creon is fully conscious of the stand he is taking. Eteocles is to be buried with honors, but Polynices 'his blood brother' (ξύναιμον 198) is to be left to the mercy of the birds and dogs. The *polis* assumes the right to punish and reward, in death as in life, without regard to the family. And it is the family especially which is injured and insulted by this prohibition of burial. "No one is to mourn over him" (κωκῦσαι 204), he says: it was of course the immemorial duty of the family and especially of the women to wash the corpse, to dress it for burial, and to sing in passionate, self-lacerating sorrow of their loss. At the funeral of one of its members the cohesion, exclusiveness, and age-old sanctity of the family was most strikingly displayed. Creon's decree strikes at the very heart of family loyalty.

But he does not expect opposition from that quarter; all that
is left of the family of Polynices is two helpless girls. The news
of the attempted burial suggests to him the existence of a
political conspiracy. He must find the culprits as soon as
possible. When he does, he also finds that the logic of his
situation demands that he go one step farther along the road
he has chosen. He began by denying burial to his sister's son
and now to enforce that decision, he must condemn his sister's
daughter to death.

In the dialogue between them which follows her passionate
defense and his furious reply, the opposition of *polis* to family
is one of the points of conflict. Her claim—the only time she
makes it—that she actually has support among the citizens, is
dismissed: "You alone of the people of Cadmus see things this
way" (508). "Are you not ashamed to think separately from
these people here?" (510). The chorus gives her no support,
and she must change her ground; she proclaims that there is no
disgrace in showing reverence for blood relatives. Creon draws
the political distinction between the brothers, enlisting the dead
Eteocles on his side. But this attempt to introduce the point of
view of the *polis*, from which they are not only separate persons
but also opposites, into her closed world of blood loyalty, in
which they are inseparable and almost identical, is a failure;
she will have none of it. "An enemy," he says, "cannot be a
friend, a *philos* [and cannot be regarded as a relative either]
not even in death" (522). But she will join in 'the love of
brothers' (συμφιλεῖν 523). Creon abandons the argument. "If
you must love, go down below and love them" (524–525).

This decision to carry out the death sentence involves him
more deeply still in the quarrel between family and state. He
forbade the burial of a nephew and found himself condemning
a niece to death. And this means he has broken off the marriage
of his son. He must face the problem now in the person of his
own flesh and blood, Haemon, whose very name emphasizes
the blood relationship between them.[54]

There is to be no compromise. He tells his son that the con-

demnation of Antigone is τελείαν ψῆφον (632)—his deliberate
political decision, officially sealed.[55] He asks whether he comes
'raging' against his father—"or am I loved by you (σοί . . .
φίλοι), no matter what I do?" (πανταχῇ δρῶντες 634). There
is no give and take here; he will maintain what he considers
the interest of the *polis* even if it means losing the love of his
only remaining son. Haemon's answer is a soft one, and Creon
congratulates him on his loyalty and himself on his good fortune in having such a son. Haemon must renounce Antigone,
"with contemptuous loathing" (πτύσας, literally 'spitting') as
if she were an enemy (δυσμενῆ 653). The claims of the *polis*
override not only loyalty to kindred blood but even the passionate love of a young man for his betrothed. The point is reinforced by the choral stasimon which follows this scene, the
famous ode on love—("Ἔρως ἀνίκατε μάχαν 781 ff.).

For Creon the family is a sort of training ground for the
exercise of political virtue. It is a sphere in which the highest
good is discipline (κόσμος).[56] Haemon, by observing family
discipline, will show his capacity to be a good citizen and
eventually a good ruler. "Whoever is a man of worth in his
relations with his family (ἐν τοῖς . . . οἰκείοισιν 661) will appear a just man in the city too." And by the same token Creon
will show his capacity to be a good ruler by enforcing discipline
in his own family. "If I bring up those who are my natural kin
to be undisciplined (ἄκοσμα 660), then I shall do so all the more
to those outside the family." The family is like the *polis*.
Loyalty to its head is the condition of membership in it; in the
family as in the *polis* obedience (πειθαρχία 676) is the key to
safety and for both the greatest danger is anarchy (ἀναρχίας
672). "This is what destroys cities, overthrows houses, and
breaks the lines in rout in the spear fight" (673 ff.).

The sequence of events has forced Creon to more and more
drastic action against the family and to justify that action he
resorts to ever more extreme arguments. To Antigone's blind,
exclusive loyalty to blood relationship he opposes an equally
blind and exclusive loyalty to the *polis* and its ruler, himself.

'My brother, right or wrong' is Antigone's position. Creon says to Haemon: 'Your father, right or wrong' (πανταχῇ δρῶντες 634), and he implies: 'Your ruler, right or wrong.' Which is exactly what he goes on to say before the scene is over: "The man, whoever he is, whom the city puts in authority, his commands must be obeyed—great and small, right and wrong" (ἀλλ' ὃν πόλις στήσειε τοῦδε χρὴ κλύειν/ καὶ σμικρὰ καὶ δίκαια καὶ τἀναντία 666–667).

The spokesman for the *polis* here reveals himself as even more extreme and narrow in his loyalty than his opponent. Antigone ignores totally the claims of the *polis*, but Creon besides dismissing the claims of family, demands unquestioning obedience to himself from all the citizens, whatever he may do, right or wrong. Creon and Antigone stand irreconcilably opposed. The discussion between them (450–525) serves only to show that in their mutual dismissal of each other's fundamental assumptions they are, for all practical purposes, speaking different languages.[57]

IV

Antigone 2

ANTIGONE'S exclusive loyalty to blood relation-
ship clashes with Creon's equally exclusive loyalty to the *polis*,
and between these two loyalties, on the specific point at issue,
there is no possibility of compromise. But the irreconcilability
of the two opponents is made even more complete by the religious
difference between them; they stand not only for radically
hostile political conceptions but also for fundamentally different views of the gods man worships. Just as it has not always
been fully recognized that, in fifth-century Athenian terms,
Antigone's loyalty to the family implies a political viewpoint,
so it has not been generally admitted that Creon, as well as
Antigone, has a religious attitude. But he does. Both adversaries appeal to gods as well as to human institutions, and the
appeals are, on both sides, sincere.

Antigone's religious feelings are clearly expressed in the prologue. They go back, like her political loyalty, to sources older
and deeper than the *polis.* She has a respect amounting almost
to veneration for the dead of her family and a pious devotion
to the gods of the underworld, those gods whose keenest wrath
was reserved for failure or refusal to bury the dead.[1] The first
glimpse we are given of her religious motives reveals an ob-
sessive concern for the dead, their existence in the world below,
and their right to burial as a requisite for respect in that world.
This is actually the first hint of a motive of any kind which
Antigone gives us. When she first describes the situation to

Ismene she tells her that Creon has "hidden Eteocles below the
earth, respected by the dead below" (τοῖς ἔνερθεν ἔντιμον
νεκροῖς 25). This respect of the other dead is something of
which Creon by his decree has deprived Polynices. The expression she uses is often illustrated by a reference to the famous
passage in the *Iliad* (23.71 ff.) where Patroclus appears in a
dream to Achilles and demands quick burial. "Bury me as
quickly as you can, let me pass through the gates of Hades.
They push me far off, the souls, the images of the dead." But
there is no such suggestion here; in fact, if we were supposed to
think of Polynices as wasting in some sort of limbo for the
unburied,[2] Sophocles would surely have made such an idea
explicit, for it would have been an even more compelling motive
for Antigone's defiance of the *polis* than what he *has* supplied.
The phrase ἔντιμον νεκροῖς implies more than a simple permission to pass through the gates of Hades, and for its implied
opposite, ἄτιμος νεκροῖς, 'unrespected by the dead,' we can find
a parallel not in Homer, but closer, in Aeschylus. Orestes in the
Choephoroe wishes that his father had been killed at Troy (345),
for then he would have left behind him fair fame in his house.
"And would have been," the chorus continues his thought,
"conspicuous below the earth, a king, august in honor"
(σεμνότιμος ἀνάκτωρ 356). "Whereas now," Verrall comments,
"his honor is impaired by the insults of his death and burial."[3]
Agamemnon's respect among the dead can be restored only by
the punishment of his murderers. Even in death's kingdom the
Greek is still obsessed with τιμή, the respect of his fellow men.
Antigone is spurred to action not by a Homeric belief that
burial is necessary if the dead man is not to linger on the
threshold of life and death but by a feeling that Polynices, if
his corpse lies unburied, will suffer the contempt of his fellow
ghosts. It is to restore his τιμή that she resolves to bury him.[4]

   The first reference to what might justly be called religious
motives is in fact really an extension of her loyalty to blood
relationship. And in Ismene's reply the same concept is implied:
"I for my part will beg forgiveness of those below the earth"

(τοὺς ὑπὸ χθονός 65). There is no ground for taking this to mean 'the gods below the earth' (as Jebb does, though he adds 'and also the departed spirit of Polynices'),[5] for the gods have not yet been mentioned, and Antigone's reply to Ismene begins with what is exclusively a reference to Polynices: "I shall bury him. . . . I shall lie beloved with the one I love most" (71, 73). But now, faced with Ismene's disapproval, she uses specifically religious terms for the first time. "I shall commit a holy crime" (ὅσια πανουργήσασ' 74), ". . . But if you feel that way, show disrespect for what the gods hold in respect" (τὰ τῶν θεῶν ἔντιμ' ἀτιμάσασ' ἔχε 77). The word 'gods' is finally pronounced, at the end of a series of ambiguous phrases. But the expression which introduces the whole statement, ὅσια πανουργήσασ', prepares our mind for the transition. It is a surprising phrase. The word πανουργεῖν—literally, 'to do anything'—smacks of the market place rather than the tragic hero. The usual translation —'crime'—blunts the edge of the Greek word;[6] a 'crime' may be magnificent in some way, but πανοῦργος has a strong overtone of contempt—it implies trickery, low cunning, unscrupulousness.[7] With this word she defiantly anticipates the worst the world can say to condemn her action;[8] it shows the same contemptuous pride which prompted her to stress the legal, constitutional basis of Creon's power rather than justify herself by calling him 'tyrant.' But with this word she couples another, ὅσια—'something in the divine domain as contrasted with the human.'[9] There is already present in this startling juxtaposition the contrast she will clearly formulate later, between divine authority and human. And in the last line of her speech she refers for the first time to the gods as her sanction; she accuses Ismene of showing disrespect for what the gods hold in respect. It is the same word she used before, of the burial of Eteocles, 'respected by the dead below.' But she has now enlarged her claim; her action is not only a restoration of the τιμή of Polynices, it is 'honored in the sight of the gods.'[10]

With Ismene she can urge now one claim, now the other (and in fact before the prologue is over she returns to the demands

of the dead brother on his blood relatives 94 ff.); for a sister
both claims are equally valid. But haled before Creon she
naturally puts her stress at once on her position as champion of
a religious loyalty which overrides man-made law; the position
already clearly implied in ὅσια πανουργήσασ'. She has 'over-
stepped these laws' (Creon's phrase for his edict) because it was
not in any way[11] "Zeus who made this proclamation" to her
(the phrase is a contemptuous barb at Creon, who did) "and
because that *Dikê* (that retributive, balancing justice), which
shares the household of the gods below, did not prescribe such
laws for mankind." He has accused her of 'overstepping'
(ὑπερβαίνειν) the laws; she uses a stronger term for his offence
—he has tried to 'outrun' (ὑπερδραμεῖν) and so 'defeat' the
divine ordinance.[12] "I did not think your proclamation so
powerful that [you],[13] a mortal man, could overcome the unwritten and unfailing *nomima* of the gods." To his *nomoi*—
'laws' (she allows his proclamation that title)—she opposes the
nomima of the gods, their 'customs, ways, usages.' These are
customs hallowed by time and religious awe, which are not
engraved on stone or ratified by an assembly. They are so far
from being written law, and hence made by man and so subject
to change,[14] that they are eternal. "They are alive, not just
today and yesterday, but for ever" and, unlike written laws,
"no one knows when and from what source they first appeared."

This noble and deservedly famous passage has been the subject of so much controversial discussion that it is difficult to see
one's way clear through the jungle of interpretation, refutation,
and generalization with which it has been overgrown. The concept of 'unwritten laws,' ἄγραφοι νόμοι, appears in many con-
texts in the literature of the fifth and fourth centuries, and there
is a natural inclination to connect this speech of Antigone's
with these passages, especially with the famous reference to
'unwritten laws' in Pericles' Funeral Speech (Th. 2. 37, 3).
Antigone's lines, from Aristotle on, have been included in the
evidence for a widespread concept of unwritten laws which

represents the stirrings of individual conscience or the first groping of the Western mind towards the idea of permanent, natural or ideal law. One of my predecessors as a Sather Lecturer has even found in this speech 'the prototypes of the supreme Ideas of Plato' and so discovered "a direct line from one of the noblest beliefs of the fifth century to that doctrine which is Plato's chief glory."[15]

A cold eye cast on the lines in their dramatic context and on the particular words they contain sees only uncertainty where others are so sure. Apart from Aristotle (of whom more later), the main basis for the inclusion of Antigone's speech in the discussion of the general problem is its resemblance to Pericles' reference to 'unwritten laws.' But the resemblance is superficial; the two passages actually show profound differences of content and expression.

In the first place, the Periclean speech distinguishes the un-written laws from the written[16] (and in many other passages the two are sharply contrasted).[17] But in the *Antigone* there is no question of Creon's law being written; it is a κήρυγμα,[18] an emergency decree announced by the voice of a herald, the normal means adopted by a general (a term applied to Creon verse 8) to announce his will to the population in conditions resembling what we would call martial law.[19] The case for considering Antigone's expression as similar to that of Pericles and the others would have been infinitely stronger if Sophocles had made Creon's κήρυγμα a written law, and Ehrenberg (to whose lucid discussion of the whole problem I am much in-debted) regrets that he did not do so. "In opposing the un-written laws to Creon's decree Sophocles made what could perhaps be called a logical mistake" (40). If Sophocles was interested in the philosophical, political, and ethical problem raised by the concepts of unwritten and written laws, he un-doubtedly *did* make a logical mistake, a bad one in fact; and it is all the harder to understand because it would have been easy for him to present Creon's edict as a written law if he had so wished. It seems more likely that the antithesis between

written and unwritten law, with all the philosophical problems
it involves in later literature, was not in his mind at all.

Secondly, in the case of the unwritten laws of which Pericles
speaks, we have no idea what they said. Endless discussion of
what they may have been leads to no agreement. Like the
Eleusinian mysteries, which have remained a mystery, the
unwritten laws of Pericles' speech have defied all efforts to read
them. Ehrenberg's careful discussion draws a blank and ends
"without any manifestation of their particular contents. . . .
We cannot expect to find them clearly formulated . . . the
very nature of the concept excludes strict definition or limi-
tation." But in the *Antigone* the context shows clearly what the
unwritten *nomima* are concerned with—[20]one thing only: the
burial of the dead. And this is one of the few things that has
not at some time or other been proposed as one of the concerns
of the unwritten laws in the Periclean speech.

According to Xenophon (*Mem.* 4. 4, 19 ff.), Socrates applied
the term 'unwritten laws' (ἀγράφους . . . νόμους) to what
have been called 'the three Greek commandments': to honor
gods, parents, and strangers. Many scholars have thought that
this definition of the unwritten laws is valid for all the passages
where the phrase occurs, including the Periclean speech (though
Ehrenberg argues convincingly against this last notion).[21] But
these three rules have clearly little or nothing to do with what
Antigone is talking about.

The ancient authority for treating Antigone's speech as a
formulation of 'general,' 'natural' law is of course Aristotle, who
in two passages of his *Rhetoric* refers specifically to her words.
In both passages he quotes them as an example of an appeal to
'natural' law; it is 'common law' which 'exists by nature'
(1375 a); her action is 'just by nature' (1373b). This is typical
of Aristotle's treatment of tragedy as a whole: he secularizes.
From his discussion of fifth-century tragedy we would hardly
know, if all the texts had disappeared, that the gods play a
vital role in it,[22] and so here he blandly ignores the source of

those *nomima* Antigone defends and which she so clearly names. They are nothing to do with what is 'universal' or 'natural'; they are *nomima theôn*, the usages of the gods.[23]

And lastly the word she uses is not *nomoi* 'laws,' but *nomima*.[24] The history of this word has not yet been written, and conclusions about it must be based on incomplete surveys.[25] But it is fairly clear that in fifth-century Greek the normal force of the adjective *nomimos* was 'customary' and that the neuter plural *nomima* meant usually 'customs.'[26] Very often (and this is true even in the fourth century) these customs are in the domain of religion rather than that of the law.[27] And the word *nomima* was often used to describe the 'customary' rites of burial. In the Euripidean *Helen*, for example, it is twice used of the fake burial at sea which Helen contrives to rescue Menelaus from Egypt (1270, 1277), and, in his *Suppliants*, Creon's refusal to allow burial of the bodies of the seven champions is twice described with this word: the Thebans are "showing disrespect for divine custom" (νόμιμ' ἀτίζοντες θεῶν 19—Antigone's phrase exactly), they are "destroying the customary usages of all Greece" (νόμιμά τε πάσης συγχέοντας Ἑλλάδος 311). In the fifth century the phrase *ta nomima* carried as one of its major connotations the 'customary rites of burial for the dead,' and even in the fourth, though then it is often used to mean 'laws,' it is still the normal phrase for such ceremonies.[28]

Antigone's appeal is not general but specific. She is not opposing a whole set of unwritten laws to the written laws of the *polis*, nor is she pleading the force of individual conscience or universal and natural law. She is claiming that the age-old customary rites of mourning and burial for the dead, which are unwritten because they existed even before the alphabet was invented or the *polis* organized, have the force of law, unwritten but unfailing, which stems from the gods and which the gods enforce. If she had defied these *nomima*, she says, she would have had to stand trial before the gods (ἐν θεοῖσι τὴν δίκην/ δώσειν

459–460). Antigone's speech, far from pointing forward to
Plato's Ideas and Aristotle's Natural Law, points back—to the
age-old reverence for the dead and their protecting gods.

In the bitter conflict of the dialogue which follows her speech
Antigone makes clearer the nature of the authority to which
she appeals. To Creon's argument that the one brother was a
patriot and the other a traitor she replies: "All the same, Hades
desires these laws." "Who knows," she cries out, "if this [the
distinction between patriot and traitor] is free of pollution
(εὐαγῆ 521) there below?" She appeals to the same authority in
her fierce exchange with her sister. "Hades and those below
know who did the deed" (542). And others recognize what gods
she worships. To Creon's accusation that everything he says
is on Antigone's behalf, Haemon replies: "and on yours and on
mine and on behalf of the gods below" (καὶ θεῶν τῶν νερτέρων
749). At the end of the scene Creon recognizes her exclusive
devotion to the gods of death: "There let her make her prayer
to Hades, the only one of the gods she feels reverence for"
("Αιδην, ὃν μόνον σέβει θεῶν 777).[29]

Antigone's religious devotion, like her loyalty to the blood
relation, is older than the *polis*. It is that reverence for the
family dead and belief in their continued existence which seems
to have been the earliest religion known to man. Rachel Levy,
speaking of the excavations in the caves on Mount Carmel,
gives us a vivid picture of the unimaginable antiquity of this
religious belief and practice. "The uncouth bodies of Mousterian
men, who hardly walked upright, who seem never to have fully
developed articulate speech, were buried in trenches laboriously
excavated in the floors of their caves, under conditions which
leave no doubt that the living believed in their continued
existence, at a period long antecedent to the coming of the
Cro-magnons to Europe."[30] These customs indeed are not just
of today and yesterday—no one knows when and whence they
first appeared.

Interestingly enough, the rites paid to the dead, like the
loyalty to the family, seem to have been regarded with a

hostile eye by the *polis* at a certain stage of Athenian development; at any rate we read of legislation by Solon against undue
expenditure on funerals, a law which has been interpreted as a
political measure directed against the influence of the great
aristocratic families. "It hindered the cult of the grave," says
Bonner, "in which the populace could not participate."[31] But
the cult of the dead and the nether gods was in any case independent of the *polis*, for the chthonian deities, unlike the
Olympians, were never closely associated with any particular
city; their worship had no part in the pageantry and ceremony
of the life of the *polis*. Athens claimed Athena as its protector
and champion, Hera was at home in Argos and Ares in Thebes,
but Hades was a name no city wished to invoke—it was in fact
a name which men tried never to pronounce. "Of all men that
we know," says Pausanias, "only the people of Elis worship
Hades."[32] The temple was opened once every year, and even
then entry was not permitted except to the consecrated priest.
The city of Hades is nowhere—and everywhere. For this god
the cities of men had no importance; before him all men were
reduced to equality in the common fate of death. Antigone's
devotion to Hades and the gods below gives her a religious
sanction which is completely independent of the *polis*.

And these are the only gods on whom she calls, the gods, not
of the *polis*, but of the world below. She mentions Zeus as the
source of the troubles of the house of Oedipus (2), but when she
names him as authority for her defiance of Creon's edict, it is
not the same Zeus to whom Creon appeals so often. She associates Zeus with "that *Dikê* which lives with the gods below";
this is "underground Zeus," Ζεὺς καταχθόνιος, that "other
Zeus" who, as the Suppliants of Aeschylus sing "judges misdeeds in a final trial among the dead" (Ζεὺς ἄλλος ἐν καμοῦσιν
Supp. 231). Her appeal is always to the gods below, and to
Hades himself; in her farewell speech she pronounces the dread
name of his consort Φερσέφασσα (894), the queen of the underworld.[33]

All this means nothing to Creon. By his decree he has set

family and *polis* at odds, and by the same decree he has ranged the *polis* in harsh opposition to the old, fearful, religious awe for death, its principalities, and powers. For Creon there is obviously nothing intrinsically awe-inspiring in the fact of death. He can look at a dead man and decide coolly whether he should be honored for service or punished for treachery, without any religious fear. Death, for him, is simply the end of life. It can be used as a political deterrent, a threat to enforce obedience, a means of punishment, even as a privilege to be withheld from the obstinate under torture (308). He can say "Hades is what will stop this marriage" (575), without any of the feeling of invoking a personal god which we sense in Antigone's use of the same word (542), and he taunts Antigone with the threat of death. "Even the bold run away when they see Death near their life"—or perhaps it means: "when they see the death of their life near" (580–581). There is no consciousness at all in these expressions of that life in and after death which Antigone takes for granted. "The dead are dead," he might say, with Euripides' Admetus (*Alc.* 541). Antigone's statement that she will enjoy Polynices' love in death makes little sense to him; "Go down below and love if love you must" (524) is bitter sarcasm. He mentions life after death again, in his speech to Haemon, only to dismiss it in a savage phrase. "Spit on her and put her aside as an enemy," he tells his son, "let the girl find a bridegroom in the house of Hades" (653–654). The hyperbole marks his disbelief; not even Antigone can think that there is marriage and giving in marriage in the country of the dead. The commutation of Antigone's sentence from stoning to imprisonment in an underground cell in the rock is an almost blasphemous expression of his defiance of all that she believes in; the champion of the gods below against the *polis* of living men is to be confined living in a tomb—so she calls her prison and so Creon describes it later. "There let her pray to Hades, the only god she reveres, and perhaps she will be granted a favor—not to die—or learn, late though it be, that reverence for Death's realm is labor lost" (777–780). The fierce irony of these words—'let her pray to Death for life'—marks Creon's utter insensitiveness to the religious aspects of death.

But this does not mean that Creon is irreligious. Like the political aspect of Antigone's stand, Creon's religious belief is not usually given a proper emphasis. But it exists, is clearly expressed, and, what is more, it would have been not only recognized, but enthusiastically shared by most of the Athenian audience which saw the play.

Creon's point of view is simply that the gods, those gods worshipped in the city's festivals and housed in the city's temples, are the champions and protectors of the city. The first line of his inaugural speech invokes them: "Gentlemen the city is safe—the gods who rocked it in a heavy swell, have righted it once more" (τὰ μὲν δὴ πόλεος ἀσφαλῶς θεοί 163). And he enforces his statement that he himself would place the city's welfare above all other things and relationships, with an appeal to Zeus "who sees all things always" (184).

All this is often interpreted (in that same modern attitude of cynicism towards the state of which we have spoken before) as the conventional religious clichés of a statesman assuming office. But there is one reference to the gods in this speech which is not conventional, but fiercely sincere. "Polynices," he says, "the exile who returned and wished to burn from rooftop to foundation stone his native land, and the gods of the race" (καὶ θεοὺς τοὺς ἐγγενεῖς 199). He sees Polynices as the enemy of the gods as well as of the *polis*. And when the chorus in the next scene suggests that the burial of Polynices was 'god-directed,' he turns on them in zealous anger. "What you say is intolerable." His passionate words express a religious point of view, which, like the political view he puts forward in his first speech, must have seemed to the audience very like their own. "Intolerable! That the gods should show concern for this dead man. Did they proceed to bury him as a supreme honor for a benefactor—this man who came to put the torch to their temples and surrounding columns, the offerings displayed there, to scatter in confusion their land and laws? Do you by any chance observe the gods respecting the wicked? It is not so" (282–289). It is clear that Creon considers his proclamation as an expression of the will of the gods, in fact, he considers himself the spokesman and champion of that will.

But these are not the gods Antigone worships. Unlike Hades, they have their temples, with colonnades of marble pillars, full of statues and dedications; their likenesses are carved in marble on frieze and pediment. They are the inhabitants and guardians of the city's most central and sacred territory—the Acropolis, the Agora; their festivals are the checkpoints of the city's calendar. They are the focal points of local patriotism, the saviors invoked in the city's hour of danger and worshipped with songs and dances of thanksgiving in her hour of victory. These are the gods invoked by the chorus in the victory hymn which follows the prologue of the play: Zeus, who hurled down the enemy champion Capaneus from the battlements of Thebes, Zeus of the battle rout ($Z\eta\nu\grave{\iota}$ $\tau\rho\sigma\pi\alpha\acute{\iota}\omega$ 143) to whom the defeated enemy left their bronze armor for a trophy, great Ares (the patron deity of Thebes)[34] who, pulling extra weight like a trace horse in the chariot, dealt out heavy blows among the city's enemies, and Dionysus, the god whose mother was a Theban princess.

Between devotion to such gods as these and Antigone's exclusive reverence for the gods below the earth there is no common ground, any more than there is between her loyalty to the family and Creon's to the *polis*. In fact the opposing religious attitudes are extensions of the political: Creon is the champion of the *polis* and its gods, Antigone of the family and those gods invoked at the funeral, the ceremony which emphasizes the family's unity and its exclusiveness.

The conflict between two individuals represents the conflict between two different complexes of social and religious loyalties, one expressing the mood of the past, the other of the present. But we are never made to feel that these programs dominate the play, that Creon and Antigone are merely spokes-men of opposing ideologies. The formulation of their different points of view is a gradual development through the swift-moving action of the first half of the play; each new partial revelation of their fundamental beliefs is provoked by dramatic circumstance and action, and appears always as the natural expression of character. And in the second half of the play an astonishing thing happens. Both Antigone and Creon, as the pressure on them becomes intolerable, contradict and renounce the general principles they have claimed as support for their actions. The defense of their position falls back on purely personal considerations, unrelated to family, city, gods. "These people," said Haemon, speaking of the heroic temper, "when they are laid open . . ." (διαπτυχθέντες): this is what happens to both of the antagonists—they are laid open for us to see, and there is nothing there but the stubborn, individual, private will.

For Antigone this surprising development is brought on suddenly by the immediate prospect of death. She made light of death before, welcomed it as a gain, claimed it as her choice, but now she is face to face with it, alone. "Even the bold," says Creon, "run away, when they see the death of their life near." Antigone does not weaken, but her mood does change. Before Creon she defiantly proclaimed her right and principle, but now she can think only of herself. She sings her own funeral lament. It is rudely interrupted by Creon, who orders his guards to take her away to her place of punishment. Her time has come; she is looking death in the face. There is no point now in explaining or defending her action to Creon or the chorus, and indeed she does not, in the famous speech which follows, address them at all. She speaks to her tomb, to her mother, to her brothers, first Eteocles, then Polynices. Her speech is addressed to the dead of her own family. She has per-formed the funeral rites for all of them, she says, last of all for Polynices, and for this her reward is death. So far she displayed the same complete loyalty to blood relationship and the rites of death she has championed all along, but at this point she makes a strange statement. "I would not, if I had been the mother of children, nor if my husband, dead, lay rotting in death, have taken this task on myself in defiance of my fellow citizens. In observance of what law do I say this? As for a husband, if he died, there could have been another, and another child from another man if I lost the first. But with my mother and father hidden in the realm of Hades, no brother could be born for me" (905–912).

This speech is of course one of the most discussed in all Attic drama. Ever since Goethe, who found it 'ganz schlecht,' expressed in his naïve and Olympian way the hope that scholars 'would find it spurious,' the argument has continued between those who find the lines intolerable and those who, most of them with various degrees of misgiving, defend the text. Opinions are still as divided as ever,[35] and no conclusive proofs are likely to be forthcoming; every reader must make up his own mind. It must however never be forgotten that to attack the authenticity of the passage is in this instance an especially radical piece of surgery, almost a counsel of despair. For the offending lines were in the text Aristotle read approximately a century after the first performance of the play, which means that our authority for this passage is better than what we have for most of the rest of the play—a manuscript written *fifteen* centuries after the performance. Not only that, but the casual manner in which Aristotle refers to the lines suggests strongly that in his time it was a celebrated passage, one everybody knew. If we are to believe that these lines were in fact inserted after Sophocles' death by some later actor, producer, or editor, we must face the consequences. And they are grave. Aristotle, the greatest scientific and scholarly intellect of the century after Sophocles, the most influential literary critic there has ever been, the head of a research school which busied itself among many other things with the history of tragedy, saw clearly the difficulties posed by the speech, and called the sentiment 'improbable' (ἄπιστον) and so demanding an explanation

by the poet, but it never for a moment occurred to him that
the lines might be an interpolation. If they are, then we are
forced to conclude that already, in Aristotle's time, the text of
the *Antigone* was so fundamentally corrupt in a crucial passage
that there was no criterion, no record, no tradition by which it
could be corrected.[36] Such a supposition deals a mortal blow to
our confidence in the general soundness of the tragic texts. If
that is possible, anything is, and we cannot object to those who
would delete and transpose right and left. We must even give
our late and reluctant blessing to the shade of August Nauck,
who, acting on a principle somewhat like that of the English
provincial dentist—"If you won't miss it, why not have it out?"
—gave the ungrateful world a text of Euripides some four
hundred lines shorter than any it had seen before.

On the other hand it is no use closing our eyes to the difficulties the speech presents. Jebb, who condemns it, states the
case against it most eloquently. "Her feet slip from the rock
on which they were set; she suddenly gives up that which,
throughout the drama, has been the immoveable basis of her
action—the universal and unqualified validity of the divine
law."[37] There can be no doubt that she does exactly that;
Hades desires the burial of a husband and a child just as much
as that of a brother.[38] She has for the moment ceased to speak
as the champion of the gods below. Only for the moment, for in
her very last speech as she is led off to her tomb she reasserts
her claim. "See what I suffer . . . for my reverent observance
of reverence" (τὴν εὐσεβίαν σεβίσασα 943). This fact has been
used (by Jebb for example) against the authenticity of the
speech in which her loyalty to the nether gods is abjured, but
it serves rather to define the nature and suggest an explanation
of that speech. In this final assertion of loyalty to the gods of
death, as in all the others, she is addressing her fellow citizens
and her enemy; she is making a claim, a defense, a protest. In
the tortured speech in which she speaks so strangely she is
talking neither to Creon nor to the chorus, but to the dead of
her family, whom she is shortly to join. She is alone with them,

oblivious of the presence of others; not one line in the speech is addressed to those present on stage. Like Ajax in his great speech of agonized self-questioning, she struggles with her own emotions in a self-absorbed passion which totally ignores the presence of those around her.[39]

This is the moment when in the face of death nothing matters but the truth. She is not trying to justify her action to others, she is trying to understand it herself. In the loneliness of her last moments in the sunlight, all that was secondary in her motives, all that was public rather than private, all that was self-comfort and hope, dissolves before her eyes, now made keen-sighted by the imminence of death. And one thing is very clear. The gods she championed have failed her. She says so herself: "Why should I in my misery look to the gods any more? Which of them can I call my ally?" (922–923). A Christian martyr, secure in his faith and remembering that Christ rebuked those who demanded a 'sign' as a 'wicked and adulterous generation,'[40] does not expect a miracle to save him or even a lesser manifestation of God's support. But the ancient Greek did. The world was full of signs and portents, omens and miracles: when Odysseus girds himself for the battle with the suitors he asks not for one sign of heaven's support, but two —one inside the house and one outside. And both are immediately sent.[41] But Antigone is given no sign of approval or support, and though she will later in her last appeal to the chorus describe herself once again as the champion of reverence for the gods, she cannot offer herself that comfort now. She is reduced to purely human feelings; all that is left her is the love she bears the dead of her own blood. As she goes to join them she tells over her claims to their love and gratitude. She has performed the burial rites for all of them, last of all for Polynices, an action which has cost her her life. For him she has sacrificed her life as a woman—the husband and children she might have had. In the almost hysterical hyperbole of her claim that she would not have run such a risk for that husband and those children she will now never live to see, she is telling Polynices that no other love, not even that she might have had for the child of her own body, could surpass her love for him. The illogicality of her explanation cannot be denied. Her words—"with both parents dead, no other brother could be born"—are better grounds for saving a live brother than burying a dead one, and of course in the Herodotean passage Sophocles is adapting it *was* said of a live brother. But the illogicality can be understood; for Antigone the distinction between living and dead has ceased to exist. She has for some time now regarded herself as dead[42] and she talks to Polynices as if he were alive; she is dead and about to be entombed in the land of the living, he is alive in the world of the dead.

She has abandoned her claim to be the champion of the nether gods, and, also, by her statement that she would not have risked as much for her own child, her position as champion of the blood relationship. In her moment of truth she is moved by nothing but her love for her dead family, not the family as an institution, a principle,[43] but those individual human beings, father, mother, brothers, whom she now goes to join forever. The source of her heroic spirit is revealed, in the last analysis, as purely personal.

And Creon too is 'laid open.' The process is slower. Antigone abandons both her political and her religious loyalties in one speech—in one sentence, in fact; Creon denies first his loyalty to the *polis* and later to its gods. Up to the point where Haemon comes to reason with him, Creon is presented as a ruler who may be mistaken in his action but who sincerely believes that he is fulfilling the will of his fellow citizens and acting in their interest. His assertion of the priority of the claims of the *polis* is accepted by the chorus and buttressed by the first two odes they sing: the hymn of thinksgiving for victory, which emphasizes the monstrous nature of Polynices' crime, and the celebration of man's conquest of his environment and its culmination, the creation of the *polis*. In the argument with Antigone he claims the unanimous support of the citizens, and though Antigone denies this the chorus gives her no word of approval.

But with Haemon's opposition, Creon's position changes. As a father he expects love from his son whatever he may do, and, very soon, in the name of 'discipline'—*kosmos*—he demands from everyone loyalty to his rule, whatever he may do, just or unjust. For "there is no evil worse than anarchy" (ἀναρχίας δὲ μεῖζον οὐκ ἔστιν κακόν 672). This is a different mood from that of his inaugural speech; opposition has turned him into an extremist. There may indeed be nothing worse than anarchy, but there is something the Greeks thought just as bad— tyranny; and Creon's statement contains the seeds of it. In the face of Haemon's continued opposition and his statement that 'the whole city' (ὁμόπτολις λεώς 733) praises Antigone, the seed springs to full growth. "Shall Thebes tell me what orders I must give?" "Am I to rule this land for others than myself?" "Yes," says Haemon, "for it is not a *polis* if it belongs to one man." To which Creon answers: "The city is the ruler's property." It is the watchword of the tyrant, and Creon immediately proceeds to act like one: Antigone is to be brought out and killed before the eyes of the man who loves her. Creon no longer speaks and acts for the *polis* as a whole; he speaks for no one but himself.

The *polis*, in the person of Haemon, has turned against him, and he defies it. Later Tiresias comes to tell him that the gods are against him too, not the nether gods, whom he scorned, but the gods above. Tiresias is their spokesman, the prophet of Apollo, son of Zeus, and he has, as Creon admits, given the *polis* good advice before. He tells Creon now that these gods demand the burial of Polynices. Their altars, all of them, are tainted with carrion brought from the corpse by birds and dogs; the gods refuse to accept sacrifice. Creon contemptuously rejects the prophet's advice and expresses his rejection in a blasphemous defiance that far surpasses Antigone's momentary and hypothetical abandonment of the gods below: "You will not bury him in the grave, not even if the eagles of Zeus wish to seize his body and carry it off to the throne on which Zeus sits—not even in fear of that defilement will I let him be buried.

For I know well that no man has the power to defile the gods"
(1039–1044). "His religious sense is temporarily confused by
his anger," says Jebb of this blasphemous defiance, which is
unparalleled for its ferocity in all Greek tragedy. This will not
do. If ever a man denied his gods, Creon does here. Jebb proceeds to describe the statement that gods cannot be polluted
by mortals as "a sophism of the kind with which an honest but
stubborn and wrongheaded man might seek to quiet his conscience." "The most orthodox Greek piety," he says, "held
that 'no mortal could pollute the gods,'" and cites as his
authority the speech of Theseus in the *Heracles* of Euripides.
But Euripidean tragedy is strange water in which to fish for
examples of orthodox Greek piety. In that speech Theseus
denies the validity of that horror of infectious pollution by
murder or death which was fundamental to the old religious
feeling, which was built into the procedure of the Attic courts
of law, and which was so strongly held by Sophocles that even
Oedipus at Colonus, who has repeatedly proclaimed his inno-
cence in the deeds that have made his name a byword, still
believes that he must not allow his benefactor Theseus to touch
him (*OC* 1132 ff.). The words of Creon must have caused a
shudder in the audience; he violently and blasphemously
repudiates that Zeus on whom he called when he was sure the
gods were on his side, and who has now, through the prophet,
made clear his displeasure. Tiresias returns to the attack, and
spells out for him where the gods he once claimed to speak for
now stand. "You are keeping here a corpse which belongs to
the gods below, unburied, unhonored, unhallowed. With the
dead you have no business, nor do the gods above; this is something you have forced on them" (1070 ff.). Antigone was given
no sign of support from the gods below, but Creon has to face
the unmistakable anger of those above and the fearsome penalties which Tiresias now predicts.

This is Creon's moment of truth, and, unlike Antigone, he
gives in at once. But if, like Antigone, he had remained stubborn, and, like her, explored his real motive, what would he

have said? It is not an idle question, for he has in fact earlier in the play shown us what else, deeper than his claim to represent the *polis* and the gods above, keeps him steady on his fatal course. It is outraged pride. The fury he feels at the successful defiance of his first public act forbids him to retreat. "Since I caught her in open disobedience, the only one in the city, I shall not prove myself a liar in the city's eyes—I shall kill her" (655 ff.). This hurt pride is made more painful and dangerous by the fact that his opponent is a woman. "I tell you, I am not the man, *she* is the man, if victory remains with her and she goes scotfree," he says when she first defies him (484–485), and this bitter refrain occurs obsessively in every reference he makes to the quarrel from now on. "While I live, no woman shall rule me," he says at the end of this same scene (525). "We must not ever be defeated by a woman," he says to Haemon. "It is better, if we have to fall, to fall at the hands of a man; then we shall not be called inferior to a woman" (678–680). "This man, it seems, is fighting on the woman's side," he says of Haemon (740), and later shouts at him: "You disgusting character, less than a woman," (746), "You woman's slave" (756).

All that sustains Creon, in the last analysis, is outraged pride and contemptuous hatred for the girl who has defied him. "When they are laid open, they are seen to be empty." Empty indeed. Unlike Antigone, he has nothing strong enough to nerve him against the ultimate threat, which Tiresias now delivers in the name of the gods.

In both Creon and Antigone the deepest motive for action is individual, particular, inexplicable in any other terms than personal, a passionate, almost irrational impulse. But they have both appealed to greater sanctions, to conflicting institutions and gods. The questions they have raised bulk large in the play, and they must be somehow answered. The answers, such as they are (for this is a play, not a philosophical dialogue), are

given to us in the concluding scenes, in what happens to
Antigone and Creon.

Creon, to enforce what he considers the good of the *polis*, has
defied in action and denied in speech the obligations imposed
by membership in the family. Not only has he exposed the
corpse of a nephew, condemned a niece to death, and broken
the marriage of a son, he has also shown, in many of his
speeches, a clear consciousness of what he is doing. His rejection of the claims of the family is deliberate. When disaster
comes on him so suddenly, it is precisely in this sphere that
the hammer blows strike in swift succession: his own family
turns against him in violence and hatred.

He has his own idea of what the family should be—a disciplined
community, a *kosmos*, like the *polis*, obedient to its head. When
Haemon professes such obedience, Creon, in his joy at the
possession of so dutiful a son, reveals his conception of the ideal
family. "That's how you should feel in your heart, my boy—
to stand behind your father's will in all things. That is why men
pray to beget obedient children to have in their house—so that
they can repay their father's enemies with evil and respect his
friends equally with their father. But a man who begets
children that are no help to him—there is nothing else to say
but that he has brought into the world trouble for himself and
something for his enemies to laugh at" (639–647). His illusion
is short-lived. Soon he is raging in anger at his son: "You villain,
arguing with your father" (742), and Haemon leaves him with
the bitter farewell: "You will never set eyes on my face again '
(764). There is much worse to come. When Creon, now re-
pentant, but too late, comes to the tomb to release Antigone,
Haemon, the messenger tells us, spat in his father's face, tried
to kill him, and then, in rage at his failure, killed himself.
Creon's wife Eurydice, who has heard the messenger's story,
kills herself in turn, and her last words are a curse on her
husband Creon 'the killer of his son' (τῷ παιδοκτόνῳ 1305).
The family, that ancient and intimate relationship which Creon

has treated with such contempt, takes an exquisite and terrible revenge.

But this is not all. Creon cannot even claim, in the end, that what he did was for the best interests of the *polis*. He has turned into a tyrant prepared to impose his own will, right or wrong, on the city which he considers his own property; and that will is clearly exposed as contrary to the interests of the *polis*. Tiresias tells him so. The exposure of the corpse has polluted the city's altars and so cut it off from communion with its gods; "the gods no longer accept prayers or sacrifice at our hands." The responsibility is Creon's. "This sickness has come on the *polis* through your ideas" (1015). There are political consequences of Creon's error, too. The exposure of the bodies of the other six champions (a detail cryptically referred to in Antigone's first speech[44] but now brought out into the open) has caused hatred for Thebes and Creon in all the cities which have sent their champions to the battle—"they are in a tumult of hatred" (1080). And this (though Sophocles does not specifically mention it) will in time produce a fresh—and successful—assault on Thebes. Creon's policy, far from guaranteeing the safety of the *polis*, will bring it once again face to face with siege and assault, and, this time, capture.

The great ode on man's progress to mastery of the world concluded with a warning. "Possessor of ingenuity of technique subtle beyond expectation, man moves now to evil, now to good.[45] If he includes[46] the laws of the land and the justice by which men swear in the gods' name, his city is exalted, and he is high in the city" (ὑψίπολις 370—the word means both things).[47] Creon has excluded the laws of the land (the word used, χθονός, suggests the earth in which the dead are buried rather than the earth, γῆ, which maintains the city's life) and also that *dikê*, that justice of the lower gods of which Antigone spoke; his city is humbled and he is brought low in it.

The messenger sums up for us the fall of Creon, his disaster both as ruler and father, in the state as in the family. "Creon was to be envied once, by my reckoning. He had saved this city from its enemies, he was given the full and sole authority over the land, and steered its course; he flourished like a tree in the noble children of his begetting. And now everything has been lost" (1160 ff.).

The gods too turn away from him. His belated amends made to the gods of death are ignored; Hades has already, through the suicide of Antigone, ensured Creon's punishment. The gods above, whose champion he once claimed to be, repudiate him, as Tiresias comes to tell him. He was wrong, wrong from the start; he does not even have the cold comfort of heroic obstinacy to sustain him. He broke, and tried to make amends, but failed to escape the consequences of his actions.

He realized his mistake at last. "I am afraid," he says, when he goes off to undo what he has done "that it is better to live out one's life observing the established ways" (τοὺς καθεστῶτας νόμους 1113)[48]—those ways, those laws, of which Antigone spoke, which are older than the *polis*, so old, that no one knows when and whence they first appeared. But he realizes too late. His punishment is already fixed. He is to live, but without any of the things that make life worth living. He has lost everything; not only son and wife, but also the respect of his fellow citizens, the chorus, who speak to him at the end in a tone of brutal severity. There is nothing left. He has hardly even an identity. "Lead me away," he says, in a terrible phrase, "I do not exist, I am nobody" (τὸν οὐκ ὄντα μᾶλλον ἢ μηδένα 1325).

And Antigone? She was the champion of the family against the *polis*, and though in her last clear vision of her action she realized that she was devoted not to the family as a theoretical principle but simply to her own existing relatives (for so she thinks of them, dead though they are), she can take comfort in the result. She is rightly confident of the gratitude of those beloved dead she goes to join. And even the last living representative of the family, the sister she rejects, shows such love for her that she tries to share her death. The family does not repudiate Antigone, as the *polis*, in the person of Haemon and later of the chorus, repudiates Creon.

But she has defied the *polis*. In the particular issue on which she defied it she was right, as the last scenes of the play make clear; the exposure of the corpse of Polynices is *not* in the interest of the *polis*. But, as Sophocles so repeatedly emphasizes in everything Antigone says, her attitude is not that higher, enlightened loyalty to the *polis* which pursues the best policy rather than the immediately expedient; it is an attitude which ignores the interests of the *polis* completely. The fact that she is right about what is best for Thebes is merely accidental; it is all too clear that if the exposure of the corpse of her brother *had* been expedient for the *polis*, she would have buried him just the same. She completely ignores the obligations which membership in the *polis* imposes, and even though Creon, their self-appointed spokesman, is wrong in the demand he makes, those obligations exist and no one in the audience for whom the play was written would have denied their force or sympathized with Antigone's refusal to reckon with them.

She has ignored the rights of the *polis*, and it takes its revenge. She is imprisoned in a tomb, condemned to inhabit that dark realm whose power she championed against the demands of the city of living men, and this sentence is described in political terms. "She shall be deprived," says Creon, "of her rights of residence as an alien here above" (μετοικίας . . . τῆς ἄνω 890). By her action she has in his eyes renounced her citizenship and become a *metoikos*, a resident foreigner, and of that status, which depends on the permission of the *polis*, he now deprives her. She has no citizenship or legal residence in the world above, but neither will she have it in the world below; she is to be a living being in the realm of death, neither dead nor alive, no full citizen even in the land of Hades, but, as she herself says, a *metoikos*, a resident alien, even there (852).

The warning at the end of the hymn to man's power and progress spoke of the man who, including in his technical and intellectual brilliance the laws of the land and the *dikê* of the gods, "is high in the city and his city high." "Cityless" (ἄπολις), it continues, "is the man who because of reckless daring, harbors thoughts that are not good" (τὸ μὴ καλόν). Antigone has shown the reckless daring (τόλμη) of which they speak; from their point of view as long-standing upholders of the government of the *polis* (165 ff.), her defiance of Creon's order and still more her slighting attitude to the demands of the city are 'bad thoughts'; and she is literally 'cityless' when she goes off to her prison—deprived of her full rights in the *polis* and, in the city of Hades, confined in a stateless limbo.

And the gods, though they make clear to Creon and to all men that she was right to bury Polynices, do not praise her. After her frank admission that she would not have done what she has done for a husband or a child, she has little claim on the gods below, and those above do not claim her for their own. When their spokesman Tiresias tells Creon he is wrong, he makes no mention of the fact that Antigone was right. He refers to her only once; her imprisonment in a tomb is an offense against the gods—she is merely one more count in the indictment against Creon. The gods punish Creon unmercifully, but they do not save Antigone.

In any case, she does not wait for them. "Which of the gods shall I call my ally?" she asked; she expects nothing. She hangs herself in the tomb. Like her father's self-blinding, it is an independent action; to the last she makes her own laws, goes her own way. She will not be what Creon's sentence made her, an outcast from the city of the dead as well as that of the living: with a noose made of her veil she makes herself a full citizen of Hades' kingdom and goes to join the family for whose love she thought the world well lost.

But though the gods do not save her life or express specific approval of her action, they complete her work. They see to it that Polynices is buried, with all due rites, and by the man who exposed his corpse. "We gave him the ritual washing of the

body," says the messenger, "plucked fresh branches and with
them burned what was left of him. And we heaped up a high
tomb of the earth of his own land" (1201–1203). And the gods
also answer her prayer.[49] "If these men are wrong," she said,
"may they suffer no more than they unjustly do to me" (927–
928). The gods punish Creon with precisely that exquisite
balance Antigone prayed for: he buried her alive, and the gods
make him, in the messenger's phrase, 'a living corpse' (ἔμψυχον
νεκρόν 1167). But his punishment can come only through
Antigone's death. If she had waited and he had released her,
he would have escaped. It is Antigone who, by her last defiant,
self-willed act, executes the sentence the gods have passed on
her enemy.

Though their action shows that she was right, the gods do
not condone her indifference to the claims of the *polis:* in the
phrase of Eliot's Fourth Tempter she is one "who does the right
thing for the wrong reason." But, as always in Sophocles, we
are made to feel that the gods recognize the hero's greatness.
In Antigone there is something else to recommend her to them,
as to us, something not always associated with the heroic
temper. Creon's deepest motive for his action was hatred—
hatred for the traitor Polynices and for the girl who defied his
power. But Antigone's was love. In the last speech where she
greets her dead mother, father, and brothers this love is revealed as the source of her heroic strength, the true justification
of her action; unlike Creon's hatred, it does not fail her in the
testing time but sustains her to the end. Earlier in the play she
has pronounced her own epitaph: "I was not born to join in
hatred, but in love" (ἀλλὰ συμφιλεῖν).

V

Philoctetes

PHILOCTETES is not only the loneliest of the Sophoclean heroes, a man who has lived, sick and without resources, on a desert island for ten years, he is also the most outrageously wronged. His comrades in arms who abandoned him had no excuse but the repugnance they felt for his sickness and their inability to stand his cries of agony.[1] He had done nothing to deserve such treatment at their hands. When they come to beg his help it is only to be expected that his refusal will be adamant, obstinately and intransigently maintained; and the expectation is not disappointed. Philoctetes lives up to all that we have come to expect of a Sophoclean tragic hero. Nothing can bend him to compliance. He resists the threats of enemies and the persuasion of friends; when deprived of the weapon which is his only means of life he chooses to stay on Lemnos and die rather than yield, and even when the weapon is restored to him, and he is promised glory and health, he still cannot be persuaded by the man who has now won the right to be called his friend.

The tragic hero hews to the pattern; but the situation in which he is placed is unique. Not only do we know that he must in the end yield to persuasion (for without him Troy cannot fall and we know perfectly well that it did), we also *want* him to give in, for this is the only way in which his terrible sickness can be healed. The drama of the assaults on the hero's will and his refusal to surrender is this time played out against

a new background: the inevitability—more, the desirability—
of his surrender. And this makes the *Philoctetes* a Sophoclean
tragedy in a class by itself.

It is a tragedy which, no matter how dramatic and painful
its episodes, is bound to have a happy ending. The same thing
might be said of the *Electra*, but the happy ending there, though
it is announced in the closing lines as the liberation of the house
of Atreus,[2] is also the murder of a mother by her son, egged on
by her daughter. When Electra, hearing her mother scream
inside the house as Orestes stabs her, shouts to him: "Strike
her twice, if you have the strength," we cannot help feeling
that the freedom the chorus celebrates has been dearly bought.
But the end of the *Philoctetes* must be the hero's departure for
Troy, where he will find not only healing from his wasting
disease but also the glory of capturing the city which has
resisted the entire Greek army for ten years. This is to be a full
compensation for his suffering; there is nothing to mar or cast
in doubt the triumph which the gods have reserved for him.
And, unlike Electra, he will win this happy outcome, not by
remaining obstinately true to his resolve, but by giving way.

In such a play, which avoids 'the incurable,' τὸ ἀνήκεστον,
we are emotionally engaged, to a greater extent than we are in
tragedy proper, in the working of the plot, the success or failure
of the intrigue. In true tragedy there can be no success, and we
do not really want it; we are watching the fatal career of a hero
whose obstinacy dooms him to defeat, but whom we do not
wish to see surrender. As we watch Antigone, Ajax, or Oedipus,
our deepest emotions make us hope that the compromises
offered the hero will fail; in the *Philoctetes* we hope for their
success. In the other plays we know they *will* fail; in the
Philoctetes we know that somehow they must and will succeed.
Consequently our attention is directed not only to the central
character but also to the methods used to influence him. With
Oedipus, the hero's reaction to the attempts to turn him from
his chosen path is more important than the nature of those
attempts; Electra's refusal is more important than Chryso-

themis' arguments; but in the *Philoctetes* the methods used by
Odysseus and Neoptolemos are just as much our concern as
the hero's reaction to them. For they must somehow succeed.
For this reason, the complications of the plot, the details of the
intrigue, demand our attention more insistently than in
tragedy of the normal type. They are in fact as vital as they
are in comedy, where the dramatic conflict is based on mis-
understandings which can be cleared up rather than on fundamental differences which can never be reconciled. The methods
used in the attempt to sway the heroic will are, in the other
Sophoclean tragedies, of secondary importance, for they serve
only to increase the hero's intransigence, but in the *Philoctetes*
they are all-important; the choice of method is crucial, for here
there are right methods and wrong ones, and somehow the
right one must be found.

There are only three methods which may be employed to
break down the heroic will—force, persuasion, and deceit,
βία, πειθώ, and δόλος. These words occur frequently in the text
of Sophocles; these are the methods attempted in all six of the
heroic plays. Against Ajax only persuasion can be used, as also
against Oedipus at Thebes, but Antigone has to face both
persuasion and force. So does Electra, who is also, in a way not
intended by its author Orestes, assailed with deceit—she has to
face the shock of the false report of her brother's death. Against
Oedipus at Colonus all three methods are deliberately used;
and against Philoctetes, too, the full armory of persuasion,
force, and deceit is brought to bear.

Force and persuasion are both dismissed as useless in
the prologue, when Odysseus briefs his young subordinate
Neoptolemos. "He will never be persuaded," says Odysseus
(103), and force is useless against the inescapable arrows of
Heracles (105). So deceit is tried first, but it fails, and then
force, but it fails, too, and in the end Neoptolemos must try
persuasion. It was obviously the right method from the beginning, for Philoctetes is to be offered not only healing but also
glory as a recompense for his long years of suffering, but when

it is tried, at last, its success is compromised by the deceit and force which have preceded it. The order in which the different methods are used and the identity of the persons who use them have an interest for us which is new in Sophoclean tragedy, for it is clear that the right method used by the right person at the right time might well have succeeded; (Neoptolemos comes within an inch of success as it is).[3] Whereas in the *Oedipus at Colonus* it would have made little difference to our feelings if the order had been reversed—if Polynices had tried to use force and Creon had limited his attempt to persuasion and deceit.

In the *Philoctetes* we are emotionally involved in the nature of the methods used to sway the heroic will and the order in which they are used, consequently we are also fully involved in the character of the persons who make the attempt. The figures of Odysseus and Neoptolemos are more fully developed, more rounded, conceived in greater psychological depth than is usual for the secondary figures in Sophoclean tragedy.[4] This is not to dismiss the secondary figures of the other plays as mere types; Ismene is a different person from Chrysothemis and Tecmessa a different woman from Jocasta. But it is still true that since their primary dramatic function is to advise the hero and fail to sway him, we are shown only those sides of them which are relevant to that function. One of the marks of literary genius is that it knows what to leave out; in these plays a strict economy of characterization is maintained because the attention of the audience must be focussed exclusively on the hero. But in the *Philoctetes*, since the methods used and their success or failure are of vital dramatic interest, the characters of those who use them must be fully realized. For the action prompts a series of questions about them. Why does Odysseus insist so strongly on deceit? And what is his real objective? Will Neoptolemos succeed in the lying policy he so reluctantly accepts and then so brilliantly executes? And what will happen to him if he does succeed? The limelight is still directed relentlessly on the hero, for every thought, word, and deed of the other two characters is concerned with him; but they have an importance of their own which is new in Sophoclean tragedy. As the play pursues its course, so full of turns and surprises, we find ourselves hoping not only that Philoctetes will indeed be rescued from his sickness and solitude, but also that Neoptolemos will somehow redeem his lapse into Odyssean treachery. And though we wish for the success of Odysseus' mission, we hope that he will somehow be personally defeated.

The two characters on whose choice of method everything depends, Odysseus and Neoptolemos, are strange bedfellows; in the prologue the cynical worldly wisdom of the older man provides a brilliant contrast with the all-too-naïve idealism of the boy. But the contrast between them is more than merely personal and dramatic. For Neoptolemos is the son of Achilles. The contrasted figures of Odysseus and Achilles had become, for the fifth-century Athenians, mythical and literary prototypes of two entirely different worlds of thought and feeling.[5] Achilles, the invincible warrior, was the ideal figure of the Greek aristocratic tradition,[6] a hero who deliberately sacrificed long life for glory, one whose passionate nature led him often to excess of violence but who was incapable of deceit. It is he who says, in the *Iliad*: "He is hateful to me as the gates of Death, that man who conceals one thing in his heart, and says another" (9.312).[7] Odysseus, the man to whom these words are pointedly addressed,[8] was, on the contrary, a man whose brain controlled his every action, for whom successful deceit was a matter for pride, and who, in the *Odyssey*, through constant vigilance, intelligence, and endurance, wins through to the end and returns home alive.[9] These two heroes are the polar opposites between which the Greek ideal of man moves in its search for the mean. The aristocratic viewpoint in Greek literature (in Pindar especially, who has no use for Odysseus)[10] is Achillean, an ideal of warlike generosity, of rigid standards of honor, of insistence on *timê*, the respect of the world—all this combined with the asceticism and physical beauty of the athlete and his all-too-frequent intellectual limitations. The democratic viewpoint (typically that of a seafaring and commercial community)[11] is Odyssean—an ideal of versatility, adaptability, diplomatic skill, and intellectual curiosity, insisting on success combined with glory rather than sacrificed for it. So, in the *Ajax* of Sophocles, Odysseus, who accepts the mutability of all things human, shows his adaptability by winning burial for the corpse of his bitter enemy; his conciliatory action and his persuasiveness present him as the type of the new democratic ideal,[12] opposed to the aristocratic intransigence of Ajax, and also to the tyrannical spokesmen of 'order,' the Atridae.

The introduction of these two figures, Odysseus and the son of Achilles (whose name is pronounced at once, verse 4) invokes for the audience the rich background of ethical and social significance with which poets and sophists had invested the contrast between the two great heroes, a contrast that was already emphasized by Homer in book 9 of the *Iliad* and book 11 of the *Odyssey*. But Odysseus' opposite number in this play is not Achilles, whom no one could move from his resolve, Odysseus least of all. It is his son, a very young man, almost a boy, new to action and debate, his great name still to win in the world. This expedition to Lemnos is in fact his first exploit. His youth and inexperience would suggest to a Greek (as we see from so many passages in Plato) that he needs an older man to attach himself to, who will guide and instruct him; this is all the more true of Neoptolemos because he has no father—the first time he saw his father, as he tells Philoctetes, was at Troy, a corpse laid out for burial. Circumstances have given him such an older associate, a teacher, a Mentor, in the person of Odysseus, under whose orders he has sailed to Lemnos.

He is clearly his father's son. He sees nothing wrong in violence. In fact, when he is told that Philoctetes is the objective of the expedition and that he must be deceived, he replies: "I am by birth incapable of action that involves double-dealing, like my father before me. But I am ready to bring him in by force, not by trickery. He has only one foot he can rely on, and could not overcome our superior numbers" (88–92). The fact

that Philoctetes is a cripple and no match for two strong men
does not deter him from the use of violence, which was his
father's native element, as it is to be his. But like his father he
will not lie. He would rather "act nobly and fail, than win by
base conduct" (94–95). In Neoptolemos we are shown the
Achillean ideal in its limitations and its essential nobility:
violent and primitive, yet, in its fierce way, honorable, and,
above all, ready to accept defeat rather than compromise that
honor. But he is young and inexperienced. Odysseus is his
commander on the first mission assigned him by the army.
Distasteful though he finds the deceitful role he is asked to
play, he hesitates to disobey orders; he is not yet grown to the
stature of his father who defied Agamemnon and the whole
Greek host. "Since I am sent to work with you, I hesitate to
earn the name of traitor" (93–94). That hesitation is the chink
in his armor, and Odysseus takes full advantage of it. By the
end of the prologue, with a deft mixture of authority, sophistic
persuasion, and appeals to his ambition, Odysseus has won
Neoptolemos over to his side. Neoptolemos consents to lie and
abandons the Achillean standard. In all he does and says from
now on, the constant reference to the name of Achilles will
remind us (and him) of the tradition he has betrayed and
prepare our minds for his return to it.[13] In fact, the lies Neoptolemos proceeds to tell present him as a sort of spurious Achilles;
words, mood, and pretended action are all a lying parody of his
great-hearted father. Achilles was deprived of his prize by
Agamemnon; Neoptolemos claims that the Atridae denied him
his father's armor. Achilles withdrew from the battle and
threatened to sail home to Phthia; Neoptolemos claims he has
withdrawn from the battle and is on his way home to Scyros
(240). And when Philoctetes asks him why he is angry with the
Atridae, he speaks with a mock-Achillean fury: "May I satisfy
my anger with this hand, so that Mycenae and Sparta may
realize that Scyros too is the mother of warlike men" (324–326).
It is a jarring reminder of the forthright and violent way of
speaking of the father he has betrayed. The figure of Achilles,

invoked so repeatedly throughout the play, is the measure of Neoptolemos' fall from heroic virtue and the ideal to which he must in the end rise again.

Over against the son of Achilles stands an Odysseus who is, in many respects, a degenerate descendant of the Homeric hero. Homer's Odysseus is a man of schemes and stratagems, and, unlike Achilles, he is devoted to life, not death, but he is still a fighting man and a hero, and there are times when he too must risk death rather than dishonor—as on Circe's island, where, urged to run away by Eurylochus, the sole survivor of the reconnaissance party, he replies stoutly: "I shall go there. A strong necessity is on me" (10.273).[14] The Odysseus of the *Ajax*, too, has his nobility, different from that of Ajax, more adapted to the world as it is, but still admirable. But the Odysseus of the *Philoctetes* is conceived along entirely different lines; he resembles the Odysseus of Euripidean tragedy, a fast-talking, cynical politician.[15] In the last years of the Peloponnesian war the Homeric hero appears often in the plays of Euripides as a type of the new political extremists, who, armed with sophistic rhetoric, dominated the Athenian assembly with their ferocious policies of repression and aggrandizement. For such a figure the old legend (not mentioned in Homer) that Odysseus was really the son of Sisyphus, the archetype of the trickster, who deceived even Hades himself and came back from the dead, seemed appropriate and was repeatedly invoked; in the *Ajax* it was an unwarranted insult,[16] but applied to the Odysseus of the *Philoctetes* (417, 624 ff.) it does not seem out of place. The Odysseus of this play has no heroic code which binds him, no standards of conduct of any kind; he is for victory, by any and every means. And victory for him cannot be anything which brings his own death; for him survival is an essential part of that success, that victory, *nikê*, which he hails as one of his protecting gods (134). For it he will do anything (he is πανοῦργος in the literal sense of the word), and he sums up his complete lack of moral standards in a revealing phrase. When Philoctetes reproaches him for his villainy and prays for his punishment, he replies calmly: "Where such men are needed, I am such a man" (οὗ γὰρ τοιούτων δεῖ, τοιοῦτός εἰμ' ἐγώ 1049). This phrase is the quintessence of moral relativism. The word 'such' (τοιοῦτος) instead of referring to something fixed and intelligible, refers to another 'such' (τοιούτων); this is the creed of the faceless timeserver: "I am—whatever the circumstances demand."[17] Behind Neoptolemos stands, as a reproach and an ideal, the figure of his heroic father, but for Odysseus there is no heroic standard, no point of reference at all, no identity.

But he can talk; he is, as he says himself, a man of words, not deeds (96–99). He needs all the skill he can summon, for his task is not easy—to turn the son of Achilles into a liar and trickster like himself. He takes the bull by the horns. "Son of Achilles," he begins, "you must be noble (γενναῖον)[18] in the mission on which you have been sent, but not in body alone" (50–51). 'Noble,' is a dangerous word for him to use, one which with its evocation of birth and parentage sums up a whole heroic tradition. Odysseus, in true rhetorical style, takes the principal argument against him and turns it into a weapon for himself. Neoptolemos must be worthy of his father, his courage, violence, and invincible audacity, but not alone in body—the son is to be as bold mentally as his father was physically. Odysseus subtly presents the deceitful role Neoptolemos is asked to play not as falling below the Achillean standard, but as rising above it, extending its narrow dimensions of physical prowess to include moral audacity. This is of course an exquisite perversion of all that the word γενναῖος means, and must have recalled to the audience precisely the kind of subtle distortion of the true meaning of words they had heard so often from sophistic teachers and ambitious demagogues, as it recalls to us Thucydides' brilliant description of the Protean variations of the meanings of words in times of revolution and civil war.[19]

The new 'nobility' is to deceive Philoctetes with words. Neoptolemos is to win the hero's confidence by means of a lying story of the wrongs he has suffered at the hands of Odysseus and the Atridae and of his intention to withdraw from Troy, and, like his father, abandon the Achaean cause. "Tell him you are Achilles' son. No need to lie about that" (57). But that will be the biggest lie of all. Neoptolemos cannot lie and be Achilles' true son. He will be the son of Odysseus. And at the end of the scene, when the young man, yielding to his teacher's authority and experience, agrees to lie, Odysseus calls him "my child" (τέκνον 130). This Odysseus is a slippery customer, and it is characteristic of him that his instructions to Neoptolemos are vague. The young man is to lie, yes, but what precisely is he supposed to *do*? There is no specific order to bring Philoctetes to Troy.[20] In fact, Odysseus repeatedly and exclusively emphasizes one thing and one thing only—the bow. It is this weapon, he says several times, which will take Troy. And with a promise (as vague as his orders) to send a sailor disguised as a sea captain to help him with a 'subtle speech' he leaves Neoptolemos to draw his own conclusions and fend for himself. The prophecy of Helenos, which is the reason he has come to Lemnos, he does not mention; he reserves that for another occasion. This matter of the prophecy has given rise to a great deal of discussion, for it seems to cause difficulties.[21] If the prophecy explicitly said that Philoctetes must be brought to Troy in person and in person fight and take the city, why, at various points in the play, do Neoptolemos and Odysseus and the chorus act as if they did not need Philoctetes at all, but only the bow? But these difficulties do not arise if we watch the play, as the audience did, without the two-edged benefit of a scholarly introduction, without preconceived notions, and take our cue from what the play reveals to us scene by scene.[22] The prophecy is not produced until later; it is clear that Neoptolemos was not sure of its exact terms until he heard them from Odysseus' disguised sailor, and that he did not realize the full significance of the prophecy until near the end of the play. Odysseus, who does know exactly what the prophet Helenos said, keeps it to himself in the prologue. He has perhaps good reasons. As the complicated intrigue,[23] set in motion and controlled by Odysseus, unrolls before us, the impression grows in our minds that

Odysseus' real objective was from the start the situation he produces three-quarters of the way through the play: the bow under his own control (he is an archer) and Philoctetes voluntarily, indeed passionately, determined to remain on the island. The glory of capturing Troy will fall not to Neoptolemos and Philoctetes, but to Neoptolemos and Odysseus. It is true of course that this is not what Helenos prophesied, but prophecies, as everyone knew, can be fulfilled in various and sometimes unexpected ways,[24] and in any case the Odysseus of this play is not the man who would stick to the letter of a prophecy when a free interpretation would suit his own book better.[25] Whatever his motive and real objective may be, the text is clear enough. He gives the young man vague orders from which only one thing stands out—the importance of the bow; "You must become the thief of the invincible weapon" is one of the few unambiguous instructions he gives. And it later emerges that both Neoptolemos[26] and the chorus[27] understood that they were to steal the bow and leave Philoctetes behind.

Neoptolemos has resolved to play the deceiver and, as he says, to "put away all sense of shame" (120). As he talks to the chorus we see that process at work; to their expressions of sympathy for Philoctetes he replies in cold egoistic terms.[28] And then he is suddenly faced with the man he is to deceive. The hero of the play is a sick, abandoned, bitter man who for ten lonely years has brooded over his wrongs and refined his hatred for those who left him on the island. To persuade him now to go to Troy, to win for those enemies the victory they have not been able to achieve by themselves, would be difficult enough already, even if the fact that Troy means health and glory for him were stressed. But as the confrontation between Neoptolemos and his intended victim develops, it becomes clear what the consequences of the decision to use deceit are: everything Neoptolemos says, truth and lies alike, feeds Philoctetes' hatred, confirms his prejudice, and hardens his mind against the leaders of the Achaean army.

Neoptolemos begins with the truth: "I am called the son of

Achilles, Neoptolemos. So—you know everything" (240–241).
He follows this immediately with his first lie, the elaborate and
well-acted pretense that he has never heard of Philoctetes.[29]
This is a terrible blow to the wronged hero's pride, which
reinforces his sense of grievance and his hatred for his enemies.
"Those who so impiously abandoned me," he says, "smile and
keep silent" (258). It provokes a description of his abandonment, his life on the island, and, to conclude, a curse on
Odysseus and the sons of Atreus (315–316). The false tale which
Neoptolemos now tells,[30] of Odysseus' refusal to hand over the
arms of Achilles and the connivance of the Atridae in this
injustice, seems all too true to Philoctetes and confirms his view
of the Greek commanders as hardened villains. The news of
the deaths of those Achaeans Philoctetes most admires, of
Achilles, of Ajax, of Patroclus, of Nestor's son Antilochus—
while Odysseus and Thersites are still alive—removes even
what little sympathy Philoctetes might have preserved for the
Achaean army and causes him to doubt the goodness of the
gods. When he finally begs Neoptolemos to take him home he
is a man who now has stronger reasons than ever before to refuse to go to Troy. The task of persuading him will be all the
harder when the time comes, as come it must, for even if he is
carried off to Troy by deceit, nothing can make him *fight* against
his will, and fight he must, if Troy is to fall. It will be harder to
persuade him. Was this in Odysseus' mind from the first? At
any rate, the disguised seaman who now comes to say what
Odysseus has taught him, completes the task and adds, if any
were necessary, fresh grounds for intractability. He reports the
prophecy of Helenos, that the Achaeans will never sack Troy
"unless they can persuade Philoctetes by words and bring him
from the island" (611 ff.).[31] But this vital information is set
in the context of a narrative which could not have been more
painful to Philoctetes if it had been deliberately designed to
enrage him—as perhaps it was, for the false merchant, as we
know, was briefed by Odysseus. Helenos, Philoctetes hears, was
captured by Odysseus, and it was Odysseus who at once, when

he heard the prophet's message, volunteered for the task: "to bring him and show him to the Achaeans" (δηλώσειν ἄγων 616), as he had already 'exhibited' (ἔδειξ' 609) his prisoner Helenos. He thought he would most likely bring him in of his own free will, "but if not, then by force." The whole thing is presented as Odysseus' action from the beginning, as an occasion for his personal glory; there is no mention of the glory reserved for Philoctetes and not one word of the healing of his sickness. Philoctetes is mentioned merely as an occasion for the triumph of Odysseus.

No wonder his reaction is fiercely negative. "Odysseus," he says, "it was he, that universal menace, who swore he would persuade me and ship me off to the Achaeans. I shall as soon be persuaded to come back from Hades to the light when I am dead, like his father" (621 ff.). The pity of it is that this wild exaggeration expresses the truth. The island, like that home he begs Neoptolemos to take him to, is a form of death, from which he is to be invited to return to life. Isolation and inactivity, first enforced and then preferred, are a kind of death for the man whose possession of the bow of Heracles marks him out for heroic labors and victory.[32] The gods have forced the Achaeans to offer him a return to life. But that offer he is now passionately resolved to refuse.

Neoptolemos has shown himself a brilliant pupil of his master. The sea captain was to be sent "if things seemed to go slowly," said Odysseus (126 ff.), but it is hard to see how Philoctetes could have been more quickly and expertly ensnared. He is now on fire with urgency to sail and goes in to the cave to collect his soothing drugs (a hint of the terrible attack of sickness which is about to come) and also any arrows for the great bow which may have been left there. Neoptolemos expresses his awe of the marvellous weapon, is allowed to touch it, and promised that it will be entrusted to him. He is now within an inch of success; once the bow is in his hands his mission is fulfilled.

As he goes into the cave with Philoctetes the chorus sings its first real stasimon. Its only activity so far has been a short, interrupted ode (391–402 and 507–518); the first strophe, like many another choral lyric in Greek tragedy, is an address to a god, in this case an oath, but it is unique in the fact that the oath is false, the god is called to witness a lie.[33] But now they sing, with heartfelt sympathy, of Philoctetes' sufferings during his long years of total isolation. The ode has a vital dramatic function. If the chorus, left to itself, momentarily free of the necessity to sustain the deceit, can sing like this, what must be going on in the mind of the son of Achilles?[34] The choral ode sets before us all those feelings of sympathy and admiration for Philoctetes which Neoptolemos has suppressed and hidden beneath the brilliant surface of his lying improvisations, all that is soon to burst out and overpower him. But not yet. The closing words of the stasimon are sung as the two men come out of the cave, and the chorus quickly puts its mask back on; they sing of the happy outcome for Philoctetes who will be taken to his home now that he has met "the son of noble men" (ἀνδρῶν ἀγαθῶν παιδί 719).

Suddenly, with the swift onset of Philoctetes' attack of pain, Neoptolemos gets what he wants: the bow is placed in his hands, and Philoctetes lies helpless, delirious, and finally unconscious. The plot has been brilliantly successful. "We must hunt for the bow," he had said to Odysseus (116) and now the hunt is over. But he cannot enjoy the victory. The agony of Philoctetes is unbearable, for others as well as for himself. At the end of his long heroic struggle, first to conceal it and then to control it, it takes complete possession of him, and he bursts out into a terrible cry of agony: ἀπαππαπαῖ, παπᾶ παπᾶ παπᾶ παπαῖ (746). This long rhythmic cry does not *mean* anything, and cannot be translated—the two translations I have looked at render it in the one case with "Oh!" and the other with "Pff!"[35] Jebb does not translate it at all, and he is right. For English, unlike Greek, has no formulaic sounds for grief and agony. There is a pitch of physical suffering which words are inadequate to express, and when human beings reach it they make sounds, like animals, which convey nothing but the extremity of their pain. In Greek these sounds are formalized; there is something to scream—not words, but sounds that one has heard others make in agony and that now offer, indeed impose, themselves as a formal pattern in which to express a suffering past human endurance. Such is Philoctetes' cry, and the only way to 'translate' it is by a stage direction: 'a scream of agony, twelve syllables, three iambic metra long.'[36]

We understand now fully why the Achaeans abandoned him. "Screaming and moaning," Odysseus said (11), but we could not have imagined anything like this. This animal scream of pain is more than other human beings can stand; we live by forgetting that such pain exists, we shut it away in sound-proof rooms and dull it with drugs. But Neoptolemos is brought suddenly and brutally face to face with it; he has to watch the momentary obliteration of personality, of all traces of humanity, under the pressure of intolerable pain. It forces from him his first expressions of sympathy. They are confused, incoherent, repetitive, unlike the smooth and skillful rhetoric of his lies. And when the great bow is handed over to him for safekeeping and he promises he will not leave without Philoctetes we have a sure sense that he means what he says. And he does. With Philoctetes asleep, and the bow in his hands, he rejects the urgent, repeated appeals of the chorus to leave the island at once. In a new meter, the hexameter, the medium of heroic poetry and of divine prophecy,[37] he states clearly what his objective has so far been as he renounces it forever. "I see that we have hunted this bow to no purpose, if we sail without him" (839–840). Faced with the unspeakable agony of the man he has come to pity and admire, he understands the real meaning of the prophecy of Helenos even though he has heard it only in the carefully calculated version of Odysseus' spokesman. It was not a promise of victory for the Greeks, with Philoctetes the instrument of their triumph; it was the recompense offered Philoctetes by the gods for all that he had suffered. "The crown [of victory] is for him . . . it is he whom the god told us to bring" (841). To the chorus' repeated exhortations to leave, fast and stealthily, he pays no heed. Philoctetes comes to his senses. The easy solution, to take the bow and leave and so avoid the reproaches of the sick man when he hears the truth, is no longer possible. Neoptolemos is now launched on a course which, as the chorus tells him, is full of insoluble difficulties (ἄπορα 854).

Philoctetes heaps coals of fire on his head. He had not expected such loyalty. The Atridae had abandoned him in exactly similar circumstances. "But you, your nature is noble, as your father's was" (874–875). But Neoptolemos is a prey to emotions that he can no longer conceal, and they force from him a sudden cry—παπαῖ (895). It is no ordinary exclamation; it is the same cry of agony we have heard Philoctetes utter in his torment. The agony of Neoptolemos is just as great, but it is of the mind. "What am I to do from now on?" (τοὐνθένδε γε 895), he asks himself. Not just, "What is my next step?"—though this is a grave question, for sooner or later Philoctetes must be told the truth about his destination—but also, "What am I to do for the rest of my life?" The glib formula of Odysseus— "Give yourself to me, for the short part of one day be shameless and then for all the future be called the most pious of men" (83–85)—he now sees as empty sophistry; what he has done in the short part of one day will be with him forever. "I shall appear ugly" (αἰσχρὸς φανοῦμαι 906). He has already told lies, and now he must suppress the truth. It is too much for him, and he tells Philoctetes where he intends to take him. To Troy.

He is now in a position halfway between the methods of Odysseus and those of Achilles. He has finally told the truth, but since he holds the bow of Heracles (without which Philoctetes cannot live on the island) he can compel the hero to go with him. The result is the same as if he had acted in Achillean fashion from the first, announced his intentions openly, and taken the bow by force. The only snag is that he won the bow not by Achillean violence but by Odyssean lies. In his speeches to Philoctetes he glosses over this weakness in his position, justifying his action by appeals to necessity, to 'justice,' to expediency (921–926).

These are strange arguments to hear from the lips of Achilles' son, and he cannot maintain them against the furious onslaught on his actions and the appeal to his pity which Philoctetes now makes. This speech hurls at him all the aristocratic terms of contempt for Odyssean double-dealing which he himself had so hypocritically used in his false tale, strips him of his feeble pretexts of necessity, 'justice,' and expediency, and shows him to himself as a degenerate son of his father, a worthy graduate of the school of deceit and treachery. Woven into the texture of the speech is the constant invocation of his father, which Philoctetes uses mercilessly to mock the young man's pretensions as a man of force. He interrupts his invective with moving appeals—"Give me back the bow. Be yourself again" (950)— and ends with a combined curse and exhortation. "May you perish—no, not yet, before I learn if you will still change your mind. If not, may you die a miserable death" (961–962).

Neoptolemos is deeply moved, and now wishes in truth what he had feigned to wish before, that he had never left his home on Scyros (969, cf. 459–460). Under the pressure of renewed appeals, he abandons his plans entirely. "What shall I do, men?" he asks the chorus, but it is evident that he answers his own question and moves to give back the bow, for Odysseus, who now breaks in, cries to him: "Let go that bow, give it back (πάλιν) to me" (975). The phrase can only mean that he catches Neoptolemos in the very act of handing the bow to Philoctetes.

And now Philoctetes meets his real enemy, who proudly admits his responsibility. "It was I, you are right, no one else. I admit it" (980). He goes on to tell Philoctetes that he must go to Troy, but in the most insulting and brutal terms he can find. The bow must go to Troy, he says, "and you must go with it, or they will ship you off by force" (982–983). "You must tread this road" (993). "You must obey" (994). Small wonder that his claim to be the agent of Zeus is rejected as a pious fraud, and his assurance that Philoctetes will be no slave but the equal of the best, with whom he must take the city, is ignored. Philoctetes is right: Odysseus *is* treating him like a slave. He tries to throw himself off the cliff, but is prevented,[38] and then, held by Odysseus' henchmen, he makes his long and passionate refusal to go to Troy. It is a speech which, as the chorus says, "does not give in to misfortunes" (1045–1046).

At this point Odysseus, instead of having Philoctetes forcibly put on board the ship, as he had explicitly threatened to do (983), renounces the use of force and, as he ironically puts it, 'gives way' (ἐκστήσομαι 1053) to Philoctetes.[39] "My nature is to wish for victory everywhere. Except in your case. Now I shall willingly give way to you. Release him."[40] Philoctetes can stay on the island. "Walk your beat on Lemnos. I wish you joy of it." The Achaeans do not need him. Teucros can use the bow or, better still, Odysseus himself. Is this unexpected manoeuver, as it has so often been explained, a mere bluff, a final attempt to bring Philoctetes round?[41] It is hard to see what its object is, if so. Whether Philoctetes is put aboard the ship by force or decides to go rather than starve on Lemnos without the bow seems unimportant—in neither case could he be described as coming to Troy 'of his own free will.' And he would still have to be persuaded to fight. The bluff, if successful, would accomplish nothing at all. And it does not sound like a bluff. Odysseus leaves at once, with final instructions to Neoptolemos: "You go, too; do not look at him, generous (γενναῖος) though you are. Don't spoil our fortunate success" (μὴ τὴν τύχην διαφθερεῖς 1069). This surely can have only one meaning. The bow is safely under Odysseus' control; the only way Neoptolemos can 'spoil the fortunate success' now is to persuade Philoctetes to come to Troy. Neoptolemos does go, but orders the chorus to grant Philoctetes' prayer and stay with him for a short time, though he knows and says that this gesture (which affords Philoctetes a last chance to change his mind) will meet with the censure of Odysseus.

And now the chorus makes the first serious attempt to persuade the hero. To his heart-rending lamentations in which he foresees his death on Lemnos they reply: "You, it was you who made the decision . . . this fortune does not come upon you from elsewhere, from a stronger power . . . This is destiny, the destiny of the gods, not any treachery at my hand" (1095 ff., 1116 ff.). But they have no right to take this tone, no right to reproach him, for they were themselves instruments in the Odyssean intrigue.[42] No wonder they cannot move him. He ends by proclaiming his inflexible resolve never to go to Troy. "Never, never, not even if the lightning bolt comes blazing to burn me. Be damned to Troy and all those beneath its walls" (ἐρρέτω Ἴλιον οἵ θ' ὑπ' ἐκείνῳ πάντες . . . 1200 ff.). He will go instead to Hades, by means of a weapon if they will give him one, if not, then by starvation and exposure on the island he now sees he was destined never to leave.

This scene, which employs the familiar situation and formulas of the attempt to persuade the hero to surrender, has a dramatic tension different from that of similar scenes in other plays. For though the chorus's self-righteous tone is contemptible, we wish for their success. Philoctetes' stubbornness condemns him not just to a spiritual death of inactivity and isolation, but now, with the bow taken from him, to death by starvation. And his heroic obstinacy also seals the triumph of Odysseus and his cynical manoeuvers. For the first time in Sophoclean tragedy we want to see the hero give in, and his intransigence, magnificent though it is, arouses our pity and the hope that another attempt to break it, made by a more honest advisor, will succeed.

We have not long to wait. Neoptolemos returns, still carrying the bow, followed by an anxious and puzzled Odysseus. The roles the two men played in the prologue are reversed; the initiative has passed to Neoptolemos, and it is now Odysseus who will have to hear "something new, something he has never heard before" (cf. 52–53). Neoptolemos is going, he says, 'to undo the mistake' he has made (λύσων ὅσ' ἐξήμαρτον 1224), the mistake he made in obeying Odysseus and the kings. He has made a clean break not only with Odysseus but also with loyalty to the army commanders; he is now ready to defy them, as his father did before him, on a point of honor. To Odysseus' argument that what he is doing is not 'clever' (σοφά 1245), he answers: "If it is right, it is better than cleverness" (τῶν σοφῶν κρείσσω 1246). He is back where he started before he became a disciple of Odysseus; he is ready to lose honorably rather than win by deceit. Against this instinctive nobility, impregnable now in its reassertion after a temporary lapse, Odysseus' sophistries are unavailing. Neoptolemos is more concerned with the restoration of his own honor, the necessity to 'retrieve his mistake' (τὴν ἁμαρτίαν . . . ἀναλαβεῖν 1248–1249), than the fate of Odysseus, Troy, and the Achaean army. With right on his side (ξὺν τῷ δικαίῳ 1251) he feels no fear of the army or its representative on Lemnos. Odysseus' threat to resort to force is a fiasco; his tongue triumphed in the prologue, but here it fails, and the resort to hands pits him against the son of Achilles on disadvantageous ground. He retreats ignominiously, and Neoptolemos calls Philoctetes out of the cave.[43]

He intends to restore the bow, but first he asks Philoctetes again to come to Troy of his own free will. The passionate refusal and the curses which accompany it he answers simply by handing the bow back to its owner. Odysseus' scheme is irretrievably wrecked, and his final appearance at this point, only to be chased off and almost killed by Philoctetes, emphasizes the fact that now neither force nor deceit can be used any more. Nothing is left but persuasion. And Neoptolemos, unlike the chorus, can make the attempt in honesty as a friend. He is now clear of guilt towards Philoctetes, as he says, and Philoctetes accepts him as Achilles' true son: "You have shown your nature, my boy" (τὴν φύσιν δ' ἔδειξας, ὦ τέκνον 1310). He can speak and try to persuade, as man to man, equal to equal.

His appeal is powerful.[44] It is what should have been said at the beginning. It starts with the most important argument: Philoctetes' sickness and the healing which awaits him at Troy. This was not mentioned in the account of the prophecy given

by Odysseus' emissary, nor by Odysseus himself, but it is
clearly implied in the prophecy of Helenos, for Philoctetes is
to *fight* at Troy, and it is obvious that the man who broke down
in such helpless agony earlier in the play must be healed before
he can use the bow of Heracles in combat. There is no other
cure for his sickness but "to go of his own free will to Troy."
There he will find release from his illness and "with these
weapons and with me you will be revealed as the sacker of
Troy's citadel." This *must* happen (δεῖ 1339); it is prophesied.
And it must happen in this present summer. What Philoctetes
is offered is 'a fine acquisition'—to be judged the bravest of
the Greeks, to come to the hands of healers, and to take Troy,
that city of sorrows, and win surpassing glory.[45]

This is how it should have been done right at the start. It
would have succeeded, for it almost succeeds now. Philoctetes
seems ready, after an initial protest, to yield. "What shall I do?
How can I fail to trust his words, this man who has given me
friendly advice? Suppose I give in then?" (1350 ff.). But the
thought of what giving in entails returns to plague him—the
fact that he will have to associate with his enemies, against
whom he has now more cause for anger than ever before. What
is he to expect from them in the future? He hardens irrevocably
against Neoptolemos' proposal and wonders how the young
man could have brought himself to make it. "You should not
go to Troy yourself . . . These are the men who treated you
with violence and insults, who stole your father's armor, his
gift of honor" (1364 ff.). The lie he told before returns to trip
Neoptolemos now. "I have come," he told Odysseus, "to undo
the mistake I made." It is not so easy; things cannot be so
simply undone. To explain to Philoctetes at this stage that the
whole elaborate and convincing story of Odysseus' refusal to
hand over the armor of Achilles was a lie from beginning to end
would not help matters now; he must try to argue his case on
the weak basis which is left him.[46] All he can do is repeat
what he has said before. But Philoctetes is adamant and

Neoptolemos gives up the attempt to persuade him. "The easiest thing is for me to stop talking, and for you to live, as you do now, without rescue" (1395–1396).

But he has forgotten something, and Philoctetes is quick to remind him of it. He promised, in his cunning attempt to win the bow of Heracles, to take Philoctetes home to Oeta. His action is no longer free; it is bound by the consequences of the lies he told. Not only is his sound argument undermined by the lying story of Odysseus and his father's arms, his present action also is hampered by a false promise he gave for a deceitful purpose. The means he used when he was the pupil of Odysseus turn in his hand; if he is fully to retrieve his mistake and restore his honor, he cannot leave things as they are, he must go all the way—fulfill his promise, take Philoctetes home, break irreconcilably with the Greek commanders, and renounce his own personal ambition and dream of glory, the sack of Troy. It is a hard decision to make; but for the man who claims to be Achilles' son it must be made, there is no other way. And he consents. "If that is what you want, let us go." Philoctetes finds the word for his decision: "That is a noble thing you have said" (γενναῖον εἰρηκὼς ἔπος 1402). It is noble indeed. In fact, Neoptolemos' decision adds a new dimension to the nobility of his great father. He sacrifices his own cherished ambition of glory to make up for his shameful conduct. Through the ordeal of his surrender to Odysseus and the triumphant reassertion of his own nature he has come to higher ideals of moral conduct than could have been expected of the boy who was averse to lying but ready to use superior force against a sick man. "You must be noble, like your father," Odysseus said to him, "but not in body only." In a way Odysseus could never have foreseen, this has come about. The renunciation of his future glory to atone for his past misconduct shows a nobility of soul which surpasses even that his father showed when he yielded to old Priam's plea and gave up the body of Hector for burial.

Philoctetes has won. The heroic will here wins a victory which outshines any that we have seen in the other plays. One man's stubbornness has defeated not only the whole Greek army but also the prophecy of Helenos and the will of Zeus, which is the pattern of history. It is an extraordinary moment in the theater of Dionysus, and we know, from the descriptions we have of the *Philoctetes* plays of Aeschylus and Euripides, that for the audience it must have been utterly unexpected. It is a theatrical *tour de force*, and we no sooner experience the shock of it than we realize that the play cannot end this way. For Philoctetes' victory is a terrible defeat. He will go home, a prey still to the monstrous pain of his sickness, to rot in idleness in Oeta as he did on Lemnos. And we know too that Troy did fall, and to Troy he must somehow go.[47]

It does not look as though he will. They move off stage now to the fast-moving rhythm of tetrameters, bound for Oeta and Scyros, as Sophocles extracts the last tense moments of suspense from the impossible situation he has created. Neoptolemos guides the cripple's steps and asks how he can escape the blame of the Achaeans. What if they come to attack Scyros? "I shall be there," says Philoctetes, "and defend you, with the bow and arrows of Heracles" (1406). It cannot happen this way. And this mention of Heracles reminds us strongly that it cannot. For if Neoptolemos throughout the play has moved in the shadow of his father, the standard from which he falls and the ideal to which he must rise again, Philoctetes too has behind him a heroic figure who serves as a measure to assesš his action and his stature: the figure of Heracles, whose invincible weapon he carries.[48] It is a name invoked often in the play. When Philoctetes first meets Neoptolemos he identifies himself proudly as the possessor of the bow of Heracles (262) and later, when he allows Neoptolemos to touch it, he tells him: "I obtained it by performing service for others" ($\varepsilon\dot{\upsilon}\varepsilon\rho\gamma\varepsilon\tau\tilde{\omega}\nu$ 670). That service, he tells him later, was to light the funeral pyre of Heracles (801–804). And when he hands the bow and arrows to Neoptolemos for safekeeping as the sickness overcomes him, he prays that they will not be a source of many labors and sorrows ($\pi o\lambda\dot{\upsilon}\pi o\nu a$), as they were for him, and the

one who owned them before him (777–778). Once he has lost
the bow, he speaks to it, imagining the shame it must feel in the
hands of Odysseus, the bow that once belonged to Heracles
(1128 ff.). And all these passages remind us that the bow of
Heracles, which he used against the giants, against monsters
and murderers, serves Philoctetes only to kill the birds and
beasts of Lemnos. He tried to use it against Odysseus and
promises now to use it against the Greeks. But it was not given
to him for such targets. In the hands of Heracles it accomplished great labors for mankind, and in the hands of Philoctetes too it is intended for great things. The heroic stubbornness
of Philoctetes is in fact devoted to a false objective. The
heroism of the great Sophoclean figures is displayed always in
action. Ajax crowns with a final magnificent act of violence a
long saga of prowess in battle. Antigone buries her brother, and
by her suicide brings about the punishment of Creon. Electra
stubbornly pursues her self-appointed task—to remind her
father's murderers of their crime and the vengeance that must
come—and helps the avenger when he at long last appears.
Oedipus at Thebes pushes on single-handed against opposition
to the discovery of the truth and at Colonus seals the doom
of his ingrate sons and by his choice of burial place gives Athens
victory over Thebes. But Philoctetes' stubbornness condemns
him to inaction, to ineffective suffering; he clings to the mood
of vengeful self-pity, which has been his comfort for ten lonely
years, and plays the role of victim rather than hero.

He must break out of his isolation, measure up to the heroic
standards of Heracles, his patron, and, like him, use the bow
not in the deathlike inaction of the island or his home but for
the purpose for which it was given him. "Pray," he said to
Neoptolemos, "that it will not be πολύπονα for you, a source
of labors and pain, as it was for me and for my predecessor."[49]
The word *ponos* means both 'labor' and also 'pain' (a linguistic
phenomenon only to be expected on the tongue of a people
whose highest ideal of life was *scholê*, leisure). The bow has been
associated with Philoctetes' pain, but in the hands of Heracles

it performed labors. And so it must in the hands of Philoctetes, and the time for those labors has now come.

But no human being can convince him of that. It takes a god come from heaven; Heracles himself appears to advise (παρῆνεσ' 1434) the hero.[50] He at once reminds Philoctetes what the bow and arrows stand for. "First I shall tell you of the labors I labored (πονήσας . . . πόνους 1419) and went through, and the immortal glory I have won." The same thing is reserved for Philoctetes—"after these sufferings (πόνων 1422) to make your life glorious." He is to go to Troy, to kill with the bow and arrows Paris, the cause of the war, and sack the city. Neoptolemos must go too. "You cannot take Troy without him nor he without you. Range like a pair of lions, guard each one the other." Neoptolemos is given at last the older man who will be his guide; not Odysseus, but Philoctetes. But he has grown to manhood in the fire of his ordeal and, though before he was Odysseus' subordinate, now he is to be Philoctetes' equal.

There can be no refusal: they both gladly accept. Philoctetes at last consents to come back from the dead, to life, to a life of activity and glory, of heroic action worthy of his great protector. But the play does not end on this note. It ends with his unexpected and beautiful farewell to the island. He is bound for Troy now, for the world of men and great deeds, the world too of his enemies—of Odysseus, of lies, craft, and stratagem, a world in which he must face the problem of living with others. And though he is content to go, the farewell to his island shows his love for it, for the scene of his lonely endurance and suffering —that island, which, like so many islands in the *Odyssey*, was a form of death, of oblivion, but also a tempting haven from the real world of men, with all its dangers, anxieties and disappointments.

> I take my last farewell of this island now.
> Farewell to the cave which shared my sleepless nights
> to the nymphs of the meadow's spring
> and the male thunder of sea on cliff.

Here was shelter for my head
yet the rainy squalls came in
and Hermes' mountain sent me back
the voice of my lamentation,
the echo of the storm in my heart.

Now stream from which I drank
now I must leave you, it comes at last
this parting I never thought to see.

Farewell, sea-circled island,
do not begrudge my leaving
send me a wind
to where destiny transports me
destiny, the wisdom of friends,
and the all-conquering divinity which shaped this decree.

VI

Oedipus at Colonus

IT IS the last play, written just before the poet's death, and not performed until five years after it. He died in 406 B.C., two years before the destruction of the Athenian fleet at Aegospotami; he did not live to see the Spartan galleys, their oarsmen paid by Persian subsidies, sail into the Piraeus and force the surrender of Athens. But he knew already, as all the world must have known, that Athens had lost the war,[1] that it faced certain defeat and, possibly—so greatly was Athens hated—extinction.[2] In the last terrible years of mounting despair, the dream of the Funeral Speech had turned into a nightmare. The government of the democracy was in the hands of violent, ignorant demagogues, the Attic soil beleaguered by a Spartan garrison at Decelea, a short day's march from Athens, the flower of Athenian manhood lost in Sicily and a score of indecisive battles on the Aegean. In the last months of his long life, Sophocles, born in the village of Colonus ninety years before, turned back to the figure of Oedipus, whom he had once portrayed as the ideal type of Athenian intelligence and daring, and wrote this strange play about the hero's old age, about the recompense he received for his sufferings, and also about Athens.

The recompense Oedipus is to receive is death—death as a human being, but power and immortality as something more than human, in fact as a protecting hero of the Attic soil. The close association of Oedipus with Athens is full of significance.

Oedipus *tyrannos* was the Athenian ideal of the days of the city's greatness, but his courage, energy, and intelligence were set in a tragic framework where their heroic impetus brought about his fall. The old Oedipus of this play is like the exhausted, battered Athens of the last years of the war, which, though it may be defeated and may even be physically destroyed, will still flourish in immortal strength, conferring power on those who love it.[3] It is no coincidence that this play contains the most moving and beautiful ode in praise of Athens that was ever written, a poem which celebrates Athens' strength, power, and beauty in images which suggest death and immortality in the same breath. The city, like Oedipus, may die, but only to become immortal.

The play is a worthy last will and testament. All the great themes of the earlier plays recur; it is as if Sophocles were summing up a lifetime of thought and feeling in this demonic work of his old age. The blind man who sees more clearly than those who have eyes is now not the prophet Tiresias but Oedipus himself, who prophesies, first in the name of Apollo and then in his own. As in the *Oedipus Tyrannus* and *Trachiniae*, the action unrolls against the background of the oracular prophecies of the gods, those cryptic, partial revelations of the divine knowledge which the human intellect cannot accept or understand until they are fulfilled. The heroic creed of Ajax, to reward friends and punish enemies, and that mutability of human fortune which mocks such a creed, reappear in this last play, but with a different emphasis. The theme of the *Philoctetes*, the hero's recompense for unmerited suffering, is used again; like Philoctetes, Oedipus, the despised and rejected, turns out to be the one man his enemies cannot do without, and they come to take him away. And death, that death Ajax and Antigone proudly claimed as their own, which Electra and Oedipus at Thebes wished for in their moments of despair, which Philoctetes preferred to the life among men which he had come, with good reason, to fear—that death is

Oedipus' declared goal from the first: he is a wanderer looking for the place where it awaits him, his promised rest.

And the play uses again the familiar situation and formulas of the heroic will and its victory over attempts to turn it aside. This is all the more astonishing because the beginning of the play seems to exclude such a possibility entirely. Oedipus is not only a blind beggar, he is also a very old man. And old men, in Greek tragedy, are not treated too kindly. With the single conspicuous exception of the prophet Tiresias (and even he is treated with a certain measure of cynical irreverence in the *Bacchae* of Euripides),[4] they are always portrayed with a keen eye for the foibles of old age. Officious and complacent like the Corinthian messenger in the *Oedipus Tyrannus*, weak and pathetic like Amphitryon in the *Heracles* or Peleus in the *Andromache*, cynical and selfish like Pheres in the *Alcestis* or Cadmus in the *Bacchae*, garrulous like Tyndareus in the *Orestes*, filled with impotent, bloodthirsty spite like the old servant in the *Ion*—they are usually either slightly ridiculous or sinister.[5] To cast an old man in the role of the hero was a bold step, and of all old men in the world this Oedipus is surely the least likely candidate. When we first see him on stage he is a repulsive sight. His son Polynices describes him for us later. "Dressed in clothes whose old disgusting filth has settled on his old man's body, irritating the flesh. On his eyeless head the hair blows uncombed in the wind. And in keeping with all this he carries what appears to be food for his wretched belly" (1258–1263). Sophocles spares us no detail of the hero's sordid condition; it is a salutary reminder, if Philoctetes' unbearable cries of agony did not suffice already, that the modern distinction between Euripidean realism and Sophoclean 'classic restraint' is, like so many such clichés, based not so much on the texts as on an ancient literary tradition which in this case owes more to Aristophanes than to Aristotle.

But this is not all. Not only is the blind, dirty, old man visually an unpromising subject for heroic treatment, he also

opens the play with a speech which is total renunciation of the
heroic temper: "Who will receive the wanderer Oedipus with
paltry gifts today? I ask little and get less, but it is enough for
me. I have been taught acquiescence (στέργειν 7) by my sufferings, by my constant companion, long time . . ." (χρόνος 7).
"We are come to learn (μανθάνειν 12), strangers from citizens,
and to perform what we hear (ἀκούσωμεν 13) from them."
This is the mood which all through Sophoclean tragedy the
advisors have tried to produce in the heroic soul, acquiescence
in the lesson of time. The humility of this speech was not to be
expected from the blinded but still demanding Oedipus we saw
at the close of the first play. The imperious figure who had to
be sharply reminded that he was no longer *tyrannos* in Thebes
has with time become humble almost to the point of self-
effacement. He is waiting, patiently and in submission, for
death.

That death, though he does not know it, is to be his recompense for his suffering. Not that he claimed or expected any
recompense, but we feel that it is his due. In the first play, he
served the gods as an example, a paradigm (παράδειγμα) as
the chorus calls him in the great ode which follows his self-
recognition (1193);[6] he was a demonstration, through his pre-
dicted destiny and his heroic action, that man's keenest sight
is blindness, his highest knowledge ignorance, his soaring confidence and hope an illusion. So Job served as the subject of a
divine demonstration, which was beyond his understanding,
and was in the end recompensed for his sufferings. "And the
Lord gave Job twice as much as he had before; the Lord blessed
the latter end of Job more than he had the beginning. For he
had fourteen thousand sheep and six thousand camels and one
thousand yoke of oxen and one thousand she-asses. He had
also seven sons and three daughters. And after this lived Job
an hundred and forty years and saw his sons and his sons' sons,
even four generations" (42.12 ff.). This is a reward which speaks
for itself; it needs no explanation. But the reward of Oedipus
includes no camels or she-asses, no long years of life, in fact no

life at all. It is death, but a death which Job and the author of *Job* could never have understood, something which the strict monotheism of the Hebrew would have regarded as an abomination. For Oedipus in death becomes a *heros*, a superhuman being, a spirit which lives on with power over the affairs of men after the death of the body. His tomb is to be a holy place; the city in whose territory he lies buried will win a great victory on the site of his grave. By his choice of a burial place he thus makes history, becomes a presence to be feared by some and thanked by others.

"We beg you," said the priest, in the earlier play, "regarding you not as one equated to the gods" ($\theta\epsilon o \tilde{\iota} \sigma \iota \ldots o \dot{\upsilon} \varkappa \iota \sigma o \acute{\upsilon} \mu \epsilon \nu o \nu$ 31). The *tyrannos* was not indeed equal to the gods (though he acted as if he were), but in this last play there is a sense in which he is. For at the end of it the gods call him to join them. "Equated to the gods." They do not show their face often in Sophoclean drama but we know by now what the gods are. They have knowledge,[7] that full, complete knowledge which Oedipus *tyrannos* thought he had. He was proved ignorant;[8] such knowledge is precisely what distinguishes god from man. Since the gods have knowledge, their action is confident and sure; they act with that swift certainty which was characteristic of Oedipus *tyrannos* but which was, in him, misplaced. Only a god can be sure; a man, never. And their action is just. Like the justice of Athena towards Ajax,[9] of the gods towards Creon in the *Antigone*, it is exact and appropriate, and therefore allows no room for mercy, though it can be angry. This full, angry, merciless justice is what Oedipus *tyrannos* tried to deal out to Creon in the earlier play, but it was based on ignorance, and was injustice. These attributes of divinity—knowledge, certainty, and justice—are the qualities Oedipus *tyrannos* assumed, and that is why he was the perfect example of the tragic inadequacy of human knowledge, certainty and justice. In this last play he assumes the attributes of divinity once again, but this time he *is* made equal to the gods. This old Oedipus, before the play is over, seems to be once more the young Oedipus we knew, fiercely angry in his administration of justice, utterly sure of himself, but this time he is justified. Now he does know surely, sees clearly; the gods give Oedipus back his eyes, but they are the eyes of superhuman vision. Now in his transformation (which is the action of this play), as then in his reversal (which was the action of the first), he serves still as the example, $\pi\alpha\rho\acute{\alpha}\delta\epsilon\iota\gamma\mu\alpha$. The rebirth of the heroic Oedipus in this tired, blind, old man emphasizes the same lesson, defines once more the line drawn between man and god, states again in images of overwhelming beauty and terror, that the possession of knowledge, certainty, and justice is what distinguishes god from man.

He has been promised, he tells us, 'rest' ($\pi\alpha\ddot{\upsilon}\lambda\alpha\nu$ 88) in a country which will be the end of his wanderings, where he will find a home and a welcome among the August Goddesses, the Eumenides. He is to find rest, but the rest must be won by great effort.[10] To win it he must summon all the qualities of heroic persistence which once were his; his road to it is to be a heroic achievement like his earlier fall. But this time the hardening of the heroic temper has a strange new meaning. In the last hours of his life as a man Oedipus gradually assumes the attributes and powers of the *heros* he is to become; the play puts on stage the mystery of his transition from human status to something greater.[11]

His opening speech shows us a man who seems to be at the end rather than the beginning. He has learned acquiescence; there is nothing more to learn. The nearby city, whose walls he cannot see, is merely one more temporary stop in his wandering existence, another place to beg for bread. He does not realize that it is the place of his reward, his grave, his eternal home. His first contact with the inhabitants of Colonus is not auspicious. He is brusquely interrupted in his appeal for information and ordered off; he has trespassed on holy ground, the grove of the Eumenides, daughters of Earth and Darkness, those august goddesses among whose dread and ancient functions was the fulfillment of a parent's curse.[12] But this rebuff brings an unexpected reaction; the humility of the beggar vanishes in a moment, and he replies with a refusal to move. He announces his decision in an absolute, determined phrase which recalls the heroic *tyrannos:* "I shall never move from this place where I have taken refuge" (45). "What does that mean?" asks the astonished native of Colonus, and he is answered with an enigma: "The watch word of my fate" (46). Oedipus has recognized his final resting place—among the august goddesses; here he is to stay forever. The patient beggar of the opening scene now demands an audience with Theseus, the king of Athens; in fact, since he has stated so emphatically that he will not leave, he is summoning the king to Colonus. He is sure that he will come. For Oedipus brings a gift to Athens. Theseus, he says, "by small service may win great gain" (72). The puzzled native of Colonus retires to talk this over with his fellow citizens, and Oedipus, left alone with Antigone, prays to the goddesses of the grove. We learn now the basis of his sudden confidence and peremptory speech. The prophecy of Apollo which foretold the deeds which have made him an outcast also promised him this resting place among the Eumenides,[13] and more than that. In this country he would end his life of suffering, and by his residence there be a benefit to those who received him and destruction to those who drove him out and so sent him there. He is to end his life by rewarding his friends and punishing his enemies. And though he has at the moment not the slightest idea how this will be accomplished, his faith in the god's word is so great that he sends for Theseus at once. He prays now to the goddesses of the grove for fulfillment of Apollo's promise, and calls on Athens to receive him, in terms that foreshadow his transition from body to spirit. "Pity this wretched ghost (εἴδωλον 110) of Oedipus the man; for this is not the body he possessed once long ago."

As a body, as a man, he is a thing to be pitied—blind, feeble, ragged, dirty—but the change has already begun. The first comer treated him with mingled pity and condescension—"You seem noble, though obviously unfortunate" (76)—but the chorus of old men of Colonus feels fear at the sight of him. "Dreadful to see, dreadful to hear" (δεινὸς μὲν ὁρᾶν, δεινὸς 141). They too order him to leave the sacred grove, and he does leave, but only when they have promised him protection in the new place of refuge to which he moves. When they extract from him his name, they go back on their promise. "Out of this country, go far away" (226). Apollo promised him 'rest' but it is a gift he must fight for. He must defend his past, and, not for the last time in this play, he rehearses the whole dreadful tale again. He acted in ignorance, he says, he killed his father in self-defense; his past is suffering rather than action. But now he comes to act, not to suffer, not in ignorance but in knowledge and power. He comes 'sacred' (ἱερός), the suppliant of the Eumenides, 'reverent' (εὐσεβής)—he is fulfilling the oracle of Apollo—and he comes "bringing advantage to this town" (287–288).

He does not yet know what advantage; he speaks with blind faith in the prophecy. In the next scene his daughter Ismene comes to tell him what he needs to know. His two sons are at war for the throne of Thebes, and a new prophecy has been delivered by Apollo at Delphi: that Oedipus, in his life and even after his death, will be sought after by Thebans, for their victory and power lie in his hands. Soon Creon, acting for Eteocles, will come to take Oedipus home. Not to Thebes, but to a place near the border, where he can be held, alive and dead, under Theban control. It is hard for the old man to understand this new prophecy, which seems to contradict the one he has just described, that he would find rest among the Eumenides, to whose grove in Athens he has been brought, as he sees it, by divine guidance (97 ff.). But gradually it becomes clear that the new prophecy supplements the old. It is his burial place that will bring victory, and the Thebans, much as they want that victory, still will not bury him in Theban soil, for he has his father's blood on his hands. "Then they shall never have me in their power" (408), he replies, and learns they will live to regret it; they will suffer from his anger when some day they take their stand in battle on the ground where he lies buried. He sees now that the two prophecies are one; it is by his choice of resting place that he can do what Apollo promised him the power to do, to hurt his enemies and help his friends. He chooses to give victory to Athens and defeat to Thebes when one day Theban armies invade Attic soil. He will deny both his sons the victory that either of them might win if he gained control of the old man's body; his anger against them is sharpened by their renewed ingratitude which appears flagrantly in their failure to invite him home to Thebes now that they have heard the prophecy (418–419).

He expresses his decision in words which show that he is still a man, no more. To reward Athens and punish Thebes by his choice of a place to die is something which *does* lie within his power as a man, and he states it as an intention, and as an offer to Athens. But the punishment of his ingrate sons is something over which the prophecy gives him no control, and that he can express only as a wish, a prayer: "May the gods not quench that fated strife between them and may the issue of their quarrel lie in my hands. If that were to be, the one would not remain king nor would the exile ever return home" (421–427). He prays for the fulfillment of the curse he has already[14] pronounced on them, that they should kill each other in the fight for his inheritance. This is no part of the prophecy of Apollo— it is his wish; but before the play is over he will restate it in the unmistakable voice of true prophecy, not Apollo's but his own.[15]

He has proclaimed himself a savior for Athens, and the chorus treats him now with respect. But if he is to stay in Colonus he must propitiate the goddesses on whose untouchable ground he has trespassed. The chorus describes for him in elaborate detail the purificatory ceremonies that must be performed. The scene is spun out far longer than is warranted by its technical (and necessary) function—to get Ismene off stage so that she can be captured by Creon. The loving care with which the ritual is described sets the tone for the religious mystery we are going to witness, and the scene also shows us the hero's docility and eagerness to be instructed in matters of religion,[16] an attitude which will be sharply contrasted with his growing assertiveness and intractability in his relations with men. The ceremony of purification will restore him to proper contact with the goddesses on whom he will later call for strength and words to curse Creon and his own sons; it is in no sense a ritual absolution from the pollution of his past actions. That will remain with him until the end.[17]

With Ismene gone to make the proper sacrifices, the chorus returns to its insistent, almost prurient, probing into the horror of his past, and it is in this atmosphere of old, terrible, crimes recalled that Theseus first comes face to face with his strange visitor. We are thus prepared for a repetition of the same outraged rejection that Oedipus has already suffered once, but that is not what happens. Theseus welcomes him, without any reference to the promise of advantage, but simply on the basis of his own experience of exile and his knowledge that all men are equal in the mutability of fortune: "I know, being a man, that I have no greater share of tomorrow than you" (567–568). It is the same tragic sense of life that Odysseus in the *Ajax* shows in his pity for his enemy; "thinking of my own case no less than his" (124). In the words and figure of Theseus we are presented with the best morality by which mortal man can live in this unstable world and a picture of the humane greatness of Athens at its best, the generosity and compassion which had long since vanished in the crucible of war and revolution but which Sophocles here recreates in all its ideal dignity and warmth. Oedipus has chosen well. *This* Athens deserves the future victory over a Thebes represented by the violence and lies of Creon, the hyprocrisy and fratricidal hate of Polynices.

His gift to Athens, the old man says, is his own wretched body. It will bring profit, but only after it is buried. It will bring trouble too, for the Thebans will come to claim it as their own property. When he learns that Thebes wants Oedipus back and that the stubborn old man refuses to go, because, as he says, they did not take him when he wished it, Theseus loses his patience and speaks to him harshly. "You fool, passion is not what your misfortunes call for" (592). The answer is a fiery rebuke from a superior. "Wait till you hear what I have to say before you reproach me" (593). His grave, he now explains, is to be the scene of an Athenian victory over Thebes at some future time. But Theseus, the statesman, cannot conceive of war between the two cities. Oedipus rebukes him in his turn. Such confidence is misplaced. "Dearest son of Aegeus, only to the gods comes no old age or death. All else is dissolved by all-powerful time. The earth's strength decays, the body's too, faith dies, mistrust flowers, and the wind of friendship does not blow steady between man and man, city and city. For some now, for others later, sweet turns to bitter, and back again to love" (607–615). These words strike the same note as the great speech of Ajax, written so many years before. In the flux of time nothing in this mortal world remains the same. No man can be confident of the future. Man's knowledge is ignorance. It is the lesson Oedipus himself learned in his own person at Thebes, and he reads it now to Theseus with all the authority of his empty eyes and dreadful name. But he does not apply it to his own knowledge. For he goes on to predict the future— war between Athens and Thebes. He prescribes for Theseus the limits of human knowledge but he is not bound by them himself; he speaks not as one subject to the law he lays down but as one of the powers that administer it. And with this confident prediction, this assumption of sure knowledge, goes anger, but the words Sophocles gives him suggest something stronger than the anger of a mortal man. As he speaks of the future defeat of Thebes on the field of his grave the words take on an unearthly quality, a daemonic wrath. "There my sleeping and hidden corpse, cold though it be, will one day drink their warm blood" (621–622).[18] There was nothing like this in the prophecy of Apollo; this stems from the growth of some new force and knowledge within himself. But the prediction is qualified: "if Zeus is still Zeus and Apollo a true prophet." He does not yet prophesy in the authority of his own name. That will be the final stage.

Theseus recognizes the authority of this speech and accepts for Athens the gift he is offered. "Who would reject the favor of such a man . . . ?" (631). The word he uses, *eumeneia*, is a word normally used of divine favor,[19] and the form of the word recalls the Eumenides, those kindly goddesses in whose grove Oedipus first recognized the watchword of his fate. Oedipus asked for a refuge, but he is given much more; Theseus makes him a citizen of Athens (ἔμπολιν 637) and assures him the full protection of his new city. Oedipus is now an Athenian; the wandering stateless beggar has a home, a city to protect him. And just in time; his enemies are close at hand. Creon has already seized Ismene and will soon be here in force, to take away Antigone, his other support (848)—like Philoctetes he is to be deprived of his means of life.

He is a citizen, and of no mean city. The ode which precedes Creon's entry sings the praise of Colonus and of Attica in those marvellous lines which recreate for us the Attic landscape as Sophocles knew and loved it: the thick shade of the trees, the nightingales in their branches, the ivy, the dew on the narcissus, the golden crocus, the river waters, the olive groves, the horses, the sea. This is Attica, not Athens; the city is not mentioned. And yet it is there. Every detail of the landscape recalls some aspect of the city's greatness.[20] The ivy of Dionysus, "who walks the land," and the narcissus, "ancient crown of the twin goddesses," remind us not only of the wine of the country and the grain which, so tradition ran, was first cultivated on Attic soil, but also of the theater which began in Athens and of the great religious center at Eleusis. The waters of the river Cephisus are associated in Attic legend with the goddess Aphrodite,[21] and, Sophocles adds, "the dancing chorus of the Muses loves them too." The olive, Athena's gift to Athens, "which flourishes most fruitfully in this land," produced the oil, the great Athenian export, carried to every quarter of the

Mediterranean world in those vases, made of Attic clay, which
men in countries where no Greek was spoken prized above all
other possessions and took with them to the grave. The horses,
Poseidon's gift, are the restive mounts of those aristocratic
Athenian youths who will soon ride to the rescue of Oedipus'
daughters and who still ride in the procession on the Parthenon
frieze. And the oar which Poseidon fitted to Athenian hands
had made the city undisputed mistress of the sea; for most of
Sophocles' long lifetime, no ship had sailed the waters of the
Aegean against Athens' will.

But under this lyric celebration of Athens' greatness through
the evocation of the landscape there runs a deep strain of
sadness. The nightingale is the bird of lamentation;[22] the
narcissus, which tempted Persephone to her doom, is the flower
of death;[23] the crocus, also associated with the Eleusinian
goddesses, was planted on graves. The power of Athens is
dying; that inviolate peace of the grove at Colonus and of the
Attic landscape had been breached and ruined. Colonus itself
had been just a few years before the scene of the last-minute
defeat of Theban cavalry *en route* for Athens;[24] the way to
Eleusis, the processional road, was barred by Spartan patrols;[25]
the olive trees of the Attic farms had been chopped down and
burned by the enemy who now occupied the northern ap-
proaches; the young horsemen of the frieze were long since
dead on the stricken fields of Delium and Mantinea; and
Athenian seapower rested now on a battle-weary fleet waging
an unequal struggle against superior forces which were soon to
annihilate it on the Hellespont. But the sadness is not despair.
For these same images speak not only of death but also of
immortality. The twin goddesses promised blessed life after
death and the olive is 'self-creating' ($\alpha\dot{\upsilon}\tau o\pi o\iota\acute{o}\nu$ 698)—the
sacred olive on the Acropolis, burned by the Persians, had put
out fresh shoots the next day.[26] The Athens Sophocles knew in
his youth is to die, but be immortal; he sings of it as he re-
membered it in its days of greatness and beauty, and this is
how we remember it still. "Even if we lose," said Pericles,

"the memory will live forever." The city of Sophocles' youth and manhood will put on immortality, like the old, blind man who has now become its citizen.

The wanderer has found a home, and now comes the attempt to dislodge him. Creon arrives, and with armed guards. The struggle of which Oedipus warned Theseus has begun. Creon has come with force, but first he tries deceit. He invites Oedipus back to the home of his fathers; we know, as Oedipus does, that this is a lie. Like Odysseus in the *Philoctetes*, Creon regards the hero as an instrument for his own purposes and does not see that the prophecy portends not advantage for Creon but recompense for Oedipus. His expressions of pity are hypocritical and hardly conceal his disgust. The answer he gets is not what he expected. We have seen Creon and Oedipus face to face before, in the earlier play, and there Creon had to bear the brunt of the hero's savage anger. So he does here. Their final interview is a repetition of their first. In both Creon is condemned out of hand, with the same swift, vindictive wrath, but this time the condemnation is just. Oedipus, blind though he is, sees through to the heart of Creon—he knows what Creon is. He taunts him with the truth. "Not to take me home, but to settle me outside the frontier so that your city (πόλις δέ σοι 785—he speaks as an Athenian) may escape from this land untouched by disaster" (784–786). But it will not happen that way. Now he prophesies, and now, face to face with the object of his wrath, he prophesies not in the name of Apollo, but in his own. "You will not have it so; what you will have is this—my avenging spirit dwelling forever in the land. And as for my sons, they will inherit of the land I ruled enough to die in, no more" (787–790).

Creon proceeds to show the justice of Oedipus' rejection by turning to force. He reveals that he has already seized Ismene; he now seizes Antigone and threatens to lay hands on Oedipus himself. Oedipus is helpless, and only the prompt arrival of Theseus saves him. This is the man in whom new strength is growing, power and knowledge which will make him equal to the gods; not the splendid *tyrannos* at the height of worldly success and bodily vigor, but a blind old man, the extreme of physical weakness, who cannot even see, much less prevent, the violence that is done him. Physical weakness, but a new dimension of spiritual strength. This Oedipus judges men justly and exactly, knows fully, sees clearly; his power is power over the future, the defeat of Thebes, the death of his sons. And this transformation of human weakness into superhuman power is conveyed to us in the familiar formulas of heroic intransigence. One thing Creon said to Oedipus throws light on the nature of the process we are witnessing: "Ill-fated man, will not even time teach you wisdom?" (804–805). Creon expected to find the Oedipus of the opening scene of the play, a man taught acquiescence by time and suffering. But what he finds seems to be the same *tyrannos* he once knew and feared. "You work evil for your own self now as you did then," he tells him, "indulging in that anger which has always been your ruin" (853 ff.). He recognizes the old man before him as equal to the young *tyrannos*. In one sense he is right, the heroic fire has been reborn in the old man, but in a greater sense the young Oedipus and the old are no more equal than man is equal to the gods.

Theseus' arrival rescues Oedipus, and his angry reproof of Creon restores the dignity of Athens, insulted by this successful attack on its suppliant and newly made citizen. But Creon is not finished yet. Deceit and force have both failed, and now he tries persuasion. Not on Oedipus, but on Theseus. His speech is a crafty attempt to alienate the city from the man it has taken in. He excuses his action on the grounds that he knew Athens would never welcome such a tainted man, the killer of his father, a man of impiety, who had been married to his mother. He appeals to the authority of the ancient court of the Areopagus "which," he says, "forbids wanderers such as this to dwell in this city" (948 ff.). It is a reproach to Theseus and a manoeuver designed to drive a wedge between Oedipus and the chorus. Oedipus must defend himself, and as an Athenian he speaks as if he were pleading before that solemn court

Creon invoked, the Areopagus, the ancestral Athenian place of judgment for cases of murder. His defense is detailed and omits no particular of the terrible events which cost him his eyes. It is a plea which the Areopagus could admit. He killed his father and married his mother in ignorance (ἄκον πρᾶγμα 977, ἄκων 987), not voluntarily. And as for his father Laius, Oedipus would have been innocent even if he had known his victim's identity, for he struck in self-defense. Not even his father, he says, if he were living, would contest this plea. The speech is intended to justify him before the high court of the city which has adopted him; and it succeeds. Theseus orders the pursuit of Creon's men, who are riding for the border with their prisoners, Ismene and Antigone; the power of Athens is engaged, at risk of war (which Creon threatens), to protect the rights of Oedipus.

With Theseus' return and the restoration of the daughters to their father's arms, the action seems to be almost complete. "I hold my dear ones," says the old man, "and now were I to die, I would not die wholly wretched" (1110–1111). But the thunder and lightning and earthquake shock which were to summon Oedipus to his death do not come yet. There is to be one more assault on his determination, one more effort to pry him loose from Athens. A mysterious suppliant at the altar of Poseidon begs for a word with him. It is a man of Oedipus' own family, from Argos. "Stop where you are!" cries the old man. "Do not ask me" (1169–1170). He knows who the suppliant is; it is Polynices, his son, come to beg for help against Eteocles and Creon. Oedipus will not listen. But the strong urging of Theseus and the reproachful pleas of Antigone wring this concession from him. Before he goes to his promised rest, he must face this last trial, hear, though he cannot see him, the son whom he has cursed, whose speech, as he said himself, would cause him "the greatest pain of any voice in the world" (1173–1174).

To the very last moment his life is to be suffering. The chorus, old men themselves, see in his helpless, harrassed, old age the proof that "not to be born is best, when all is reckoned in. But once a man is born, the second best is to go back quickly to where he came from. For after youth with its lightheaded folly is past, come trouble, sorrow, hatred, faction, strife, battle, murder, and, last of all, old age" (1224 ff.). Oedipus has known them all, and his rest is overdue, but "like some sea cape in the north, the storm waves beat on him from every quarter" (1240 ff.). And now comes the last, Polynices, his son.

There is not much Polynices can say. He can only beg pardon for his neglect, promise to atone for his misdeeds, and invoke the name of mercy (Αἰδώς 1268).[27] Oedipus remains obstinately silent; he promised to listen, he did not promise to speak. Polynices turns from the past to the future, and tells why he has come. His allies, ready for the attack on Thebes, have sent him to win Oedipus to their cause, for the oracle promises victory to the side which Oedipus will join. He is a foreigner in a strange land, like his father, like him a beggar, like him expelled from Thebes. "Both of us live by fawning on others, our fate is the same." And he promises, if victorious, to restore Oedipus to his home.

These words stir Oedipus to answer. All the years of brooding on the ingratitude of his sons bear their bitter fruit now in this terrible denunciation, which sweeps from accusation through malediction to prophecy in language that seems to transcend the nature of human speech altogether and become the medium of a daemonic, superhuman wrath. He repudiates his sons: "You are some other man's sons, not mine" (1369). He prophesies again, this time not the content of the oracle of Apollo but the fulfillment of his own curse: "You shall not sack that city, but first will fall soiled with your brother's blood and he with yours" (1372 ff.). And in a final passage which clangs and rattles with massed, bristling consonants, an explosion of hate and fury, he curses his son: "Get out. I spit on you. I am not your father. You vilest of all vile things, take this curse with you, which I call down on you. Never may you win with the spear the land where you were born, nor return to the vale of Argos, but die and in dying kill the brother who drove you out. This is my curse, and I call on the hateful darkness of Tartarus where my father lies to prepare a place for you. I call on these divinities of the grove, on the war-god who planted such dread hatred in you both. Now you have heard me, go" (1383 ff.). The content can be translated, but not the sound of it. This is a superhuman anger welling from the outraged sense of justice not of a mortal man and father but of the forces which govern the universe.

Creon could argue and resist, but to this dreadful speech no reply is possible. There can be no doubt of its authority. Polynices tries to make light of it (though he will not tell his allies what he has heard); he will go to Thebes all the same. When Antigone tries to dissuade him she finds the right word for Oedipus' speech. "Do you not see that you are fulfilling his oracles?" (μαντεύμαθ' 1425). "Who will dare to follow you when they hear what he has prophesied?" (οἳ ἐθέσπισεν 1428). These are the words used of divine prophecy; Oedipus who once tried to escape prophecy, and cast scorn on it, now speaks with its voice. And his son now starts on the same road his father trod. He dismisses the prophecy,[28] and does so in a phrase that is a startling echo of something his mother said long ago. "For all prophecy can say," Jocasta said to Oedipus, "I would not in future look this way or that" (οὐχὶ μαντείας γ' ἂν οὔτε τῇδ' ἐγώ/ βλέψαιμ' ἂν οὕνεκ' οὔτε τῇδ' ἂν OT 857–858). And her son says now: "All this is in the power of the *daemon*, it may turn out this way or that" (καὶ τῇδε φῦναι χἀτέρᾳ 1443–1444). "In the power of the *daemon*"—a god, does he mean, or Fortune? Whatever he means, he does not realize the sense in which the words are true. The *daemon* in whose power it lies is Oedipus himself. He had prayed that the result of the battle between his sons should lie in his hands; the prayer has been granted and he knows it—he both foresees and determines the future.

Oedipus has put on power which does not belong to human kind; such power should not walk the earth in mortal shape. And as the chorus in bewilderment tries to understand what it has just heard, the thunder crashes. Oedipus' time has come. But first he must fulfill his promise to Theseus, and as the thunder and lightning summon him ever more imperiously he calls for the king to come before it is too late. To Theseus, who now recognizes him as a true prophet, he gives his last instructions: to keep secret for himself and his royal descendants the place where his body will lie. And then in a scene which must be seen for its tremendous effect to be appreciated, the blind old man, whose every painful step had to be guided since the beginning of the play, leads his daughters and Theseus off stage with surefooted certainty. "Follow me . . . I will lead you now as you led me . . . Do not touch me, let me find by myself the holy burial place . . . This way, come this way . . . this is the way Hermes the guide leads me, and the goddess below" (1542 ff.).

The chorus prays to the gods of death that Oedipus may leave this life not in pain, nor in deep-toned lament. And the prayer, as we learn from the messenger, is granted. "The manner of his death was not in lamentation, nor in sickness or suffering, but miraculous, if ever man's death was" (1663 ff.). And before he went to his mysterious end, the gods, at last, spoke to him. They reproached him for his slowness. "You, Oedipus, you there, why do we hesitate to go? You have delayed too long" (ὦ οὗτος οὗτος Οἰδίπους τί μέλλομεν/ χωρεῖν; πάλαι δὴ τἀπὸ σοῦ βραδύνεται 1627–1628).

These strange, almost colloquial words are all that the gods say to Oedipus in either of the two plays.[29] But as we have a right to expect of so long-delayed and august a summons, the words are complete and final. The hesitation for which they reproach him is the last shred of his humanity, which he must now cast off; where he is going, vision is clear, knowledge certain, action instantaneous and effective—between the intention and the act there falls no shadow of hesitation or delay. And the divine "we" completes and transcends the equation of Oedipus with the gods; his identity is merged with theirs.

The last of the Sophoclean heroes, the most fiercely angry of all those intractable figures who defied the limits set to human power and assumed the attributes of divinity, is here recognized by the gods as their peer and welcomed to their presence. The gods of Sophoclean tragedy, the most remote and mysterious creation in all Greek literature, here show their respect for the hero in unmistakable terms; they gave Ajax his burial, Antigone her revenge, Electra her victory, Philoctetes his return to life—but to Oedipus, who suffered most and longest, they give, in the death he longed for, immortal life and power.

NOTES

NOTES TO I
(Pp. 1–27)

[1] An important addition to the literature on this subject is E. M. Waith's *The Herculean Hero*. See especially 48, 63, 88, 104.

[2] John Jones, in his *Aristotle on Greek Tragedy*, argues (11–20), with considerable effect, that "we have imported the tragic hero into the *Poetics*, where he has no place" (13). He also believes, and makes a good case for his belief, that we have imported the tragic hero into Aeschylean tragedy, where the concept has no place either. Of the *Agamemnon* he says, "There is something wrong in our critical isolation of the protagonist" (82), and interprets the play, and the trilogy, "in the light of Aeschylus' intention to dramatize the troubles of the *house* of Atreus" (90, italics mine). The '*oikos*,' not the 'hero,' is the theme. This is a challenging book, full of new ideas, which will be the subject of much discussion.

[3] Arist. *Po.* 1453e.

[4] See the brilliant discussion in Gerald F. Else, *Aristotle's Poetics: The Argument*, 304–307. "Aristotle's 'practical' world," he says (306), "which is also his poetical world, is the world as we know it from day to day: the realm in which we strive for happiness through 'virtue' and sometimes achieve it and sometimes fail, in which we are what we are because of the choices we have made and what we have done or failed to do. God or Fate do not break into the charmed circle." Cf. also 73: "because poetry is a portrayal of the life of action the closest affinities with the *Poetics* will turn up in the other works that deal with the 'practical' sphere: the *Rhetoric*, the *Politics*, and especially the *Ethics*."

[5] The reader will at once object that the *Prometheus Bound* is a play of this type; he is referred to the discussion in pages 45–50.

[6] The nearest thing to it is the tantalizing formula of Theophrastus (G. Kaibel, *Comicorum Graecorum Fragmenta* I, 57): τραγῳδία ἐστιν ἡρωικῆς τύχης περίστασις. This last word is used in Aristotle (e.g., *Mete.* 364b, 14, *Pr.* 942b, 27) to mean 'a change in the direction of the wind,' and so here may mean something like Aristotle's *peripeteia* and *metabolê*; in later Greek it often means, 'crisis, critical situation.' For discussion see Konrat Ziegler's article in *Pauly-Wissowa*, *Tragoedia*, 'Die Definition des Theophrastos' (2050). Recent discussion in Jones 276, Else, 386–388. The *Etymologicum Magnum*, 764.1 has a similar definition: τραγῳδία ἐστι βίων καὶ λόγων ἡρωικῶν μίμησις.

[7] The titles which appear in Aristophanes (e.g., *Ra.* 53, 1021, 1026, *Th.* 770, 850) show that in the last quarter of the fifth century the plays were easily identifiable by title, and it is probable that these titles are the ones preserved by the Aristotelian lists.

[8] H. D. F. Kitto, *Greek Tragedy, A Literary Study*,[3] 188, n. 3.

[9] Once again the reader is referred to pages 45–50.

[10] An inscription from Aexone (published in 1929) records a trilogy of Sophocles which dealt with the story of Telephos. It is possible, as Albin Lesky (*Tragische Dichtung der Hellenen*, 138) says, that there were others. "One can only say that Sophocles, in general, abandoned the trilogic combination for the single play." For Lesky's discussion of the Telephos trilogy, see *ibid.* 135–136.

[11] This is a sharply controversial question, and unfortunately the evidence is almost nonexistent. The view expressed here is based on the only evidence we have: the notice in the *Souda* that Sophocles "began the practise of competing play against play, not by trilogy," πρῶτος ἦρξε τοῦ δρᾶμα πρὸς δρᾶμα ἀγωνίζεσθαι ἀλλὰ μὴ τετραλογεῖσθαι. This statement has been treated with suspicion not only because Aeschylus' *Persians* is obviously not part of a trilogy, but because, it is claimed, the statement of the *Souda* is obscure almost to the point of unintelligibility. But the *Persae*, with its contemporary theme, was obviously incompatible with trilogic form, unless Aeschylus had written a whole trilogy on the Persian war—which would have been absolutely unprecedented (whereas the single play at least had a precedent, though an unfortunate one), and in any case what would he have chosen for the subject of the satyr play? The statement of the *Souda* is surely not so baffling as many have claimed. It refers to the fact that presentation of three separate tragedies instead of a connected trilogy changed the nature of the tragic competition. Whereas, before, the judges gave their verdict on what were in essence three long plays by three different poets, they now had to award the prize after consideration of three offerings of three separate tragedies which might vary greatly in quality in the case of each poet. The judges who awarded the second prize to the *Oedipus Tyrannus*, for example, may have been influenced by the inferiority of the other two plays which accompanied it as compared with the plays of Sophocles' competitors. They could no longer judge between whole trilogies, but had to reckon play against play, which is what the δρᾶμα πρὸς δρᾶμα of the *Souda* notice means.

[12] See B. M. W. Knox, 'The Hippolytus of Euripides,' *YCS* 13, 3–6.

[13] This is of course to dismiss the fashionable classification of the *Ajax* and *Antigone* as 'diptych' plays. In the *Ajax* the stage, after the hero's death, is still dominated by his corpse, which is the sole subject of discussion in all the scenes which follow. (See B. M. W. Knox, 'The *Ajax* of Sophocles,' *HSCP* 65, 1–2). In the *Antigone* (see pages 74, 75) the collapse of Creon's resolution, his abject surrender, casts into strong relief the heroism of Antigone, and the end of the play, his punishment, is the fulfillment of her prayer to the gods.

[14] A. *A.* 182: δαιμόνων δέ που χάρις βίαιος.

[15] The most recent discussion is Ivan Linforth, *Electra's Day in the Tragedy of Sophocles*, 121 ff.

[16] *Hipp.* 5–8, 47 ff., *Ba.* 1347, *Tr.* 69 ff., *HF* 840 ff.

[17] *HF* 1227–1228. Cf. *Tr.* 726 ff.

[18] This view of the Sophoclean hero and situation is of course not new; in particular Karl Reinhardt (*Sophokles*) and Cedric H. Whitman (*Sophocles: A Study of Heroic Humanism*) explore similar views with great subtlety and eloquence. Much earlier, C. R. Post ('The Dramatic Art of Sophocles,' *HSCP*, 23, 71–127) described the Sophoclean plays (except the *Trachiniae*, 83) as possessing "the same architectural framework. . . . From the very beginning the principal character is marked by an iron will centered upon a definite object; and the drama, according to Sophocles, consists to a

certain extent of a series of tests, arranged in climactic order, to which the will is sub-jected and over all of which it rises triumphant" (81). This is too rigid a formula; the 'climactic order' of the 'tests' is hard to prove. G. M. Kirkwood (*A Study of Sophoclean Drama*) attempts to create a 'synthesis' in the chapter entitled 'The Character of the Tragic Hero' (169-180); he lays particular stress on the heroic concept of εὐγένεια. Georges Méautis (*Sophocle, Essai sur le héros tragique*) also develops a general concept of Sophoclean heroism, which, however, though it claims as its basis the Greek religious 'hero,' is expressed in Christian terms throughout. His critical vocabulary abounds with such words and phrases as 'résurrection' (35, 225, 243, 244, 251), 'la nuit obscure' (87, 129 and *passim*), 'le calvaire' (133, 134), 'la nuit de son âme' (133), 'la couronne des épines' (211). There is much to be learned from this book, but the insistence on Christian parallels sometimes leads to formulations which would have made Sophocles stare and gasp; good examples are the comment on Antigone and Haemon (202): "nous pouvons bien pressentir que ce couple sera réuni comme le sont dans la Divine Comédie Francesca da Rimini et l'être qu'elle aimait" and the generalization (293), "Ajax, Oedipe, Héracles doivent passer par la croix de la souffrance, de l'abandon, de la solitide, pour parvenir à la rose claire lumineuse de la résurrection, cette rose dont Dante a fait le symbole même du Paradis."

[19] Witness the astonishing diversity of assessment of the Sophoclean characters in the critical literature.

[20] For example σωφροσύνη, which since J. T. Sheppard's chapter 'Sophrosyne' in *The Oedipus Tyrannus of Sophocles*, lix-lxxix, has been a commonplace of Sophoclean criticism. Though it is fairly frequent in Euripides, the word σωφροσύνη does not occur in the extant text of Sophocles, and even σώφρων and σωφρονεῖν are comparatively rare; and, besides, they are often used to describe not what the hero should be but what he should not—see Knox (2), 16-17. Similarly ἀρετή, which bulks large in Whitman's book (cf. also John A. Moore, *Sophocles and Aretê*), is a fairly rare word in Sophocles (six occurrences in the extant plays, and those only in *Ajax*, *Trachiniae*, and *Philoctetes*).

[21] Cf. *Ant.* 97: καλῶς θανεῖν.

[22] Cf. also *OT*: 138 ἀποσκεδῶ, 145 δράσοντος, 265 ὑπερμαχοῦμαι, . . . ἀφίξομαι.

[23] Eduard Schwyzer, *Griechische Grammatik* Vol. II, translates this (409) "oboedien-dum est"—he is discussing 'intransitiva.' (Cf. Alphonse Dain and Paul Mazon, *Sophocle*, Vol. II, *ad loc.*). But there is no grammatical necessity to take this as a form of ἄρχεσθαι rather than of ἄρχειν. If Clytemnestra in Euripides (*IA* 1033) can say ἄρχε, "Rule⁶", Oedipus can say ἀρκτέον, "I must rule." Jebb's defence of this meaning is cogent.

[24] *El.* 1029: οὔ ποτ' ἐξ ἐμοῦ γε μὴ πάθῃς τόδε.

[25] Cf. *Ph.* 1274: πότερα δέδοκται σοι μένοντι καρτερεῖν;

[26] Cf. also *OC* 1309: λιτάς.

[27] αἶνον 'advice,' so Jebb, rightly. *LSJ⁹* gives 'tale' for this passage s.v. αἶνος, and 'counsel' s.v. αἰνέω. But what 'tale' has Neoptolemos told? W. J. Verdenius (*Mnemosyne* IV, XV, 4, 1962, 389) says: "Neoptolemos has not given an advice; he has expressed an intention (1373 βούλομαι)." But this is a quibble; Neoptolemos' whole speech is advice. And the meaning Verdenius proposes—'allusive tale,' 'tale containing an ulterior purpose'—still does not meet the objection that nothing Neoptolemos has said can be called a 'tale' in any sense of the word, and further demands an interpre-

tation of αἰνέσας as "used in the sense of αἰνίσσομαι, 'to speak in covert terms,' " for which Verdenius cites A. *A.* 1482 (on which, however, see Eduard Fraenkel, *Aeschylus Agamemnon, ad loc.* and note 2).

[28] The 'advice' is described by the word συμβουλεύειν at *OT* 1370 and the advisor as σύμβουλος at *Ph.* 1321.

[29] Cf. also *El.* 529, 1048, 1056.

[30] Cf. *OT* 1066: τὰ λῷστά σοι λέγω (Jocasta), to which Oedipus replies (1067): τὰ λῷστα τοίνυν ταῦτά μ' ἀλγύνει πάλαι. Cf. also *Ph.* 1381.

[31] These lectures had already been delivered when I came across the brilliant article of Hans Diller, 'Über das Selbstbewusstsein der sophokleischen Personen' (*Wiener Studien*, LXIX 70-85). It anticipates my argument on this and several other important points and is frequently referred to in the notes below.

[32] Cf. Ellendt–Genthe, *Lexicon Sophocleum*, Berlin, 1872, s.v.: "ceteri tragici eo verbo abstinuerunt."

[33] A. *Pr.* 320: οὐδ' εἴκεις κακοῖς; cf. S. *Ph.* 1046, *Ant.* 472. The other instances in Aeschylus are addressed to the chorus (*Supp.* 202), to Cassandra (*A.* 1071), and by one section of the chorus of the *Agamemnon* to another (*A.* 1362). For an analysis of the Aeschylean use of the word see Diller 73–74.

[34] See below, pages 45–50 for a detailed discussion of the 'Sophoclean' character of the *Prometheus Bound*.

[35] All other occurrences of the word in Euripides (*HF* 300, *Ion* 637, *Supp.* 167, *Hel.* 80, *Heracl.* 367 and ὑπείκω *Or.* 699, *IA* 140, *IT* 327), are in peripheral and incidental situations.

[36] Add to the demand that the hero 'yield' *OT* 625, ὡς οὐχ ὑπείξων οὐδὲ πιστεύσων λέγεις, which must be assigned to Creon. In the mouth of Oedipus πιστεύσων does not make much sense, but it is appropriate for Creon (cf. 603–604); the word φθονεῖν in 624 is appropriate for Oedipus—he has already (382) accused Creon of φθόνος. A line must have dropped out here. This assignment of the lines is due to Lewis Campbell, *Sophocles, Plays and Fragments*. It is adopted by I. Errandonea, *Sofocles Tragedias* and by H. D. F. Kitto in his recent Sophoclean translations—*Sophocles, Three Tragedies*, 68 and note.

[37] Cf. also *Aj.* 1243: οὐδ' ἡσσημένοις/ εἴκειν (Agamemnon to Teucer).

[38] A similar formula of the advisor is θέλω ("of consent rather than desire" *LSJ*[9] s. v. ἐθέλω). Cf. *OC* 757: θελήσας ἄστυ καὶ δόμους μολεῖν (Creon to Oedipus); *OT* 649: πιθοῦ θελήσας (chorus to Oedipus); *Ph.* 1343: συγχώρει θέλων (Neoptolemos to Philoctetes); *El.* 330: χοὐδ' . . . διδαχθῆναι θέλεις (Chrysothemis to Electra).

[39] Cf. *Ph.* 817.

[40] Cf. *Aj.* 428, 754.

[41] The advisors talk to the hero 'in vain,' μάτην. Cf. *Ph.*: 1276 μάτην γὰρ ἄν εἴπῃς γε πάντ' εἰρήσεται, 1280 πάντα γὰρ φράσεις μάτην: *OT* 365: ὡς μάτην εἰρήσεται.

[42] Cf. *Ant.* 38: εἴτ' ἐσθλῶν κακή.

[43] Cf. also *OT* 582: κακὸς . . . φίλος.

[44] Cf. also *OC* 1173: παῖς οὑμὸς ὤναξ στυγνός.

[45] The hero's attitude to his advisors is described by them with the words μέμφομαι (*El.* 384, *OT* 337, *Ph.* 1309) and ψέγω (*El.* 551, *OT* 338).

[46] Cf. *Ph.* 1323: στυγεῖς, πολέμιον δυσμενῆ θ' ἡγούμενος, *OT* 546: δυσμενῆ γὰρ καὶ βαρὺν σ' ηὕρηκ' ἐμοί, *Ant.* 93: ἐχθαρῇ μὲν ἐξ ἐμοῦ.

[47] Cf. *Aj.* 744.

[48] And cf. *OT* 807.

[49] Ellendt-Genthe's 'inexputabilis' (unbegreiflich) is surely wrong here; 'ill-calculating' (*LSJ*⁹) is the right sense.

[50] Cf. *Aj.* 355: ἀφροντίστως.

[51] *Ant.* 220, οὐκ ἔστιν οὕτω μῶρος ὃς θανεῖν ἐρᾷ, tells us in advance what the chorus will think of Antigone.

[52] Cf. *Ant.* 248.

[53] σκληρός is opposed to ἔμπληκτος 'veering' at *Aj.* 1361 and 1358.

[54] Cf. *Ph.* 219.

[55] Cf. *Aj.* 650.

[56] Cf. Antipho Soph. *Fr.* 132 (Blass): . . . βίος . . . οὐδὲν ἔχων περισσὸν οὐδὲ μέγα καὶ σεμνόν, ἀλλὰ πάντα σμικρὰ καὶ ἀσθενῆ.

[57] See Knox (2), 17 and note.

[58] Cf. B. M. W. Knox, *Oedipus at Thebes*, 191–193.

NOTES TO II
(Pp. 28–61)

[1] On εὐγένεια and the Sophoclean tragic hero see Kirkwood 177–180.

[2] Tecmessa (520 ff.) opposes his argument with a different conception of εὐγένεια, on which see Kirkwood (105–106), who sympathizes with it, and Méautis (29–30), who emphatically does not.

[3] In *Aj.* 710 ff. the chorus, misled by his speech, celebrates his return (πάλιν 711, αὖ 712) to εὐσέβεια (σέβων 713).

[4] Cf. *OT* 145 and see Knox (3) 14 ff.

[5] *Ph.* 1384. So Ajax (465 ff.) rejects the idea of death in battle against the Trojans because it would benefit his enemies, the Atridae.

[6] *Cra.* 419e. This derivation is accepted by *LSJ*.⁹ H. Frisk, *Griechisches etymologisches Wörterbuch*, says: "sekundäre Anknüpfungen an θύω 'einherstürmen' kann allerdings den Sinn beeinflusst haben."

[7] The *Platonic Definitions* (415e) define θυμός as: ὁρμὴ βίαιος ἄνευ λογισμοῦ.

[8] Cf. also *OC* 768 (the past), 1193, 1198.

[9] Cf. Lesky (1), 122 on the θυμός of Oedipus *tyrannos*. "Dieser Träger höchster Aktivität, die der Grieche θυμός nennt, ist jeden Augenblick zum Aufwallen bereit. . . . Der θυμός kann den Intellekt des Königs auf falsche Bahn reissen, so wenn er Kreon und Teiresias im Komplott gegen seine Herrschaft glaubt, aber aus derselben Wurzel kommt auch der hohe Mut, mit dem er unbeirrbar auf das Ziel der furchtbaren Entdeckung zuschreitet, die ihn vernichten muss."

[10] Cf. also *OC* 49.

[11] Cf. also *Ant.* 5: οὔτ' αἰσχρὸν οὔτ' ἄτιμον.

¹² Jebb's translation.

¹³ Cf. Méautis (57): "Le rire des médiocres, les sarcasmes de la foule sont un élément essentiel de la tragédie, une des conditions même qui *crée* parfois le héros tragique."

¹⁴ Cf. Σ *Aj.* 382: τοῦτο μάλιστα αὐτοῦ ἅπτεται, τὸ τῷ ἐχθρῷ καταγέλαστον εἶναι.

¹⁵ Cf. also *El.* 277, 1295.

¹⁶ Jebb's portrait of Creon (xxix)—"a good type of Scottish character"—is too magnanimous. Méautis, however, goes too far in the opposite direction; he speaks of "froide cruauté" (133), "un dernier raffinement de cruauté" (136).

¹⁷ Polynices, however, associates his father with himself as an object of the laughter of Eteocles (κοινῇ καθ' ἡμῶν ἐγγελῶν 1339).

¹⁸ He invokes 'Zeus of the curses' (πρὸς 'Αραίου Διός 1181); see Jebb's note on this title of Zeus. For ἀρά, cf. also *Ph.* 1120, *El.* 111, and *OC* 154, 865, 952, 1375, 1384, 1389, 1406, 1407.

¹⁹ Cf. also *Ph.* 314–316.

²⁰ Cf. *Ph.* 2: ἄστιπτος, *OC* 126: ἀστιβὲς ἄλσος.

²¹ This is Jebb's interpretation. For the phrase μηδὲν μέγ' εἴπῃς cf. *Aj.* 386, 422.

²² Cf. also the bitter tone of *OC* 385–386.

²³ The first example in Greek literature of such an address to the landscape seems to be A. *Pr.* 88 ff. (For discussion of the problem of the *Prometheus Bound*, see pages 45–50). Wolfgang Schadewalt (*Monolog und Selbstgespräch*) whose thesis is that "Aischylos kennt im grossen und ganzen nur eine Form der Selbstäusserung: den Anruf an eine Gottheit oder gotterfüllte Wesen" (38), explains the monologue of Prometheus as follows: "Aber auch dieses wechselvolle Selbstgespräch beginnt mit Anrufungen an göttliche Mächte, wie alle anderen Selbstäusserungen bei Aischylos. . . . Der Dichter lässt ihn die unpersönlichen göttlichen Mächte anrufen, welche die Einsamkeit um ihn her erfüllen. Das Göttliche ist also auch hier das Gegenüber" (52). This does not seem entirely convincing. It is true, as Schadewalt points out in the same passage, that Prometheus can hardly call on the Olympian gods, but the careful enumeration of the four elements in his address seems to hint at a philosophical rather than a religious background for his expressions. The address to the landscape is clearly unlike any other "Selbstgespräch" in Aeschylus, and its resemblance to similar Sophoclean passages makes it one more of the many problematical elements in the play.

²⁴ Cf. also *Ph.* 952, 986, 1087, 1146.

²⁵ Cf. also *Aj.* 412 ff., 418 ff.

²⁶ This is strictly what Schadewalt classifies as "Rufe an Entfernte" (42) like A. *A.* 1157. But for a blind man all landscapes, near and far, are in the imagination; Oedipus addresses those places which witnessed the key incidents of his life. Similarly, at Colonus (though he has a supernatural sense of direction when he goes to his death, cf. 1590 ff.), he speaks not to the landscape but to 'the rayless light' (φῶς ἀφεγγές 1549).

²⁷ For ἐρᾶν and the heroic temper cf. also *Ant.* 90, 220, *OC* 436.

²⁸ Cf. *OC* 1662: εὔνουν διαστὰν . . . βάθρον.

²⁹ See A. J. A. Waldock's witty and destructive discussion of 'the documentary fallacy' in his *Sophocles the Dramatist.* This chapter is brilliantly right, but when Waldock starts to examine the Sophoclean plays he falls victim to what might be called the 'theatrical fallacy'—he insists that Sophocles was a theatrical technician and nothing more. Consequently the plays have no meaning, no significance, they are not 'universal.' "There is no meaning in the *Oedipus Tyrannus*," he says. "There is

merely the terror of coincidence" (168). "The questions raised by the play [the *Electra*] are essentially technical, not moral" (193). "We do wrong to press for a point," he says of the *Trachiniae*. "No doubt every play should have its point, but the fact is that many plays lack one" (102). Sophocles is left nothing but a genius for constructing a theatrically effective play. One sometimes gets the impression, reading Waldock, that he is writing not about Sophocles but about Sardou, of whom the *Oxford Companion to the Theatre* uncharitably remarks (290): "he brought to all of them [his subjects] the same technical ability and the same poverty of thought. In his hands any subject lost whatever depth it might have had, and became simply a vehicle for a series of complicated intrigues." But Waldock's Sophocles in not even up to this standard; he has trouble with his plots. He "unduly spins out the ending" of the *OC* (226), and he has trouble with the middle of the play too (219). In the *Philoctetes* he makes one blunder after another: in his handling of the chorus "in one place he appears to have been guilty of a quite extraordinary lapse" (209); the scene with the sailor disguised as a merchant is "not very good drama . . . a thoroughly unsound piece of action" (204); and his structure is so bad that before the entrance of Heracles "the drama, as such, is bogged down—that is the plain fact of the matter . . . and something desperate must be done" (206). The *Ajax* is another botched piece of work; the ambiguous speech is a theatrical failure: "Sophocles could not resolve this problem; it was a veritable impasse" (79). One can only wonder why Waldock took the trouble to write a book about a dramatist who according to him had nothing to say and said it so badly.

30 Lesky (1), 143.

31 Albin Lesky, *Die griechische Tragödie*,[2] 162.

32 The highpoint of intellectual arrogance in this school of thought was reached by W. Zürcher, *Die Darstellung der Menschen im Drama des Euripides*, who says (10): "für Sophokles die Konzeption eines wirklichen Charakters *aus geistesgeschichtlichen Gründen* gar nicht möglich ist." (Quoted by Victor Ehrenberg, *Sophocles and Pericles*, 51; the italics are his.)

33 Jones' comparison of the *Electra* and the *Choephoroe* (141–159) discusses with great insight what he calls "provisionally, the personalising of the dramatic individual in Sophocles."

34 Cf. *OC* 794: ὑπόβλητον στόμα (Oedipus to Creon).

35 Cf. Whitman, 88 "her knowledge of her own difference."

36 Ajax, too, uses this word of himself (364).

37 Cf. also *El.* 339, 1256, 1300, 1509.

38 Cf. also *Ant.* 517.

39 Cf. also *Aj.* 1102, 1107, and 483–484: δὸς ἀνδράσιν φίλοις γνώμης κρατῆσαι.

40 Cf. *OC* 883: ὕβρις, ἀλλ' ἀνεκτέα (Creon to chorus). In *Ph.* 411 Philoctetes asks how Ajax could have borne (ἠνείχετο) Odysseus' refusal to give Neoptolemos his father's armor.

41 Phaedra, Jocasta (in the *Phoenissae*), Evadne (in the *Suppliants*), and Menoeceus (in the *Phoenissae*), though he is rather a voluntary sacrifice to save Thebes than a suicide. See now Appendix E ("A Note on Suicide") in W. B. Stanford, *Sophocles, Ajax*, 289–290.

42 Cf. *El.* 140.

43 Cf. also *Aj.* 322: ταῦρος ὡς βρυχώμενος.

[44] Cf. also *El.* 785 (Electra as a serpent, cf. *Ant.* 531 ff.).

[45] Cf. Robert F. Goheen, *The Imagery of Sophocles' Antigone*, 30, 134.

[46] Similar suggestions in *OC* 950, 1026, *Ph.* 1005, 1007.

[47] See Knox (3), 159 ff.

[48] The *Trachiniae* does not conform to the pattern. Heracles, though certainly cast in the heroic mold, comes on late in the play, and dying; there is no question of heroic resolve or action (though some of the heroic formulas occur: ψυχὴ σκληρά 1260, ὠμόφρονος 975, ἐᾶτε 1004). Deianira uses *anti*-heroic formulas: 543 θυμοῦσθαι μὲν οὐκ ἐπίσταμαι, 552 οὐ γάρ . . . ὀργαίνειν καλὸν, 583 τάς τε τολμώσας στυγῶ. But when she resolves to die the heroic formulas appear: 719 δέδοκται . . . συνθανεῖν, 721 ζῆν κακῶς κλύουσαν οὐκ ἀνασχετόν.

[49] Gilbert Murray, *Aeschylus, The Creator of Tragedy*, 143: "Eteocles fits curiously well into Aristotle's famous description of the tragic hero: the noble character with the fatal flaw." See also Kitto (1), 44, 52.

[50] This is not to deny that it is action; see Kitto's brilliant treatment of the long scene in (1), 48 ff.

[51] In fact only one: πιθοῦ γυναιξί 712.

[52] It is interesting to note that the final scene of the *Septem* (which has often been explained as a later addition based on the *Antigone*), presents a Sophoclean situation (the attempt to persuade Antigone to obey the edict, 1042–1053) but exhibits practically no sign of the formulas Sophocles habitually employed in such a case.

[53] It is remarkable that there is practically no resemblance between the language of the *Choephoroe* and that of the *Electra*.

[54] Lesky (1), 77: "wie schwierig es war, einer Folge von Besuchen bei der zur Passivität verurteilten Hauptfigur dramatisches Leben zu verleihen." It is a good description of the *Oedipus at Colonus* too. On the resemblance between these two plays, see S. M. Adams, *Sophocles the Playwright*, 160–161.

[55] So Diller (84): "in allem oder fast allem, was wir hinsichtlich der Äusserungen des Selbstbewusstseins als unterschiedlich für Aischylos und Sophokles festgestellt hatten, stellt sich der Prometheus auf die sophokleische Seite."

[56] Cf. *Ph.* 305.

[57] Cf. *Ph.* 692. Σ A. *Pr.* 2.

[58] Jones (271–272), like Schadewalt, attempts to distinguish this address to the landscape from the Sophoclean passages, but on different grounds. "Prometheus stands over against Nature in massive stability . . . whereas Philoctetes broods amply upon the fluid love-hate relationship of the cave and the other natural features of the island to himself. Nature exists *for*—in the eye of—Sophoclean man with entirely new reference to self." But he does not quote the Aeschylean passage in full; he omits the last line, ἴδεσθε μ' οἷα πρὸς θεῶν πάσχω θεός 92, which puts the landscape, or rather here the elements, into the most direct 'relationship' and 'reference' to self imaginable—they are called on for sympathy. Jones seems to imply in the preceding sentences ("the articulate figure's power—and frequent disposition—to address the Universe"), that other Aeschylean figures too address the landscape. I have not been able to find any such examples.

[59] Oceanus is of course intent on negotiating a surrender: "der bedächtig wägende und ausweichende Vater Okeanos," Lesky calls him (1), 77. He swiftly accepts Prometheus' advice to leave when he sees that a surrender is out of the question.

[60] Cf. *Ant.* 83: τὸν σὸν ἐξόρθου πότμον.

[61] H. Weir Smyth's translation. Cf. αὐτόγνωτος *Ant.* 875.

[62] For ἴδοιμι in the same context cf. *Aj.* 384: ἴδοιμι δή νιν . . . , *Ph.* 1113: ἰδοίμαν δὲ νιν.

[63] Cf. page 11 (δέδοκται).

[64] For this meaning of παρά, cf. X. *Cyr.* 1.2, 15.

[65] See F. Heinimann, *Nomos und Physis*, 44, n. 5.

[66] *Pr.* 336, 1080.

[67] Lesky (1), 77–82; cf. also Lesky's *Geschichte der griechischen Literatur*,² 284.

[68] See Wilhelm Schmid, "Untersuchungen zum Gefesselten Prometheus," *Tübinger Beiträger* and "Epikritisches zum Gefesselten Prometheus," *Phil. Woch.* 51, 218; Schmid-Stählin *Geschichte der griechische Literatur*, I, 3, 281–307. Few have followed Schmid all the way to his conclusion (281), "dass es weder inhaltlich noch sprachlich den Dichter der sechs übrigen erhaltenen Aischylosstücke zugeschrieben werden kann." But most scholars are impressed by at least some of his observations. F. R. Earp, *The Style of Aeschylus*, 87–88, rejects Schmid's thesis but admits that "the study of the style and especially of the structure of the sentences confirms the belief that there is a real question." (Cf. Earp, *JHS*, 1945, 11 f.). More recently, Walter Jens, "Die Stichomythie in der frühen griechischen Tragödie," *Zetemata* 11, concludes after a careful examination of Aeschylean stichomythy as a whole: "Dies alles lässt den Schluss zu, dass der Prometheus kaum vom Dichter der Hiketiden und der Orestie stammen kann. Es ist schon rein äusserlich nicht einzusehen, warum Aischylos, der noch in der Trilogie am archaisch-strengen Bau festhält, vorher, im Prometheus, so unglaublich 'sophokleisch' frei verfahren sein sollte" (33).

[69] Certain resemblances between the *Prometheus Bound* and Sophoclean drama have of course been discussed in the dispute over the *Echtheitsfrage*; see Schmid, *Untersuchungen etc.* for verbal echoes and vocabulary analysis. An interesting independent confirmation is provided by Kirkwood 201: "the *Prometheus Bound*, the one play of Aeschylus in which the choral technique resembles Sophocles' at all closely . . ."

[70] Diller's concluding sentence suggests a similar view (though he does not make an explicit statement). "Der Prometheus lebt von dem, was Sophokles *zuerst* [my italics] auf die Bühne gebracht hatte: die Darstellung des auf sich selbst gestellten, seiner Art, seines Auftrages und seiner damit gegebenen Einsamkeit bewusst gewordenen Menschen" (85).

[71] Cf. Albin Lesky (3), 282: "ein später Ansatz des Stückes ist allerdings wahrscheinlich, und neuere Versuche, es unter die *Orestie* in den letzten sizilischen Aufenthalt des Dichters zu rücken, verdienen Beachtung."

[72] Lesky (1), 79: "man versteht dass sich die Stimmen derer mehrten die für einen der Schergen lieber mit einem dritten Schauspieler rechnen." As Lesky points out, the use of a dummy figure for Prometheus in the first play would have made the second difficult to stage. See also Lesky (3), 284, Kitto (1), 54.

[73] Prometheus does not have to fear time either. Though it is the medium of his suffering (23–25), it is his servant, not his master; through his foreknowledge he has more control over time than his otherwise all-powerful adversary, who, he says, will be 'taught by time' (981).

[74] Cf. Lesky (3), 87.

[75] See Cedric H. Whitman's brilliant chap. 9 'Achilles: Evolution of a Hero' in his *Homer and the Heroic Tradition*.

[76] *Ant.*: 73 φίλη μετ᾽ αὐτοῦ κείσομαι, 76 ἐκεῖ γὰρ αἰεὶ κείσομαι, 502 καίτοι πόθεν κλέος γ᾽ ἂν εὐκλεέστερον . . . ;

[77] *Ath.* 8.347e.

[78] A. J. Festugière, *Personal Religion among the Greeks.*

[79] *Vita* 12. For the other details cf. *ibid.* 11, 17.

[80] *Et. Mag.* 256.6: ἡρῷον αὐτῷ κατασκευάσαντες, ὠνόμοσαν αὐτὸν Δεξίωνα, ἀπὸ τῆς τοῦ Ἀσκληπιοῦ δεξιώσεως.

[81] See Lesky (1), 103. For the decree see *I. G.* II² 1252 and 1253, two fourth-century inscriptions honoring two brothers from the Piraeus for their services to the ὀργεῶνες, the association of worshippers of Amynos, Asclepios, and Dexion. From line 16 of 1252 it is clear that though the three heroes were celebrated by the same ὀργεῶνες, the shrine of Dexion was a separate building.

[82] This is disputed by Lesky (1), 50; he agrees with Ludwig Radermacher, *Aristophanes' 'Frösche'*, 269, that Aeschylus' invocation of Demeter in *Ra.* 886 ff. is merely a prayer to the goddesses of the deme where he was born and does not refer to the Eleusinian mysteries. This is hard to accept. The play is filled with references to the mysteries, the initiates, the divinities of the mysteries—in fact the main chorus is a chorus of dead initiates enjoying the blessed existence the goddesses promised their worshippers. In such a dramatic context Aeschylus' specific reference to the mysteries in an address to Demeter—a speech moreover which presents him as the champion of the mystery religion against the strange new gods invoked by his rival—surely suggests that Aristophanes thought of him as an initiate. The case against Aeschylus' initiation rests on a cryptic reference of Aristotle (*EN* 1111a) which does not of itself settle the question. The story that he was tried for impiety for revealing ἀπόρρητα may be, as Lesky calls it, a 'nicht schlecht bezeugte Geschichte,' but the crucial detail that he pleaded ignorance as a noninitiate rests on the testimony of Clement of Alexandria (*Strom.* II. 60) alone. Aristotle's remark might just as well allow us to suppose (as H. J. Rose suggests in his *Handbook of Greek Literature*,⁴ London, 1951, 148, n. 61) that "Aeschylus was an initiate but had not quite grasped the distinction between the secret and the open parts of the ritual (ἀπόρρητα, φανερῶς δρώμενα)."

[83] A recent and ambitious addition to the voluminous literature on the subject is Angelo Brelich, *Gli Eroi Greci*, Rome, 1958. Through a thorough examination of the ancient sources and modern interpreters Brelich seeks order in the chaos of conflicting information about hero cult. His purpose is to "constatare la connessione organica esistente tra i vari aspetti del culto e della mitologia eroica" (223), "delineare una morfologia del fenomeno 'eroe,' independentemente dalle singole figure" (312). His definition of the hero is worth quoting here: "un personaggio la cui morte ha un rilievo particolare; ha stretti nessi con il combattimento, con l'agonistica, con la mantica e la iatrica, con l'iniziazione nell' età adulta o nei misteri; è fondatore di città e il suo culto ha carattere civico; è antenato di gruppi consanguinei ed è rappresentante prototipico di certe attività umane fondamentali e primordiali; tutti questi caratteri mostrano una sua natura sovrumana, mentre d'altra parte egli appare anche mostruoso, gigante e nano, teriomorfo e androgino, fallico o sessualmente anormale o deficiente, portato alla violenza sanguinaria, alla follia, all' inganno, al furto, al sacrilegio e in generale a quella trasgressione dei limiti e delle misure che gli dei non permettono ai mortali; perciò anche la sua carriera, pur partendo da una discendenza privilegiata e sovrumana (ma che contemporaneamente porta il segno dell' illegalità) è sin dall' inizio minacciata

di situazioni critiche, di modo che pur raggiungendo le vette di magnifiche prove superate, di nozze memorabili, di trionfi e conquiste, nella sua connaturata imperfezione e smisuratezza, resta votato al fallimento e alla tragica fine" (313–314). This impressive sentence is the first attempt, as far as I know, to define the Greek 'hero,' and it is remarkable that many of the salient features of it correspond with the figure of the Sophoclean dramatic hero. Brelich's book, whatever may be thought of the 'morphological method,' is immensely learned, stimulating, and full of new insights into the vexed problems of the subject.

[84] Martin Nilsson, *A History of Greek Religion*, 194.

[85] Martin Nilsson, *Geschichte der griechischen Religion*, I, 189–190.

[86] VI, ix, 6–8.

[87] *Rom.* 28, 4–6.

[88] Plato (*R.* 391a-d) rejects the stories told about Achilles and Theseus; the poets must not be allowed to persuade young men that "heroes are no better than men."

[89] Pl. *Ap.* 41b (Ajax), 28c-d (Achilles). It is interesting that when Socrates half quotes, half paraphrases Achilles' reply to Thetis, he adds something which, though not to be found in the text of Homer, perfectly suits the spirit of Sophoclean tragedy; the adjective καταγέλαστος.

[90] Adams (135–136) makes a similar suggestion but with a different emphasis. He sees Sophocles as the *defensor fidei* of the hero cult; he mentions his "desire to defend the heroes" (135) and remarks that "he was fighting in a losing cause" (136). Jane Harrison's remark (which Adams quotes) that "Sophocles as a hero was not a success . . . he was in his own precinct completely submerged by the god he received" is based on a misunderstanding of the decree mentioned above, which makes it clear that the shrine of Dexion was a separate building from that of Amynos and Asclepios.

[91] See Georges Méautis, *L'Oedipe à Colone et le culte des héros*.

[92] Oedipus in Sparta, in Athens on the Areopagus, at Colonus, and at Eteonos in Boeotia—cf. Nilsson (2), 188; Philoctetes in Italy (at Makalla and Sybaris); Ajax on Salamis, at Athens, and elsewhere.

[93] The play was revived at the time of Essex' conspiracy and at the instigation of the conspirators. Later, the Queen, shown a document of the reign of Richard the Second by an antiquary, said to him: "I am Richard II; know ye not that?" See J. E. Neale, *Queen Elizabeth I*, chap. 22.

[94] His Athena predicts the increasing greatness of Athens. *Eu.* 853–854: οὐπιρρέων γὰρ τιμώτερος χρόνος/ ἔσται πολίταις τοῖσδε.

[95] Th. 2.63.

[96] See Albrecht von Blumenthal, *Ion von Chios, Fr.* 8.

[97] See Knox (3), chap. 2.

[98] For a personification of Athens in heroic terms, see E. *Supp.* 321–323: ὁρᾷς, ἄβουλος ὡς κεκερτομημένη/ τοῖς κερτομοῦσι γοργὸν ὄμμ' ἀναβλέπει/ σὴ πατρίς; ἐν γὰρ τοῖς πόνοισιν αὔξεται. See also *id.*, *Heracl.* 199 ff. where the heroic spirit of the Athenians is described.

[99] Not only in the *strategia* with Pericles, but also the other (later?) *strategia* against the Aenei (*Vita* 9). Service as *Hellenotamias* (443–42) and as one of the *probouloi* in the emergency caused by the disaster in Sicily; the *Vita* tells us also that he frequently (ἐξητάζετο—imperfect) served as ambassador.

NOTES TO III
(Pp. 62–90)

[1] For this meaning of κουφίζω, cf. *Aj.* 1411 (where also a burial is spoken of) and *Tr.* 1025 (of a dying man).

[2] *Aj.* 479.

[3] Adams, who attributes the first burial to a dust storm sent by the gods (49), is at some pains to explain away this apparent admission of responsibility for both burial attempts. Antigone, he says, "took the stand of making no denial of anything; she owed no answer to these men." It is of course literally true that, as he says, "the Greek does not mean and cannot mean that she confessed to both burials." But in the context —the guard's statement that "We charged her with the former and the present actions" (434)—what else was the audience supposed to think when he continued, "she denied nothing"? Adams stresses the 'inferences' the spectator must make from what he hears. "The dramatist . . . knows how far he can expect an audience, duly guided, to draw an inference" (47); "Little effort is needed to infer that . . ." (49). But in this case the spectator would have to have an acute legal mind to 'infer' that the guards 'inference' from Antigone's silence was a 'misinterpretation' (49, n. 11).

[4] Pearson's γοῦν λῆμ' for the manuscript reading is rightly ignored by Dain in the new Budé text (Paris, 1955).

[5] Her strong words (ἀρεστὸν οὐδὲν μηδ' ἀρεσθείη ποτέ 500) confirm the impression of her distaste for him already expressed in the sarcastic τὸν ἀγαθὸν Κρέοντα (31) of the prologue.

[6] Adams (52) points out that Creon's use of θιγοῦσαν (771) recalls Antigone's use of it in 546 and is "a deft and not too subtle indication that she did indeed save Ismene then: her words have stayed in Creon's mind."

[7] τοῦδε γὰρ σὺ κηδεμών: The bitterness of this remark is smoothed down by the parallel Jebb quotes (X. *An.* 3.1, 17) and his suggestion that it alludes to verse 47; though he correctly translates it ("all thy care is for him"), his note interprets the phrase as a charge that Ismene is a *spokesman* for Creon, one who pleads his cause. Antigone's words are much more cutting. The word κηδεύω in Sophocles refers to devoted care, that of his daughters for the blind Oedipus (*OC* 750), of the care for him which the blinded Oedipus recognizes in the chorus (*OT* 1323); κηδεμών itself is used in a description of the abandoned Philoctetes' lack of people to 'care' for his sickness (*Ph.* 195, cf. 170). Later in the *Antigone* Haemon uses a similar word to describe his 'care' for his father (*Ant.* 741). The word in Antigone's taunt suggests that Ismene devotes to Creon the 'care' she should have shown for Polynices; the suggestion is strengthened by the fact that (as Jebb points out) κηδεμόνες at *Iliad* 23.163 means the chief mourners for the dead (and κηδευθείς at *El.* 1141 refers to funeral rites).

[8] 817 ff. οὐκοῦν κλεινή etc. presents a problem which seems to have been largely overlooked. "Glorious, therefore . . ." Jebb translates; but Antigone has just lamented the fact that she is to be taken living to a tomb, that she has not been married, that she will be the bride of Acheron. "Jebb's 'therefore' is inappropriate," says Denniston

(*The Greek Particles*², 436), and he turns the speech into a question: "Well, are you not dying a glorious death?" But the trouble is that the sentence does not stop there in the Greek, in fact no punctuation is possible until 822 and the interrogative tone can hardly be held that long through such a complicated sentence, segmented by οὔτε, οὔτε and ἀλλά. In any case how can she be described as 'glorious' and 'having praise' (ἔπαινον ἔχουσ')? Who is praising her? Not the chorus. Jebb does not comment on ἔπαινον, but Dain-Mazon, in their introduction to the play (63) seem to see a problem. "Il est probable, d'autre part, que les vieillards du choeur ne promettraient pas louange et gloire à Antigone mourante (817) si Sophocle avait été le premier à imaginer le personnage et son conflit avec Créon. Il serait même surprenant s'ils se fussent exprimés ainsi s'il s'était agi d'une simple légende locale peu familière au public athénien." In other words, the chorus speaks of Antigone as 'glorious and receiving praise' here only because the subject was well known on the Attic stage. This will hardly do. The chorus can scarcely be referring either to the praise which Haemon claims the citizens gave to Antigone's action, for all too clearly they do not share that opinion—they reproach her sharply for her "rashness" (853) and uphold the claims of the state's power (κράτος 873). Ivan Linforth, *Antigone and Creon*, 222, refers the phrase to the future: "Thus strangely to pass alive to the hiding place of the dead will win her fame and praise, the chorus responds, thinking of the story that will be told of the manner of her self-chosen death." But ἔχουσ' refers to Antigone *now*, as she goes to her death. Méautis (1), 211, sees the chorus' remark as bitter sarcasm: "cette gloire le choeur la lui accorde avec les mêmes gestes dérisoires qu'eurent les soldats romains en face de celui qu'ils saluaient . . . Tu voulais la gloire, tu l'as maintenant, de quoi donc te plains-tu?" There is clearly a problem here. Is it possible that Sophocles wrote (or rather that his chorus was taught to sing, for the distinction could not be made in writing before the invention of accents) not οὐκοῦν but οὔκουν? (Cf. *Aj.* 79, where all mss. read οὐκοῦν and the editors almost unanimously print οὔκουν.) "Not glorious, nor with praise you go away to this hiding place of the dead, neither struck by wasting disease, nor receiving the wages of the sword, but self-willed, alive, alone of mortals, you will go down to Hades." Surely this makes much better sense. She goes to her death 'not with glory or with praise' because she is deprived of the occasion on which that glory and praise were celebrated, a funeral. (For ἔπαινος as a part of the funeral rite, cf. E. *Supp.* 858, 901, 929, Th. 2.34, 6.) She has no funeral because her death is no normal death (disease and war are cited as the normal ways to die, as indeed they still are); "By your own law you go to Hades alive in a way no other of mortal kind has passed" (Jebb). For the sequence οὔκουν . . . οὔτε . . . οὔτε . . . ἀλλά, cf. *OC* 924 ff.

⁹ Though Jebb categorically rejects it, the word also surely suggests the strange manner of her death. This is one of the interpretations offered by the scholia: ἰδίῳ καὶ καινῷ νόμῳ περὶ τέλος χρησαμένη. M. A. Bayfield, *The Antigone of Sophocles*,² suggests (*ad loc.*) that it refers to Antigone's peculiar method of punishment. "Such a victim enters the tomb independent, 'mistress of herself.' She can take as much or as little of the food as she will: she can die when and how she chooses."

¹⁰ Jebb tones this down; he is intent on demonstrating the sympathy of the chorus for Antigone. "There is no element of reproof in their words here." The interpretation which justifies this statement is very involved. Everything depends on the tone of the sentence beginning with καίτοι. Jebb takes it as comforting. "But it will be a great glory for thy memory that thy fate was as the fate of a goddess in death as in life."

But it can just as well be reproving. "And yet, it is a big thing for a dying girl to hear that she has shared the fate of those who are equal to the gods," i.e., 'we forgive you for talking like this.' This seems to follow more logically on the opening lines, and also gives a clearer motive than the involved one Jebb has to construct for her angry cry that she is mocked. Wunder-Wecklein, *Sophoclis Tragoediae*,[4] reads it this way. "Negat chorus . . . Antigonam recte se comparare mortalem et ex mortalibus genitam cum Niobe dea et dis nata, concedit tamen magnum esse mortuo eandem cum diis sortem nactum esse dici. Quibus verbis cum immodestiae Antigona argueretur, respondit illa οἴμοι γελῶμαι."

[11] So Electra, Νιόβα, σὲ δ' ἔγωγε νέμω θεόν, in a passage which suggests her own likeness to Niobe (150 ff.). The following lines make clear the point of the comparison in the *Antigone* passage: ἅτ' ἐν τάφῳ πετραίῳ αἰαῖ δακρύεις. Whitman (1), 93–94, has a brilliant discussion of the Niobe comparison.

[12] So both Jebb and more recently Dain-Mazon understand προσέπεσες. Pearson's προσέπαισας has the same meaning. However, Wolff-Bellermann *Sophokles Antigone*[6], understand προσέπεσες as 'throw yourself down in supplication at the altar of Dikê' (warfst du dich an die hohe Stufe [des Altars] der Dike nieder d.h. du flüchtetest dich in ihren Schutz). This interpretation is emphatically upheld by Lesky (1), 115, n. 3; "Sachlich und sprachlich ist nur die Deutung *supplex procubuisti* möglich." It is true that the parallels quoted by Wunder and Jebb for the meaning 'strike heavily against' (Jebb so translates in his note but in his translation prints, "against that throne . . . thou hast fallen") do not use the key word προσπίπτειν. But even if we accept the interpretation of Wolff-Bellermann and Lesky, the speech as a whole is still a reproach (softened in the last line by the mention of πατρῷον . . . ἆθλον).

[13] *Il.* 1.277 ff. (Nestor to Achilles).

[14] See Adams 47–50 for the theory that it really was divine intervention. H. D. F. Kitto, *Form and Meaning in Drama*, 138–158, in an eloquent discussion, sees in the 'illogicalities' of the burial a strong hint that "Antigone and the gods are working on parallel paths, μεταίτιοι" (154).

[15] See Ellendt-Genthe, s. v., for the definitions of this word by Photius and in the *Souda*. At *OT* 255 it means 'imposed by the god.' Cf. also Hdt. 7.18, 3.

[16] τοῦ παντὸς ἡμῖν Ζηνὸς Ἑρκείου 487. For a full discussion of the implications of this phrase see page 82.

[17] Cf. *Aj.* 594–595.

[18] διαπτυχθέντες. "The image," says Jebb, "might be suggested by various objects— a casket, tables, fruit or the like," but he quotes no parallel to show what the image is. (E. *Hipp.* 985 is metaphorical like *Ant.* 709.) The scholiast glosses with ἀνακαλυφθέντες which is not very helpful either. Bruhn compares Plu. *Quaest. Conviv.* 1.5, 2 (518c)— cloth held up to the light so that its quality may be examined ὑπ' αὐγὰς διαπτύσσομεν—; but this idea does not fit the word κενοί. A better parallel is E. *IT* 727: δέλτου μὲν αἵδε πολύθυροι διαπτυχαί, which refers (proleptically) to the 'unfolding' of the tablets on which the letter is written. So Orestes later, given the letter, 'dispenses with opening it,' παρεὶς δὲ γραμμάτων διαπτυχάς 793. (There is no need to adopt Badham's ἀναπτυχάς to get this meaning; Wecklein rightly points out that διαπτύσσω means 'unfold, spread out.') In *Ant.* 709 the image is that of a δέλτος, a bundle of πίνακες, tablets, which when opened (by breaking the seal and cutting the string), are spread out, but contain no

writing. They are 'empty,' κενοί, because the writing was thought of as '*in*' not '*on*' the tablets (cf. E. *IT*, 760: τἀνόντα κἀγγεγραμμέν' ἐν δέλτου πτυχαῖς).

[19] See Bayfield's interesting discussion (note on 775); his suggestion was approved by Frazer.

[20] Cf. Kitto (2), 166: "We are at liberty to reflect, after what Haemon has told us, that the people would refuse to stone one whom they thought worthy of a crown."

[21] Creon is on stage throughout; cf. Kitto (2), 146–147.

[22] So Diller 82: "Er ist die einzige sophokleische Figur, die im Grundsätzlichen schliesslich nachgibt."

[23] See Knox (3), Chap. V.

[24] This has of course been fully recognized and much discussed since Hegel first pointed it out. He discusses the matter in several places; the clearest statement is perhaps that in *Asthetik* II, 2. "The public law of the State and the instinctive family-love and duty towards a brother are here set in conflict. Antigone, the woman, is pathetically possessed by the interest of family; Creon, the man, by the welfare of the community." (Trans. by Anne and Henry Paolucci, *Hegel on Tragedy*, 178). Cf. also *ibid.*, 133.) See now the stimulating discussion of the whole problem by L. A. MacKay, "Antigone, Coriolanus and Hegel," TAPA 93 (1962) 166–174.

[25] E. M. Walker in *Cambridge Ancient History*, Vol. IV, Cambridge 1926, 144–145. On page 147, speaking of the *trittyes*, he mentions "the desire of Cleisthenes to weaken the influence of the old Eupatrid families, an influence which was mainly local and found its centre in the clan." Cf. also Paul Cloché, *La Démocratie Athénienne*, 21, "l'affaiblissement de la cohésion du *genos*." C. Hignett, *A History of the Athenian Constitution*, 132 ff., takes a skeptical view of all this, based partly on his critical attitude towards the reliability of the *Athenaion Politeia*.

[26] Arist. *Ath.* 21, 4. This is denied by Hignett (138 ff.) though accepted by Cloché (21). The discussion of the matter by Kurt von Fritz and Frank Kapp, *Aristotle's Constitution of Athens*, 164 seems to find a good middle ground. "As Attic literature shows, people of 'good family' continued to call each other by their fathers' names even after Cleisthenes, but, in all official and public affairs, they now were called by their first names and the name of their deme. Gradually, however, it became customary to call people officially by their fathers' names *and* their demes' names and this is found to be the established practice in the inscriptions of the fourth century."

[27] E.g., αὐτογέννητος 864, συμφιλεῖν, συνεχθεῖν 523.

[28] Repeated at 696.

[29] Elsewhere in tragedy only at A. *Th.* 890 (to describe Eteocles and Polynices).

[30] 3, 13, 21, 50, 58, 61, 62.

[31] Electra uses it of herself and Chrysothemis only in the speech where she tries to win her sister over to her side for the attack on Aegisthus (fourteen dual forms in *El.* 977–985).

[32] 13, 21, 55, 56.

[33] Cf. Arist. *EN* 1161b: ἀδελφοὶ δ' ἀλλήλους [φιλοῦσι] τῷ τε ἐκ τῶν αὐτῶν πεφυκέναι. ἡ γὰρ πρὸς ἐκεῖνα ταυτότης ἀλλήλους ταὐτὸ ποιεῖ. ὅθεν φᾶσι ταὐτὸν αἷμα καὶ ῥίζαν καὶ τὰ τοιαῦτα.

[34] Even the chorus, at first, uses these forms for the brothers (143–145). Creon never does.

[35] Cf. also, e.g., *Od.* 8.233: φίλα γυῖα, *Il.*: 22.58 φίλης αἰῶνος, 7.271 φίλα γούναθ'.

[36] A. W. H. Adkins, " 'Friendship' and 'Self-sufficiency' in Homer and Aristotle" *CQ*, XIII, 30–45, provides an interesting discussion of φίλος and φιλεῖν in Homer. He defines those things that were φίλα to the Homeric ἀγαθός ('a warrior-chieftain in charge of his own οἶκος') as follows: "He has his own limbs and psychological functions, his tools, weapons, possessions and portions of land: and he has his wife, children, servants, and other dependants" (33).

[37] For this sense of φίλος, φιλία, cf. Arist. *Po.* 53b, 20 ff.: ὅταν δ' ἐν ταῖς φιλίαις ἐγγένηται τὰ πάθη, οἷον ἢ ἀδελφὸς ἀδελφὸν ἢ υἱὸς πατέρα ἢ μήτηρ υἱὸν ἢ υἱὸς μητέρα ἀποκτείνῃ. Else translates ἐν ταῖς φιλίαις "within the bonds of family ties" (229) and comments (349): "in our passage φιλίαν (52a, 31) is not 'friendship' or 'love' or any other feeling, but *the objective state* of *being* φίλοι 'dear ones' by virtue of blood ties." Jones (58, n. 2) quotes this passage with approval and points out later (117–118) that "Orestes uses the superlative *philtatos* of the mother who hates him and whom he hates," and that the brothers, Eteocles and Polynices, the mortal enemies of the *Seven against Thebes*, are called *philoi*, each in relation to the other (971). Cf. also Bacchylides 5.131 (Snell).

[38] Adams (45) remarks that she does not speak here as the champion of the right of all dead men to burial. "Rightly or wrongly, burial is or has been denied to enemies; what she will not tolerate is its denial to her brother."

[39] Jebb prefers, "truly dear to thy friends," i.e., both to the dead brother and the loving sister. But, as he himself points out, in the identical phrase in E, *IT*, 610, τοῖς φίλοις δ' ὀρθῶς φίλος, the word φίλος is active in sense.

[40] He means, of course, "let her call on Zeus of the kindred blood in an appeal to me for mercy"; nothing is further from her thoughts. But this title of Zeus (apparently not found elsewhere) draws attention (like the similar Διὸς ἑρκείου in 487) to the nature of Antigone's loyalty. It is possible also that he means, "let her call down Zeus of the kindred blood on me"; later in the play the same word is used of the curses Eurydice calls down on Creon, κακὰς/ πράξεις ἐφυμνήσασα τῷ παιδοκτόνῳ, 1304–1305.

[41] ξύναιμος is a favorite Sophoclean word (cf., in addition to its appearances in the *Antigone*, *Aj.* 727, 977, *El.* 156, *OC* 943, 1355, 1374). Surprisingly enough it does not seem to occur in any other classical author. (Even συναίμων is attested mainly for inscriptions.)

[42] On this subject, see Ehrenberg 105 ff.

[43] Jebb's 'last night' is supported by parallels like νυκτὸς τῆσδε, νυκτὶ τῇδε, etc. which do not contain the precise νῦν. 'Εν ἡμέρᾳ τῇ νῦν would mean "this present day," cf. *OT* 351–352, *Aj.* 801–802. The dramatic time of the prologue is night; the sun rises, dramatically speaking, at verse 100, ἀκτὶς ἀελίου . . . ἐφάνθης ποτ'. Antigone pours the dust on Polynices' body before dawn, before the guards take up their position for the first time; ὁ πρῶτος . . . ἡμεροσκόπος (253) is, as Jebb says, "the first who had watched at all." (Jebb has his timetable confused; he describes the time of the prologue as 'daybreak,' which would not allow Antigone time to get to the body before the πρῶτος ἡμεροσκόπος stood to his post.) If the time of the prologue is before dawn, this disposes of one of the 'difficulties' raised by critics in the wearisome business of the two burials. Adams for instance makes much of the difficulties resulting from a dawn prologue. "It requires little thought to see that this first burial cannot have been carried out by Antigone. The burial took place in the night; it was not noticed

until the first day-watchman went on duty. But the prologue presents a scene occurring when there was at least some light" (47, n. 6). Night scenes on the Attic stage are simply indicated by a verbal reference (as here, ἐν νυκτὶ τῇ νῦν); the prologue of the *Agamemnon* is a good example (νυκτός 22); cf. also E. *Rhesus:* 13 νυκτῶν, 17 νυκτῶν, also *IA* 6: τίς ποτ' ἄρ' ἀστὴρ ὅδε πορθμεύει; also *El.* 54: ὦ νὺξ μέλαινα, cf. *ibid.*, 78–79: ἐγὼ δ' ἅμ' ἡμέρᾳ . . . σπερῶ. A. T. von S. Bradshaw, "The Watchman Scenes in the *Antigone*," *CQ* (Nov. 1962), 203–204 (a masterly reëxamination of the whole vexed problem which clears away much dead wood), comes to the same conclusion about the time of the prologue.

[44] His bloodthirsty intentions are referred to by Creon later (199 ff.). It is hard to see why Adams (46) speaks of "intentions that even the traitor could hardly have entertained." Polynices' allies Tydeus and Capaneus were proverbially men of violence, and according to Aeschylus the latter attacked the city armed with a shield which was inscribed 'I shall burn the city' (*Th.* 434). In the *OC*, both Oedipus (1373) and Antigone (1421) assume that Polynices' object is the destruction (ἐρείψεις, κατασκάψαντι) of Thebes.

[45] See Lesky (1), 114, for discussion and literature.

[46] *What I Believe.*

[47] *Th.* 2.60.

[48] 190: ταύτης ἔπι πλέοντες ὀρθῆς.

[49] 189: ἥδ' ἐστὶν ἡ σῴζουσα. On these resemblances Jebb is excellent. Rejecting the suggestion of Dobree that Thucydides knew the Sophocles passage or vice versa, he says, "What is really common to both poet and historian is the general sentiment of Periclean Athens."

[50] That these famous lines are not only a history of human progress but also express confidence in its future (which is not to say that Sophocles shared the sentiment), is clear from 360: ἄπορος ἐπ' οὐδὲν ἔρχεται τὸ μέλλον. There is still too much attention paid to the nineteenth-century dictum that the 'Greeks had no word for Progress.' They may not have had a specific word for it but they invented the idea.

[51] See Jebb's notes on these words. His comment however that "σύγκλητος is one of those words which, though a technical term at Athens, could still be used by Attic poets without any prosaic local allusion being felt" now sounds very quaint.

[52] Demosthenes (19.247) has lines 175–190 read out in court as part of his attack on Aeschines (who, having played the part of Creon in the *Antigone*, knew them only too well). This does not show "a complete lack of irony on the part of Demosthenes," as Ehrenberg says (59); no one could be more ironic than Demosthenes when the occasion called for it. What it does demonstrate is the "general acceptability" (C. M. Bowra, *Sophoclean Tragedy*, 68) of the sentiments expressed, even in the century after the words were written.

[53] It is used again at *OC* 1262. It is frequent in Plato.

[54] The verbal play on Haemon's name is brought clearly to our attention by 794 νεῖκος ἀνδρῶν ξύναιμον (a reference to the quarrel between father and son) and 1175 Αἵμων ὄλωλεν. αὐτόχειρ δ' αἱμάσσεται.

[55] Cf. Σ 632: τοῦτο δέ φησιν ὡς μὴ μεταβουλευσόμενος.

[56] Cf.: 677 κοσμουμένοις, 730 ἀκοσμοῦντας, 660 ἄκοσμα.

[57] They mean different things by κόσμος for example: whereas κόσμος and its congeners means to Creon the 'discipline' of sons and citizens, it always refers, in connec-

tion with Antigone, to the burial rites for her brother (cf.: 396 τάφον κοσμοῦσα, 901 ἕλουσα κἀκόσμησα, and see Goheen, *Imagery*, 17, "The recurrent split of the two protagonists over certain common words."

NOTES TO IV
(Pp. 91–116)

[1] This too was recognized by Hegel. Cf. *Hegel on Tragedy*, 178: "The gods however, whom she thus revered, are the *Dei inferi* of Hades"; 68: "Antigone reverences the ties of blood relationship, the gods of the nether world."

[2] See Kitto (2), 147–148. He is especially good on 'the doctrine of tacit assumption.'

[3] A. W. Verrall, *The Choephoroe of Aeschylus*. This conception is not of course Homeric (there is no sign of Agamemnon being unrespected among the dead in *Od.* 11.387 ff. or *ibid.* 24.20 ff.—though 24.30 ff. is obviously the model for A. *Cho.* 345 ff.). But such an idea (the dead deprived of τιμή) also lies behind the expressions in *Cho.* 485 (cf. Σ) and *Eum.* 97 (ὄνειδος ἐν φθιτοῖσιν). Cf. also E. *Hec.* 550 ff.

[4] Cf.: 904 'τίμησα, 913 ἐκπροτιμήσασ'.

[5] Σ. ἢ τὸν Πολυνείκη ἢ τοὺς χθονίους δαίμονας. For the plural φίλους referring to Polynices, cf. πρὸς τοὺς φίλους 10.

[6] "Sinless in my crime" (Jebb), "pieusement criminelle" (Méautis 176), and so forth.

[7] πανοῦργος etc. in Sophocles is applied to the deceit of Neoptolemos (*Ph.* 927), to the rascality of Odysseus (*ibid.* 408; cf. also 448, a reference to Thersites), to the murder of Agamemnon (*El.* 1387)—which was accomplished by δόλος (cf. *El.* 197)—to Aegisthus (*El.* 1507). There is always a suggestion of trickery and lies, and this is the usual connotation of the word in Aristophanes, for example in the *Knights* where it is a *leitmotiv* (cf. especially 247 ff.). The Horatian phrase which is so often cited to illustrate the oxymoron, *splendide mendax*, is closer in content than has usually been realized.

[8] And Creon does indeed use this word to describe the burial of Polynices (300).

[9] *LSJ*[9] s. v.

[10] An unusual phrase. Ἔντιμος is usually constructed with the dative (cf. *Ant.* 25, *El.* 239). "The honoured things of the gods," says Jebb in his note, which is certainly unobjectionable, but his translation reads, "the laws which the gods have stablished in honour.' τὰ παρὰ θεοῖς τίμια ἀτίμαζε says the scholiast. τετίμηται γὰρ παρὰ θεοῖς καὶ ὅσιον νενόμισται τὸ θάπτειν νεκρούς.

[11] This is the force of τι which is neglected in most editions and translations. So also is the μοι which, like λέγω γὰρ κἀμέ 32, emphasizes Antigone's feeling that the proclamation was aimed at her personally, as the sister of the dead man and thus responsible for his burial.

[12] Cf. Wunder-Wecklein *ad loc.* "verbum ὑπερτρέχειν non valet ὑπερβαίνειν sed, ut

recte iam Schaeferus monuit, 'superiorem esse, superare.' " He compares E. *Ph.* 578, *Ion* 973.

[13] To be understood from τὰ σά.

[14] Arist. *Rh.* 1375a: τὸ μὲν ἐπιεικὲς . . . οὐδέποτε μεταβάλλει, οὐδ' ὁ κοινὸς [νόμος] . . . οἱ δὲ γεγραμμένοι πολλάκις.

[15] Festugière, 52.

[16] τῶν τε αἰεὶ ἐν ἀρχῇ ὄντων ἀκροάσει καὶ τῶν νόμων, καὶ μάλιστα αὐτῶν ὅσοι τε ἐπ' ὠφελίᾳ τῶν ἀδικουμένων κεῖνται καὶ ὅσοι ἄγραφοι ὄντες αἰσχύνην ὁμολογουμένην φέρουσιν.

[17] E.g., D. 18.275 *id.* 23.70, Pl. *R.* 563d, *Plt.* 295e.

[18] His edict is repeatedly referred to by this word or its cognates. Cf. 8, 27, 32, 34, 192, 203, 447, 450, 454, 461.

[19] See, for example, Th. 2.2, 4: the proclamation made to the inhabitants of Plataea by the Thebans after their successful *coup de main.*

[20] When Ehrenberg says (46), "He [Pericles] had no clearly defined notion of an unwritten law, nor, as to that, had Sophocles," he is speaking, in the case of Sophocles, of the general notion of divine law which he extracts from the *Antigone* speech, the choral ode at *OT* 865 ff., and other passages (cf. 34). The remark is certainly not applicable to *Ant.* 455 ff.; there it is quite clear what the unwritten law says.

[21] 48 and Appendix A (167–172).

[22] Cf. Else 474–475. "Plato's polemic against the depictions of the gods in Homer and the other poets makes it clear that he regarded them at least as serious attempts to portray the divine nature. In other words he recognized that Greek poetry was a representation of men *and gods.* One half of this world has disappeared from Aristotle's field of view. . . . The gods are gone, except as a curtain raiser, and there is nothing to replace them except an Aristotelian Prime Mover sitting forever beyond the heavens."

[23] Isocrates understood the passage better. In the *Panathenaicus,* describing the Athenian intervention in favor of the dead champions at Thebes, he says (169—a passage where he refers specifically to tragic performances), that Adrastos asked Theseus μὴ περιιδεῖν τοιούτους ἄνδρας ἀτάφους γενομένους μηδὲ παλαιὸν ἔθος καὶ πάτριον νόμον καταλυόμενον, ᾧ πάντες ἄνθρωποι χρώμενοι διατελοῦσιν οὐχ ὡς ὑπ' ἀνθρωπίνης κειμένῳ φύσεως ἀλλ' ὡς ὑπὸ δαιμονίας προστεταγμένῳ δυνάμεως.

[24] Though she calls them νόμοι at 519 (where Ehrenberg is right to defend the ms. τούτους).

[25] Unfortunately E. Laroche, *Histoire de la racine NEM—en grec ancien,* is only incidentally concerned with this word (199–200).

[26] E.g., Hdt. 1.65, 2.79, 3.2, 7.136. For the same sense in the fourth century cf. D. 7.13, 23.81, 20.106 etc. Its only other appearance in Sophocles is *El.* 1096 ff.: ἃ δὲ μέγιστ' ἔβλαστε νόμιμα, τῶνδε φερομέναν ἄριστα τᾷ Ζηνὸς εὐσεβείᾳ. This is translated "greatest laws" by Ehrenberg, who links it with *Ant.* 455 ff. and other passages. Erik Wolf, *Griechisches Rechtsdenken,* Vol. 2, 245–246, takes a different view. "Auch diese νόμιμα darf man weder alttestamentlich-christlich als 'Gesetz Gottes' auffassen . . . noch als Inbegriff naturgesetzlicher Regeln, auch nicht als konstitutive Ideen einer harmonischen Welt-Ordnung, wie es dem aristotelischen und platonischen Denken entspricht. Diese νόμιμα sind wohl 'den Göttern wohlgefällige Bräuche,' aber keine 'göttlichen Gebote,'; es sind ungeschriebene Richtschnuren des Verhaltens der ἀγαθοί, woran sie sich halten." On the Antigone speech, his position is orthodox; but it is re-

markable that he does not quote exactly what Antigone says—his pages (262–266) are studded, like those of so many others who have written on this speech, with expressions such as ἄγραφος νόμος, νόμος θεῖος, νόμος ἄγραφος Θεῶν, νόμοι ἄγραφοι, none of which appear in the text of Sophocles.

²⁷ E.g., the common phrase εἴργεσθαι τῶν νομίμων, used of the ritual seclusion of those accused of φόνος from ἱερῶν καὶ ἀγορᾶς. Cf. also D. 23.65, *ibid.* 73.59, 117.

²⁸ Cf. D. 60.8 (the Seven against Thebes again), *ibid.* 37, Din. 2.8; Men. *Her.* 34 (Körte). Similar context Th. 3.58, 4.

²⁹ The chorus, 601 ff., speaks of her as 'mowed down' ἀμᾷ by the dust, κόνις, of the gods below the earth, θεῶν τῶν νερτέρων. The right reading here is κόνις. The νιν refers not to φάος (which would make the already bold metaphor almost unintelligible) but to ῥίζα. "Over the last root the daylight was spread (ἐτέτατο Brunck, Pearson) in the house of Oedipus. But in its turn (αὖ) the bloodstained dust of the gods below cuts it down," that is, the dust Antigone sprinkled on the corpse of Polynices in the service of the gods below has brought her own death. Κοπίς is inappropriate. Bruhn is good on this suggestion: "das zum Hauen verwandte Schlacht-und Küchenmesser und ein von Barbaren getragener Säbel." Jebb's reference to E. *El.* 837—"Euripides did not think it out of keeping with the tone of a tragic *rhesis*"—does not help his case, for that *rhesis* is remarkable for its unheroic tone and its careful technical description of the butchering of an animal. Jebb does not mention the fact that the only other occurrence of the word in Attic drama is E. *Cyc.* 241, where Polyphemus is preparing to eat Odysseus and his crew—a reference which Wolff-Bellermann strangely include in the discussion with the translation 'Opfermesser.' Another argument for κόνις is that it takes up again a constant theme of the first part of the play (cf. 247, 256, 409, 429).

³⁰ G. Rachel Levy, *The Gate of Horn*, 6.

³¹ R. J. Bonner, *Aspects of Athenian Democracy*.

³² Paus. 6.25.

³³ Cf. *Il.* 9.457 Ζεύς τε καταχθόνιος καὶ ἐπαινὴ Περσεφόνεια.

³⁴ For the close connection of Ares with Thebes, see A. *Th.* 104–107, 135–136.

³⁵ Though most critics now accept the speech as genuine, conspicuous exceptions are Schmid-Stählin II, (355 n. 2), and Whitman (92).

³⁶ This pessimistic view is in effect that of Denys Page in his cogently reasoned *Actors' Interpolations in Greek Tragedy*. He has little faith in the efficacy of the measures taken by Lycurgus to restore the genuine texts. The statement of Plutarch (*Vit. Dec. Orat. Lycurgus*, 841f) to the effect that Lycurgus passed a law "that the plays of Aeschylus, Sophocles and Euripides should be written down and that this official text should be read to the actors" certainly proves that the texts had been extensively tampered with in performance, but it also surely indicates that there *was* a good text in existence which could be used as a corrective.

³⁷ Appendix, p. 259.

³⁸ As she said herself: ὅμως ὁ γ' Ἅιδης τοὺς νόμους τούτους ποθεῖ (519).

³⁹ See Knox (2), 12 ff.

⁴⁰ *Ev. Matt.* 16.4.

⁴¹ *Od.* 20.100 ff., cf. also *ibid.* 3.173 ff.

⁴² Cf. 559: ἡ δ' ἐμὴ ψυχὴ πάλαι/ τέθνηκεν.

⁴³ Which would apply in hypothetical cases.

⁴⁴ Verse 10. τῶν ἐχθρῶν κακά. See Jebb's note.

[45] Jebb's punctuation, not Pearson's. So Ehrenberg 62, n. 1.

[46] παρείρων, 'weaving in,' 'inserting,' 'including,' does not seem too violent a metaphor. The description of man's rise to civilization has been so far completely 'secular' in tone, unlike the similar Aeschylean account in the *Prometheus Bound* and that in the *Protagoras* of Plato—which however cannot in this respect represent the views of the historical Protagoras; cf. Knox (3), 110 and 256, n. 11. The gods have so far been excluded. Now comes the moment to 'insert' them. This is the meaning of παρείρω in all three of its occurrences in classical Greek (one of them is in Aeschylus—*Fr.* 281, 3; cf. also X. *Smp.* 6.2; Plb. 18.18, 13). It is the opposite of ἐξαιρῶ 'to exclude'—what Oedipus and Jocasta do to the oracles about Laios (*OT* 908 θέσφατ' ἐξαιροῦσιν) and what Protagoras, in Plato, states he does to the gods: θεούς τε εἰς τὸ μέσον ἄγοντες (cf. παρείρων) οὓς ἐγὼ ἔκ τε τοῦ λέγειν καὶ τοῦ γράφειν περὶ αὐτῶν, ὡς εἰσὶν ἢ ὡς οὐκ εἰσίν, ἐξαιρῶ (*Tht.* 162d). Dain-Mazon rightly retain παρείρων. "Il s'agit ici d'introduire dans le savoir humain la morale civique et religieuse."

[47] ὑψίπολις: "high in his city" (Dain-Mazon, Bruhn and, emphatically and exclusively, Ehrenberg 64). "High is his city" (Bowra 85, Wolff-Bellermann, Jebb). Ehrenberg appeals to analogy with other ὑψι- compounds to exclude the meaning "high is his city"; they seem to me to suggest the opposite. There is no good analogy for ὑψι- meaning 'high in'; ὑψίζυγος, for example, does not mean that the rower sits high in, or on, or in any relation to, the bench, but that the bench he sits on is high. (How do you sit high on a bench in the same way as a man is high in his city? On a cushion?) Phrases such as A ὑψι-B do not mean that A is high in relation to B (except possible ὑψινεφής but that is better understood the other way), but that B is high. (By analogy with Ehrenberg's interpretation of ὑψίπολις, νόμοι . . . ὑψίποδες [*OT* 865–866] should mean laws which are "high in the feet" and δρύες ὑψίκομοι would mean oaks that are high in the leaves). Bruhn, who insists on the meaning "hoch in der Stadt," admits that "es gibt wohl kein anderes Adjektiv, bei dem πόλις als zweiter Teil so in lokativem Sinn zu nehmen wäre." Ehrenberg's further objection to "high is his city," that "no single good citizen can make a city ὑψηλή," loses sight of the fact that the subject of ἔρπει is not a single citizen but is still the τοῦτο of verse 334, 'this creature,' 'man.' (So, rightly, Linforth (2), 197: "ὑψίπολις and ἄπολις are in the singular to agree with the collective ἄνθρωπος which has governed the whole poem from the beginning.") Man, then, if he inserts into the framework of his intellectual achievement the laws of the earth and the Dikê of the gods, is high-citied, that is, his city is high. So far so good; but with ἄπολις the emphasis changes. It is true that the Greek language could use ἄπολις of a whole people, not a single individual (and so could use it of the whole human race); Wolff-Bellermann appositely quote Plato *Lg.* 766d: πᾶσα δὲ δήπου πόλις ἄπολις ἂν γίγνοιτο, ἐν ᾗ δικαστήρια μὴ καθεστῶτα εἴη κατὰ τρόπον. But the next word after ἄπολις, ὅτῳ, must refer to a single individual. (One can continue the construction with 'man,' τοῦτο, as far as ἄπολις, but one cannot say: "Man is cityless, I mean the man to whom . . ."). In other words ὅτῳ breaks the continuity and forces us to reroute our understanding of the passage along new lines (and with the next lines μήτ' ἐμοὶ παρέστιος etc. the transition from ἄνθρωπος to a particular individual is complete). I suggest that the effect of this grammatical trick is to throw back the new meaning (a single individual) retroactively on ὑψίπολις, so that in one breath, as it were, we understand "man's city is high; he is cityless" and then with ὅτῳ perceive that the poet also means: "the man who inserts . . . is high in his city" (of a single individual it can mean only

this); "he is an outcast from the city, the one whose intimacy is with evil because of daring." In other words both interpretations of ὑψίπολις are right. The passage is a good example of the richness of meaning Sophocles packs into the notoriously elliptical style of his lyrics.

[48] As opposed to νόμους . . . τοὺς προκειμένους (481) the laws he had ordained (τιθέναι) himself. The νόμοι καθεστῶτες were there long before him.

[49] As Zeus grants the prayer of Ajax (cf. *Aj.* 825 ff. and 998 ff.).

NOTES TO V
(Pp. 117–142)

[1] *Ph.* 8–11, 1031–1034. Kitto (2), 103–104 makes the point that the Greek commanders "had no reason whatever for marooning him as they did on this uninhabited island, instead of sending him home as an honourable ally who had become incapacitated." Philoctetes mentions (though Odysseus delicately omits it) the smell of his festering wound (δυσώδης 1032).

[2] *El.* 1508–1510.

[3] Cf. 1350–1351.

[4] This has led to the fairly wide-spread feeling (stated most unequivocally by J. T. Sheppard, *Greek Tragedy*, 119) that "Neoptolemos, not Philoctetes is the hero." Cf. Méautis 58. Neoptolemos is of course one of Sophocles' greatest creations, but he is still secondary in the play. Everything he says and does is concerned with Philoctetes; Philoctetes, even when off stage is, like Ajax dead and alive, the sole subject of the speech and object of the action of the other characters.

[5] See for example the discussion in Plato *Hippias Minor* 365b, where Achilles and Odysseus are distinguished by the sophist Hippias as the types of the ἀληθής τε καὶ ἁπλοῦς and the πολύτροπος τε καὶ ψευδής.

[6] So he appears in Pi. *N.* 3.70 ff.

[7] These lines are appositely quoted by the scholiast on *Ph.* 94: εἰσάγει δὲ αὐτὸν ὁ Σοφοκλῆς τὸν τοῦ πατρὸς λόγον λέγοντα κτλ.

[8] Cf. Whitman (2), 192.

[9] ἀρνύμενος ἥν τε ψυχήν are the words used of him in the proem to the *Odyssey* (5).

[10] Cf. Pi. *N.* 7.20 ff., *ibid.* 8.26.

[11] Cf. Goethe's brilliant characterization of the *Odyssey* as opposed to the *Iliad*, quoted by Albin Lesky (3), 59: "Hört nicht aber dagegen Ulyssens wandernde Klugheit/ Auf dem Markte sich besser, da wo sich der Bürger versammelt?"

[12] See Knox (2), 24–26.

[13] Cf. Kitto (2), 114.

[14] *Od.* 10.273 αὐτὰρ ἐγὼν εἶμι, an Achillean phrase, cf. *Il.* 18.114.

[15] In the *Hecuba* and (though he does not appear in them), the *Troades* (721 ff.) and *IA* (524 ff., 1362). Cf. also *Orestes* 1404 ff. and (if it is Euripidean) the *Rhesus*. On this see W. B. Stanford *The Ulysses Theme*, 102–117.

[16] *Aj.* 189.

[17] His attitude is the exact opposite of the heroic steadfastness, and recalls the traditional comparison of the crafty timeserver to the polypus (i.e., the octopus, cf. D'Arcy Wentworth Thompson, *A Glossary of Greek Fishes*, 204), which was supposed to change its color to match the rocks in which it moved. Cf. S. *Fr.* 307 (attributed to Odysseus by Jebb), Thgn. 215 ff., Pi. *Fr.* 43 (Snell), etc.

[18] This is illustrated by Jebb with a reference to Arist. *HA*. I.1 (488b): " 'τὸ γενναῖον' is as Aristotle defines it, τὸ μὴ ἐξιστάμενον ἐκ τῆς αὑτοῦ φύσεως." The context of Aristotle's definition is however not too favorable for Jebb's explanation of the passage in Sophocles. The phrase is a sort of Prodican parenthesis distinguishing between εὐγενές (τὸ ἐξ ἀγαθοῦ γένους) and γενναῖον (as above). It applies to a previous sentence in which the lion is cited as the type of the ἐλεύθερα καὶ ἀνδρεῖα καὶ εὐγενῆ whereas the example of τὰ . . . γενναῖα καὶ ἄγρια καὶ ἐπίβουλα(!) is—λύκος, the wolf. Aristotle makes the same distinction between τὸ εὐγενές and τὸ γενναῖον again in the *Rhetoric* (1390b) and then goes on to say that generally those who are εὐγενεῖς are not γενναῖοι, in fact they are mostly worthless (εὐτελεῖς). All this has little to do with Sophocles, for whom εὐγένεια is one of the mainsprings of heroism. In any case Jebb's particular interpretation "Odysseus calls on Neopt. to prove himself a true son of his sire . . . by complete loyalty to his mission" neglects the awkward fact that the last thing in the world Achilles thought of was "loyalty to his mission." All Odysseus means is "You must act nobly, like your father."

[19] *Th.* 3.82, 4 ff. In 3.83, 1 he speaks of the disappearance of τὸ εὔηθες, οὗ τὸ γενναῖον πλεῖστον μετέχει.

[20] It is in fact Neoptolemos who speaks of 'bringing' him (τὸν ἄνδρ' ἄγειν 90, πείσαντ' ἄγειν 102, cf. also τοῦτον εἰς Τροίαν μολεῖν 112). Odysseus speaks of the bow alone (the contrast between 112 and 113 is striking) except in four phrases (σόφισμα τῷ νιν αὐτίχ' αἱρήσειν δοκῶ 14, δόλῳ Φιλοκτήτην λαβεῖν 101, οὐκ ἂν λάβοις 103, and δόλῳ λαβόντα 107), all of which are ambiguous, for to 'take' or 'capture' Philoctetes might be necessary to get the bow, but the words used by Odysseus do not necessarily imply taking him to Troy as Neoptolemos' ἄγειν does.

[21] Kitto (2), 95 ff. states and analyzes these difficulties with his customary brilliance and wit, and finds (94) that "they are essential parts of a coherent plan, very carefully designed, to the minutest detail." On them he bases his interpretation of the play—which is, he says, "almost the opposite of what is suggested by Bowra" (13)—the idea "that the Atridae and Odysseus are frustrated by what they themselves have done . . . that men like Odysseus with their apparently clever arguments and schemes are morally repulsive and politically disastrous; and that they are this because what they do, or attempt to do, runs counter to the will of the gods, or the whole order of things, which is *Dikē*" (136). With this interpretation, as will be seen, I am fundamentally in agreement; Kitto's argument is cogent and the conclusion follows inexorably from the premises. But I do not find the 'illogicalities' which play so great a part in Kitto's discussion quite as glaring as he does, in fact, most of them seem to me nonexistent.

Kitto's main point is that Neoptolemos, at various moments in the play, knows more than he can possibly be expected to know, about the past and about the future (the prophecy of Helenos). The passages in question are: 194 ff., the fact that Philoctetes' sickness comes from Chryse; 839 ff., τοῦδε γάρ ὁ στέφανος κτλ. ("This is quite unintelligible" Kitto says); and 1314 ff., where he tells Philoctetes that "he is destined to take Troy with the bow, with the help of Neoptolemos; also that he will be healed if he comes to Troy, not otherwise; also that Troy is destined to fall this very summer. All this, says Neoptolemos, was explicitly declared by Helenos. Moreover he now knows the picturesque detail that Helenos offered to stake his life on the accuracy of this prophecy" (p. 99). To this redoubtable bill of attainder is to be added the fact that he "finds himself empowered, at v. 1326, to explain to Philoctetes that the serpent bit him because he was trespassing on Chryse's domain, of which the snake was the guardian" (100). These problems spring, it seems to me, from an exaggeration of the initial ignorance of Neoptolemos. "The first scene implies that Neoptolemos has only the vaguest idea of why he has been brought to Lemnos," says Kitto (95). Yet it is he (as Kitto indeed points out, 96) who speaks of 'bringing' (ἄγειν) Philoctetes, though Odysseus studiously avoids this word, and he even speaks of 'bringing' him 'by persuasion' (102). He seems in other words to know the general nature of his mission all right; and he seems too to have a notion of the nature of Helenos' prophecy (cf. 102 and 611 ff.). We have no reason to think, in other words, that he does not know the general gossip of the Greek camp. The prophecy of Helenos was delivered in public (Ἀχαιοῖς ἐς μέσον 609), and though Neoptolemos had not yet arrived at Troy when it was delivered, he will surely have heard a more or less accurate version of it. More or less, because there is one important thing about it he does not know, that Philoctetes was *essential* if Troy was to be captured (112 ff.). All the rest, the details of the past, the snakebite in the precinct at Chryse, and so on, he will surely have heard discussed *ad nauseam* round the Greek campfires. All this of course is taking us deep into the territory of Waldock's 'documentary fallacy,' but there is no other way to make the point. The things Neoptolemos later shows knowledge of are common knowledge in the Greek army (except, as we shall see, for some which are natural inferences from what he does know). At the risk of laboring the point (which Kitto's challenging argument tempts one to do) I suggest a modern analogy. Suppose a modern dramatist to open his play with the arrival on the shore of St. Helena of two French soldiers, one a major of the Old Guard and the other a young lieutenant; their object is to persuade the ailing Napoleon to return to France. The major tells the lieutenant only that Napoleon was put there by the English, that his return is essential for France, that he is suffering from stomach ulcers and unwilling to go, and that he will have to be tricked. Shall we be surprised if in the next scene the lieutenant shows knowledge of the fact that Napoleon lost the battle of Waterloo? And that he divorced his first wife Josephine?

Neoptolemos' second-hand knowledge of Helenos' prophecy (suggested by his reference to 'bringing by persuasion') is naturally overborne by the authority and arguments of Odysseus (who does not mention the prophecy at all). But it helps to explain the passage which Kitto finds 'unintelligible,' for what Neoptolemos hears from the false merchant (and therefore, as he knows, from the mouth of Odysseus) is a version of the prophecy which in this important respect exactly coincides with his vague knowledge of it—Philoctetes must be "brought to Troy by persuasion." His statement that "the crown is his; it is he whom the god said we must bring" is a natural consequence. While acting out his lie, he has been struck by the nobility of his victim, and what is more natural for the son of Achilles than the realization that the prophecy is concerned, not with the fulfillment of his own ambitions or the Greek victory at Troy, but with the recompense and rehabilitation of Philoctetes?

The fact that he tells Philoctetes later that he will be healed at Troy is a natural inference from the prophecy. For it is clear as day (especially after the terrifying break-down of Philoctetes under the onset of pain) that he cannot use the arms of Heracles against Troy unless he is first healed. (In fact Neoptolemos hints obscurely at this healing earlier: σῶσαι κακοῦ . . . τοῦδ' 919.) And since he will have to be healed at Troy naturally it will be done by the physicians of the Greek army, the sons of Ascle-pius (1333). This statement is clearly an inference, for it is inexact; we are told later by Heracles that the healing will be done not by the sons of Asclepius but by Asclepius himself, who will be sent to Troy for the purpose, presumably from heaven. The state-ment that Philoctetes can be healed only if he goes to Troy is also common sense—he cannot be healed on the island, and Neoptolemos does not yet foresee that he will eventually feel obliged to take Philoctetes back to his home at Oeta. (Would we be surprised if later in the hypothetical Napoleon play the young lieutenant told the Emperor, in an attempt to convince him that he should come to Paris, that he was to be cured of his stomach ulcers, and that only in Paris would he find the right specialists for the job?)

The other two pieces of information Neoptolemos produces, that Helenos said Troy would fall this very summer and that he staked his life on the truth of this prophecy, are again perfectly reasonable if we credit Neoptolemos with the general knowledge of the prophecy current in the Greek camp. The first has been prepared for; when he counters the chorus' sympathy for Philoctetes with the callous statement that all this has come on Philoctetes from the gods, he says the purpose of it was "so that this man would not draw the invincible bow of the gods against Troy until this time should come round [ὅδ' ἐξήκοι χρόνος] at which, it is said [λέγεται] Troy should be overcome by them" (197–200). This can only be a reminiscence of the prophecy of Helenos, and if he knew that much there is no reason why he should not have known that Helenos staked his life on the outcome.

It comes down to this: why *should* we assume that Neoptolemos knows only what he is told in the prologue? Is it implausible to assume that he knew what anyone at Troy could have told him: that Philoctetes trespassed on the shrine of Chryse, was bitten by its guardian the serpent, and marooned on Lemnos by the Greeks; that Helenos said that Troy must fall this summer and that Philoctetes must be persuaded to come to Troy and use the bow of Heracles against it, and that Helenos staked his life on the truth of his prophecy? Everything else he says is easy inference from what he already knows.

All this has taken us far from the performance and Kitto, whose alertness to Sopho-clean dramatic skill is second to nobody's, points out that the spectators would not have bothered about such matters: "they were not intended to, any more than those who admired the new Parthenon were expected also to admire the careful placing and tilting of the columns" (95). But I am at least one *reader* who is not bothered by the 'illogicalities' either, and I am not alone. As Kitto himself says of the complex nest of problems he has dealt with in the play: "It has been there all the time since 409 B.C. and yet until Bowra's book on Sophocles appeared no one seems to have given any but the most perfunctory attention to what is a most unconventional piece of stage-craft" (101).

Adams (157, n. 15) sees no difficulty in 1326 ff., but his explanation partly depends on his theory that Neoptolemos, when he speaks the hexameter lines, is "inspired by the god of prophecy himself" (150). "He has realized by inspiration the need for bringing Philoctetes to Troy. With that realization he understands the oracle fully. It may be asked how he knows that Philoctetes' sore will be healed by the sons of Asclepius. But surely he has always known this; we have always known it." (This neglects the awkward fact that it is not true.) "As for the time decreed for the fall of the city, this is by comparison a minor matter; it may be taken as common knowledge or as something added to round out the prophecy" (157). (But Neoptolemos referred to it earlier, in verses 197 ff.)

[22] Adams' treatment of the play is influenced by a preconceived idea of what 'the legend' was. Discussing Odysseus' insistence on the bow in the prologue, he says: "But we know from the legend that Helenos . . . proclaimed the need for both Philoctetes and the bow" (137; cf. also 147: "we, who know the legend . . ."). This statement is hardly likely to be true of the majority of the audience who watched the play in 409 B.C., and it is not even true of us in our studies today. What *was* 'the legend'? All we know of what was presumably the original source, the *Little Iliad*, is that Photius in the ninth century said that Proclus in the second century A.D. (or the fifth) said that it described how "Odysseus ambushed Helenos, he prophesied about the capture, and Diomedes brought Philoctetes back from Lemnos." All this (which is a very different picture from that we find in Sophocle's play) happened, according to the *Little Iliad*, *before* Odysseus brought Neoptolemos from Scyros. The *Little Iliad* then would not have given Sophocles' audience the 'knowledge' Adams speaks of and the other early sources reflected (presumably) in Apollodorus (*Ep.* 5.8) and Quintus Smyrnaeus (9.325 ff.) would not have helped them either, for in both these accounts it is not Helenos who recommends bringing Philoctetes back, but Calchas. There was no 'legend' to which Sophocles' audience could compare his treatment, looking for pointers; they took the play, as we must, as it comes. All they 'knew,' probably, was that somehow Philoctetes was brought to Troy in the end.

[23] The complexity and excitement of the action inspires in Waldock a strange vision; "Sophocles Improvises" is the title of his chapter on the play (196 ff.). The obscurities in Odysseus' instructions in the prologue "were essential . . . as the play progresses, Sophocles can give himself elbow-room for fruitful developments. Depending, as he must, here, on inspirations . . . he must have opportunity for happy variations . . . the grand object of it all is to keep the drama afloat" (199). And later (205): "So, from moment to moment, cleverly inventive, Sophocles eases his play on its way." Even Waldock finally felt misgivings at this picture of an expert but harassed juggler keeping two oranges and a plate in the air at the same time, for he added a cryptic footnote: "I do not mean that the play lacks planning, but that the very planning is a kind of improvisation." What that means I have not the remotest idea, unless we are to imagine Sophocles giving their lines to the actors just before they go on stage in a sort of premature Attic *commedia dell' arte*. Or perhaps, like Sheridan, Sophocles (who had been busy in the assembly) was writing the last act back stage while the first act was being played.

[24] See Knox (3), 35 ff.

[25] Cf. Bowra 265 ff.

[26] Cf. *Ph.* 840.

[27] Cf. *Ph.* 835 ff.

[28] *Ph.* 191 ff. The underlying thought is that the gods prevented Philoctetes from

taking Troy until the appointed time, that is, when Neoptolemos arrived. See Kitto's perceptive remarks on this speech (2), 111 ff.

[29] This lie is enough to shatter Adams' case that Neoptolemos "may not actually lie" (142) and verse 253 destroys also the case that "literal untruths have been avoided in his first words with this man." It does not mean, as Adams translates it, citing Jebb's note, "regard me in the light of one who knows nothing" ("this is not an actual denial of knowledge" says Adams—140n.5); it means what Jebb prints in his translation: "Be assured that I know nothing of what thou askest." Since what Philoctetes is asking about are ὄνομα τοὐμόν and τῶν κακῶν κλέος his statement is as bald and literal a lie as could be imagined. In any case, Neoptolemos later admits that he lied (cf. 842 ψεύδεσιν).

[30] Adams, who is committed to the position that Neoptolemos refrains from "actual untruth," will have it that the story is true. If it is, the psychological situation of the prologue is wildly implausible. How can Neoptolemos take orders from and treat so respectfully a man who had so wronged him, and had insulted him (cf. 379 ff.) into the bargain? If the story is true, how can Odysseus use such a phrase as κυρίως αἰτουμένῳ (63) in his instructions to Neoptolemos? And above all, if the story is true, why does Neoptolemos not mention the refusal to give him his father's arms when he comes to words and almost to blows with Odysseus near the end of the play? (This last point bothers Adams; cf. 142, n. 7.) The main argument advanced by Adams for the truth of the story is that "it is not credible that the familiar story of the award to Odysseus . . . should be contradicted, even by implication, in this play (137)." No such contradiction is expressed or implied; of course Odysseus was awarded the arms of Achilles, but he handed them over to Neoptolemos when the young man came from Scyros. "Certain epic stories," Adams continues, "apparently said that on his arrival at Troy Neoptolemos was given his father's armor; but this account at least slurs over the more familiar version." *What* more familiar version? The *Little Iliad*, according to Proclus, said that Odysseus handed over the armor: καὶ Νεοπτόλεμον Ὀδυσσεὺς ἐκ Σκύρου ἀγαγὼν τὰ ὅπλα δίδωσι τὰ τοῦ πατρός (Allen 106). And both Quintus Smyrnaeus (7.445) and Apollodorus (*Ep.* 5.11) say the same thing. (Cf. Philostr. Jun. *Im.* 10 and the magnificent Douris cup [fine illustration in Ernst Pfuhl, *Masterpieces of Greek Drawing and Painting*, pl. 61–63], which shows on the outside the quarrel of Odysseus and Ajax over the arms and the judgment of the Achaeans, on the inside Odysseus handing over the arms to Neoptolemos.) This is the 'familiar version'; the only story that Odysseus kept the arms is "the tale told by the Aetolians who afterwards inhabited Ilium," recorded by Pausanias (1.35, 4)—that when Odysseus was shipwrecked the arms of Achilles were cast ashore near Ajax' tomb. (This version turns up again in an anonymous epigram in *Anth. Pal.* 9.115.)

The story in the play must be false; if Sophocles wanted us to think of it as true he would surely have indicated it clearly. He does the opposite. Odysseus tells Neoptolemos he must deceive Philoctetes with words and follows immediately with the suggestion that he describe the refusal to surrender his father's armor. Neoptolemos answers (100; cf. 108): "What do your orders mean, but to tell lies?" (ψευδῆ λέγειν). If the story about the arms is true, what on earth are they talking about?

[31] How can we possibly know, with Adams (147) that "the 'merchant' has disclosed too much"? That he has "unwittingly imperilled Odysseus' trickery"? The 'merchant'

is the emissary Odysseus promised to send in the prologue; what he says now has been carefully dictated to him by Odysseus.

[32] Cf. Whitman (1), 181 ff.

[33] For Adams of course it is sincere. But even if the arms of Achilles were kept by Odysseus, this ode has nothing to do with that; the chorus is talking about the original award of the arms to Odysseus. The chorus, who are Scyrian subjects of Neoptolemos (139 ff.) cannot have been present as they claim, for this happened long before Neoptolemos was called from Scyros. Bowra is right (274): "He tells his false tale; the chorus testify to it with what is very like an oath."

[34] See Kitto (2), 118.

[35] David Grene (*Sophocles II* in *The Complete Greek Tragedies*, 223) and E. F. Watling (*Sophocles: Electra and Other Plays*, 188), respectively.

[36] Cf. Adams (149): "In Greek drama stage directions are practically unknown. There is no parenthetical 'Philoctetes gives a cry of agony' or the like; the dramatist must incorporate this sort of thing in his text."

[37] Adams sees in the hexameter meter a hint that Neoptolemos "is inspired by the god of prophecy himself. . . . It is a revelation induced by his own pity but decreed by the god of Delphi" (150). This seems an overstatement; Apollo is not mentioned in the play.

[38] Kitto cites this quick reaction of Odysseus to the suicide attempt as an indication that Odysseus' later announcement that he does not need Philoctetes but only the bow is not sincere: "if the presence of Philoctetes at Troy were not necessary, Odysseus would not have been so swift to prevent him from doing away with himself" (124). But he prevents the suicide at 1003, just after he announces that Philoctetes must go to Troy; the decision to abandon him comes after Philoctetes' long furious tirade (at 1054) which establishes clearly that his mind is set forever against going to Troy. In any case, Odysseus is no fool; it would be one thing to come back with the bow alone and explain that Philoctetes, because he hated the Greeks so much, refused to come, and quite another to have to explain that Philoctetes committed suicide.

[39] For this word, cf. *Aj.* 672, *Ant.* 1105.

[40] 1054: ἄφετε γάρ αὐτόν. Whitman's description of Philoctetes as 'manacled,' during the lyric scene which follows (1) 184, overlooks this line. The scholiast (1004) does say δεδεμένος φησι but ξυλλάβετε (1003) means merely that he is held by Odysseus' men.

[41] E.g., Kitto (2), 124. Lesky (1), 130, takes the opposite view: "Odysseus (1055) ohne ihn [Philoctetes] allein mit dem Bogen gegen Troia ziehen will . . ." and adds in his note: "Nur unter der Voraussetzung, Odysseus könnte wirklich mit dem Bogen allein fort wollen, hat seine Rückgabe durch Neoptolemos volles Gewicht."

[42] Cf. Kitto (2), 125: "To call this Fate is nonsense; to disclaim guile is useless; to offer friendship is mockery."

[43] See Kitto's excellent analysis of this scene (2), 126.

[44] Kitto (2), 132, remarks on Neoptolemos' final attempt at persuasion: "Sophocles carefully avoids the argument that by going to Troy Philoctetes would be setting free the Greek army. This would be an argument which Philoctetes could not easily withstand." But 1200 ff.—"Be damned to Troy and *all* of those who beneath its walls" (οἵ θ' ὑπ' ἐκείνῳ πάντες)— shows that on the contrary Philoctetes would not have been moved by that argument at all; like Ajax, like Achilles, he includes in his wrath and wish for revenge the whole army as well as those who have wronged him.

[45] For the 'illogicalities' Kitto finds in this speech, cf. n. 20, above.

[46] This is why he says: λέγεις μὲν εἰκότ' 1373, "What you say is reasonable" (on which both Kitto and Adams lay stress for their differing interpretations). If he is not now to explain to Philoctetes that the whole elaborate story of Odysseus and his father's arms was a lie from beginning to end (and so revive Philoctetes' suspicions of him by revealing the full extent of his former duplicity), he must admit that Philoctetes' objections are 'reasonable.'

[47] As Kitto (2), 136, wittily remarks: "This is an occasion in which history is not so philosophic as poetry; Troy did fall."

[48] See P. W. Harsh, 'The Role of the Bow in the *Philoctetes* of Sophocles,' *AJP*, LXXXI, 408–414.

[49] For Heracles as πολύπονος, cf. P *N*. 33, E *HF* 1192.

[50] παρῆνεσ' 1435. The advice the Sophoclean hero will not accept from his fellow men, Philoctetes here accepts from a god. Cf. also οὐκ ἀπιθήσω 1447.

NOTES TO VI
(Pp. 143–162)

[1] Cf. Lesky (2), 168: "Athen, vor dessen Fall er die Augen schliessen durfte . . . Dass dieser Fall kommen wurde, hat er wohl geahnt."

[2] X. *HG*, 2.2, 19. The Corinthians and Thebans especially were for destroying Athens (ἐξαιρεῖν).

[3] Cf. Whitman (1), 210. It will be clear to the reader how much I owe to Whitman's brilliant and eloquent discussion of the play.

[4] See the judicious discussion in E. R. Dodds, *Euripides Bacchae*,[2] 91.

[5] Cf. also the comic treatment of Iolaus in the *Heraclidae* (esp. 686, 692 with its suggestion of sexual impotence and the grotesque exit of the *therapon* and Iolaus 723 ff.).

[6] Jones remarks (265) on the fall of Oedipus in the *OT* that "the word *exemplum* is inadmissible because it declares a distinct moralising intent and a way of looking at the stage-figure which Sophocles' play is without." He seems to have overlooked this passage, in which the Greek equivalent of *exemplum* is so heavily emphasized.

[7] Cf. *Aj*. 13, *OT* 499, *El*. 658.

[8] See Knox (3), 127–128.

[9] Cf. Knox (2), 7–8.

[10] Cf. Lesky (1), 132. "Der Weg des Dulders führt in den Frieden aber noch einmal greift mit Lockung und Gewalt die Unruhe dieser Welt nach ihm, ehe er dem Rufe der Gottheit folgen darf."

[11] This is of course Bowra's interpretation (310 ff.), which is severely criticized by Linforth (*Religion and Drama in the Oedipus at Colonus*, 75–192). Neither of them pays sufficient attention to the salient feature of Oedipus' transformation, the growth in

him of prophetic power. Lesky (1), 133, emphasizes the point that the hero does not undergo a transformation of *character*, the 'hero' has the same characteristics as the man. This is not a 'transformation' in the Christian sense, but an 'elevation.' "Nicht um eine Verklärung handelt es sich wohl aber um eine Erhöhung die den Menschen mit seinem ganzen Wesen in das Sein des Heros hinübernimmt; aus diesem wird er Segen und Fluch mit der gleichen Kraft eines heissen Willens senden, mit der er einst als sterblich Lebender seiner Umwelt begegnete."

[12] Adams states (165) that the Eumenides of the grove "are not, as in Aeschylus, Erinyes transformed from 'Furies' into 'Kindly Ones' . . . there is no suggestion of Erinys where these goddesses are concerned . . . when in this drama Oedipus calls on revenge, he does not call on the Eumenides." In his note he explains that when Oedipus, in his curse on Polynices, calls on the Eumenides (καλῶ δὲ τάσδε δαίμονας 1391) his curses are his own; "these powers [i.e., Tartarus, the Eumenides and Ares] are invoked to seal his curses not to make them." However Oedipus also calls on the goddesses of the grove when he curses Creon (864 ff.). It seems difficult to believe that in a play which has as its climactic scene a wronged father's curse on his son, the connection between the Eumenides and the Erinyes should be neither intended by the poet nor felt by the audience. This connection may well have been, as Adams says, an Aeschylean invention, but it clearly took root fast; in the *Orestes* of Euripides for example the Eumenides are four times named as avenging goddesses (321 ff., 836, 1650, and 38, where Electra calls them θεὰς εὐμενίδας because she is restrained by religious fear, αἰδοῦμαι, from pronouncing their name).

[13] There was of course no word of this part of the oracle when it was described by Oedipus in the earlier play (*OT* 791 ff.). This promise has been grafted on to the original oracle. This is one of the many ways in which Sophocles deliberately throughout this play refers to the *Oedipus Tyrannus*. (After all, the prophecy in the *OC* could easily have been presented as an independent utterance of the god.) Other points of connection between the two plays are the Creon scene which recalls the confrontation of the two men in the earlier play, and Polynices' echo of Jocasta's speech on prophecy (see page 160).

[14] Jebb (followed by most critics) refers the πρόσθε of 1375 to Oedipus' words against his sons in 421–427 and 451 ff. He rejects Campbell's suggestion that it refers to a curse already pronounced on the sons before the beginning of the play. But πρόσθε speaks eloquently for Campbell. It makes no sense for Oedipus to say to Polynices, "Such curses I sent forth against you before, and now I call on them to come to me as allies, "unless Polynices had heard (or heard of) the curses. Which is not true of the passages to which Jebb refers the words. In any event those passages are not curses, (what a curse is like we can see all too clearly from 1383 ff.), they are in the first case a wish and in the second a prophecy.

[15] On the growing definiteness of Oedipus' pronouncements and its significance, see Kitto (1), 388.

[16] Note the words, usually associated with the hero's intractability, which here emphasize his willingness to coöperate: παραινέσαι 464, διδάσκετε 468, δίδασκε 480, ἀκοῦσαι 485.

[17] Cf. *OC* 1132 ff.

[18] See Bowra 312–313 for the hint of hero cult in these lines.

[19] Cf. *OC* 486, *Ant.* 1200.

²⁰ Cf. Errandonea 153: "La primera estrofa con su antístrofa elogian principalmente a Colono, la segunda a Atenas, cuyos majores timbres de gloria se cifran en el olivo, el caballo y el mar."

²¹ Cf. E. *Med*. 835 ff. with Page's note (Euripides *Medea*, Oxford, 1938).

²² This needs no illustration but it may be pointed out that μινύρεται (671—used of the nightingale's song) is a variant form of μινυρίζω which originally (in Homer) was associated with sadness and complaint. Cf. Dain-Mazon *ad loc*.

²³ Cf. *OC* 684, *h. Cer*. 8, 428; crocus, *ibid*. 6, 178, 426.

²⁴ Diodorus 13.72–73; and cf. Aristides ὑπὲρ τῶν τεττάρων 172 and the scholium. But it is too much to see in this the genesis of the play, as Dain-Mazon do (69–70).

²⁵ Cf. Plu. *Alc*. 34.3.

²⁶ Cf. Hdt. 8.55.

²⁷ So Jebb, Bowra (325), Dain-Mazon (la Pitié). Adams dissents: "Antigone [sic] is not appealing to Oedipus in the name of mercy, but in the name of duty, duty of father to son" (173, n. 10).

²⁸ In a previous short discussion of the play (*Tragic Themes in Western Literature*, ed. Cleanth Brooks, New Haven, 1955, 28) I rashly accepted the suggestion of the scholiast (χρησμῳδεῖ) and translated χρῇξει as 'prophesy.' This of course cannot be maintained (if only because of γάρ) but the lexical separation of χρῇζω into two different words in *LSJ*⁹ is surely wrong. What a god wishes (χρῇξει) becomes without effort a fact (cf. A. *Supp*. 100 ff.); in expressing his wish, therefore, he 'prophecies' (χρῇξει). The word means exclusively 'prophesies' at E. *Hel*. 516, and there are several instances where the meaning is somewhere in between 'wish' and 'prophesy.' For example A. *Ch*. 340: ἀλλ' ἔτ' ἂν ἐκ τῶνδε θεὸς χρῄζων/ θείη κελάδους εὐφθογγοτέρους. Cf. Σ. χρῄζων. ὁ χρησμῳδῶν Ἀπόλλων. E. *Ion* 428: ὅσον δὲ χρῇξει—θεὸς γάρ ἐστιν—δέξομαι.

²⁹ The impatient tone is the regular formula for Death summoning the hesitant mortal. Cf. E. *Alc*. 255, where Alcestis in her final delirium hears Charon calling to her: τί μέλλεις; ἐπείγου. σὺ κατείργεις.—appropriate words for the Hermes who on the lekythos of the Phiale painter (illustrated in Arias-Hirmer, *A History of 1000 Years of Greek Vase Painting*, pl. XLI, XLII) summons the dying woman with an impatient, imperious gesture. But the summons to Oedipus is made more solemn by the preceding silence (1623), the repetition of the god's voice (πολλὰ πολλαχῇ 1626) and, above all, by the mysterious μέλλομεν χωρεῖν, which emphasizes what Jebb finely calls "the companionship of Oedipus with the unseen."

BIBLIOGRAPHY

BIBLIOGRAPHY
OF MODERN BOOKS AND ARTICLES CITED

ADAMS, S. M., *Sophocles the Playwright* (Toronto, 1957).

ADKINS, A. W. H., " 'Friendship' and 'Self-sufficiency' in Homer and Aristotle," *Classical Quarterly* (May, 1963), 30–45.

ALLEN, THOMAS W., *Homeri opera* (Oxford, 1912), vol. 5.

ARIAS, P. E. and MAX HIRMER, *A History of 1000 Years of Greek Vase Painting* (New York, 1962).

BAYFIELD, M. A., *The Antigone of Sophocles*[2] (London, 1935).

VON BLUMENTHAL, ALBRECHT, *Ion von Chios* (Stuttgart-Berlin, 1939).

BONNER, R. J., *Aspects of Athenian Democracy* (Berkeley and Los Angeles, 1937).

BOWRA, C. M., *Sophoclean Tragedy* (Oxford, 1944).

BRADSHAW, A. T., "The Watchman Scenes in the Antigone," *Classical Quarterly* (Nov., 1962), 200–211.

BRELICH, ANGELO, *Gli Eroi Greci* (Rome, 1958).

BRUHN, EWALD, *Sophocles, Antigone* (Berlin, 1913).

CAMPBELL, LEWIS, *Sophocles, Plays and Fragments* (Oxford, 1879).

CLOCHÉ, PAUL, *La Démocratie Athénienne* (Paris, 1951).

DAÍN, ALPHONSE and PAUL MAZON, *Sophocle* (Paris), Vol. I, 1955; Vol. II, 1958; Vol. III, 1960.

DENNISTON, J. D., *The Greek Particles*[2] (Oxford, 1950).

DILLER, HANS, "Über das Selbstbewusstsein der sophokleischen Personen," *Wiener Studien* LXIX (1956), Festschrift Albin Lesky, 70–85.

DODDS, E. R., *Euripides, Bacchae*[2] (Oxford, 1960).

EARP, F. R., *The Style of Aeschylus* (Cambridge, 1948).

EHRENBERG, VICTOR, *Sophocles and Pericles* (Oxford, 1954).

ELSE, GERALD F., *Aristotle's Poetics: The Argument* (Cambridge, Mass., 1957).

ERRANDONEA, IGNACIO, *Sofocles, Tragedias* (Barcelona, 1959).

FESTUGIÈRE, A. J., *Personal Religion among the Greeks* (Berkeley and Los Angleles, 1954).

FORSTER, E. M., *What I Believe* (London, 1939).

FRAENKEL, EDWARD, *Aeschylus, Agamemnon* (Oxford, 1950).

FRISK, H. *Griechisches etymologisches Wörterbuch* (Heidelberg, 1960).

FRITZ, KURT VON, and FRANK KNAPP, *Aristotle: Constitution of Athens and Related Texts* (New York, 1950).

GOHEEN, ROBERT F., *The Imagery of Sophocles' Antigone* (Princeton, 1951).

GRENE, DAVID, *Sophocles: Philoctetes* in *The Complete Greek Tragedies* (Chicago, 1957).

HARSH, P. W., "The Role of the Bow in the *Philoctetes* of Sophocles," *American Journal of Philology*, LXXXI (October, 1960), 408–414.

HEGEL, G. F., *Hegel on Tragedy*, trans. by Anne and Henry Paolucci (New York, 1962).

HEINIMANN, F., *Nomos und Physis* (Basel, 1945).

HIGNETT, C., *A History of the Athenian Constitution* (Oxford, 1952).

JENS, WALTER, *Die Stichomythie in der frühen griechischen Tragödie* Zetemata 11 (Munich, 1955).

JONES, JOHN, *Aristotle and Greek Tragedy* (Oxford, 1962).

KAIBEL, G., *Comicorum Graecorum Fragmenta* I (Berlin, 1899).

KIRKWOOD, G. M., *A Study of Sophoclean Drama* (Ithaca, N. Y., 1958).

KITTO, H. D. F. (1), *Greek Tragedy, A Literary Study*[3] (New York, 1961).

———— (2), *Form and Meaning in Drama* (London, 1956).

———— (3), *Sophocles, Three Tragedies* (Oxford, 1962).

KNOX, BERNARD M. W. (1), "The *Hippolytus* of Euripides," *Yale Classical Studies* 13 (New Haven, 1952).

———— (2), "The *Ajax* of Sophocles," *Harvard Studies in Classical Philology* 65 (Cambridge, Mass., 1961).

———— (3), *Oedipus at Thebes* (New Haven, 1957).

LAROCHE, E., *Histoire de la racine NEM—en grec ancien* (Paris, 1949).

LESKY, ALBIN (1), *Die tragische Dichtung der Hellenen* (Göttingen, 1956).

———— (2), *Die griechische Tragödie*[2] (Stuttgart, 1958).

———— (3), *Geschichte der griechischen Literatur*[2] (*Bern*, 1963).

LEVY, RACHEL, *The Gate of Horn* (London, 1948).

LINFORTH, IVAN (1), *Electra's Day in the Tragedy of Sophocles* (Berkeley and Los Angeles, 1963).

———— (2), *Antigone and Creon* (Berkeley and Los Angeles, 1961).

———— (3), *Religion and Drama in the Oedipus at Colonus* (Berkeley and Los Angeles, 1951).

MacKay, L. A., "Antigone, Coriolanus and Hegel." *Transactions of The American Philological Association* 93 (1962), 166–174.

Méautis, Georges, (1), *Sophocle, Essai sur le héros tragique* (Paris, 1957).

———— (2), *L'Oedipe à Colone et le culte des héros* (Neuchâtel, 1940).

Moore, John A., *Sophocles and Aretê* (Cambridge, Mass., 1938).

Murray, Gilbert, *Aeschylus, the Creator of Tragedy* (Oxford, 1940).

Neale, J. E., *Queen Elizabeth I* (London, 1934).

Nilson, Martin P., (1), *A History of Greek Religion* (Oxford, 1949).

———— (2), *Geschichte der griechischen Religion* I (Munich, 1955).

Page, Denys, (1), *Actor's Interpolations in Greek Tragedy* (Oxford, 1934).

———— (2), *Euripides, Medea* (Oxford, 1938).

Pfuhl, Ernst, *Masterpieces of Greek Drawing and Painting* (London, 1955).

Post, C. R., "The Dramatic Art of Sophocles," *Harvard Studies in Classical Philology*, 23 (1912), 71-127.

Radermacher, Ludwig, *Aristophanes' Frösche*, Oesterreichische Akademie der Wissenschaften, Sitzungsberichte, 198:4 (Vienna, 1954).

Reinhardt, Karl, *Sophokles* (Frankfurt am Main, 1933).

Schadewalt, Wolfgang, *Monolog und Selbstgespräch* (Berlin, 1926).

Schmid, Wilhelm (1), "Untersuchungen zum Gefesselten Prometheus," *Tübinger Beiträger* (Stuttgart, 1929).

———— (2), "Epikritisches zum Gefesselten Prometheus," *Philologische Wochenschrift*, 51 (1931).

Schmid-Stählin, *Geschichte der griechischen Literatur* (Munich, I:3, 1940).

Schwyzer, Eduard, *Griechische Grammatik I* (Munich, 1950).

Sheppard, J. T. (1), *The Oedipus Tyrannus of Sophocles* (Cambridge, 1920).

———— (2), *Greek Tragedy* (Cambridge, 1920).

Smyth, H. W., *Aeschylus* (London, 1927), Loeb Classical Library.

Stanford, W. B. (1), *Sophocles, Ajax* (London, 1963).

———— (2), *The Ulysses Theme* (Oxford, 1954).

Thompson, D'Arcy Wentworth, *A Glossary of Greek Fishes* (Oxford, 1947).

VERDENIUS, W. J., "ΑΙΝΟΣ," *Mnemosyne* IV, XV, 4 (1962), 39.

VERRALL, A. W., *The* Choephoroe *of Aeschylus* (London, 1893).

WAITH, E. M., *The Herculean Hero* (New York and London, 1962).

WALDOCK, A. J. A., *Sophocles the Dramatist* (Cambridge, 1951).

WATLING, E. F., *Sophocles: Electra and Other Plays* (London, 1953).

WHITMAN, CEDRIC (1), *Sophocles: A Study in Heroic Humanism* (Cambridge, Mass., 1951).

——— (2), *Homer and the Heroic Tradition* (Cambridge, Mass., 1958).

WOLF, ERIK, *Griechisches Rechtsdenken*, vol. 2 (Frankfurt am Main, 1952).

WOLFF-BELLERMANN, *Sophokles, Antigone*[6] (Leipzig, 1900).

WUNDER-WECKLEIN, *Sophoclis Tragoediae* (Leipzig, 1875).

ZIEGLER, KONRAT, "Tragoedia" in Paully-Wissowa, *Real-Encyclopädie der Classischen Altertumswissenschaft.*

ZÜRCHER, W., *Die Darstellung der Menschen im Drama des Euripides* (Basel, 1947).

INDEXES

INDEX

OF NAMES AND SELECTED TOPICS

INDEX
OF GREEK WORDS DISCUSSED